Assessment in Early Childhood Education

Assessment in Early Childhood Education

Fourth Edition

Sue C. Wortham

Professor Emerita
University of Texas at San Antonio

PEARSON

Merrill
Prentice Hall

Upper Saddle River, New Jersey
Columbus, Ohio

Library of Congress Cataloging in Publication Data

Wortham, Sue Clark
  Assessment in early childhood education / Sue C. Wortham.—4rd ed.
    p. cm.
  Includes bibliographical references and index.
  ISBN 0-13-140194-7
    1. Educational tests and measurements—United States. 2. Psychological tests for
  children—United States. 3. Ability in children—United States—Testing. 4. Early childhood
  education—United States—Evaluation. I. Title.

LB3060.217.W67 2005
372.126—dc22   2003069005

Vice President and Executive Publisher: Jeffery W. Johnston
Publisher: Kevin M. Davis
Editor: Julie Peters
Editorial Assistant: Michelle Girgis
Production Editor: Sheryl Langner
Production Coordination: Linda Zuk, WordCrafters Editorial Services, Inc.
Design Coordinator: Diane C. Lorenzo
Photo Coordinator: Lori Whitley
Cover Design: Ali Mohrman
Cover Image: Corbis
Production Manager: Laura Messerly
Director of Marketing: Ann Castel Davis
Marketing Manager: Autumn Purdy
Marketing Coordinator: Tyra Poole

This book was set in Berkeley Book by Carlisle Communications, Ltd. It was printed and bound by
R. R. Donnelley & Sons Company. The cover was printed by Phoenix Color Corp.

Photo Credits: pp. 1, 175, 180, 187: Barbara Schwartz/Merrill; pp. 12, 20, 29, 38, 108, 114, 147, 153, 227: Anne
Vega/Merrill; p. 61: David Mager/Pearson Learning; p. 87: Karen Mancinelli/Pearson Learning; p. 119, 192, 208: Scott
Cunningham/Merrill; p. 202: Pearson Learning, p. 239: Anthony Magnacca/Merrill.

Pearson Education Ltd.   Pearson Education Australia PTY, Limited
Pearson Education Singapore, Pte. Ltd.   Pearson Education North Asia Ltd.
Pearson Education Canada, Ltd.   Pearson Educacion de Mexico, S.A. de C.V.
Pearson Education—Japan   Pearson Education Malaysia, Pte. Ltd.

10 9 8 7 6 5 4 3 2 1
ISBN: 0-13-140194-7

Preface

Students preparing to become elementary school teachers take a course in tests and measurement as part of their undergraduate curriculum. Many textbooks for such courses describe both standardized and teacher-designed tests and how they are used to assess and evaluate students.

Students preparing to become teachers of young children—those from infancy through the primary grades—must be prepared to measure or evaluate children who are in the period of development called *early childhood*. Tests and other types of assessments designed for young children are different from those intended for children in later grades in elementary school. Because infants and children under age 8 have developmental limitations different from those of older children, a textbook that includes discussion of assessment in the early childhood years must be written from a developmental perspective.

TRADITIONAL AND AUTHENTIC ASSESSMENT STRATEGIES

This book is written especially for teachers and future teachers of young children. It includes information about standardized tests and, more important, other types of assessments that are appropriate for young children, such as observation, checklists, and rating scales. Assessments designed by teachers are explained both for preschool children and for kindergarten and primary grade children who are transitioning into literacy. With the ever-growing trend toward performance assessment, portfolios, and other methods of reporting a child's performance, chapters describing these strategies have been expanded and enhanced. The approach of this edition is the development of an assessment system that includes both traditional and authentic assessment strategies in a comprehensive plan. Thus, in this edition of the text, I seek to inform the reader about all types of assessments and their appropriate use.

HOW TO ASSESS YOUNG CHILDREN

Earlier editions of this book were developed in response to the expressed needs of teachers and graduate students who must understand and use current trends in assessment and put them into perspective within the reality of public schools that are required to focus intensively on standardized tests. Fortunately, commercial publishers of curriculum kits and textbooks for public schools are increasingly including performance as well as traditional assessments in their guides for teachers. Portfolios are becoming common as well. Nevertheless, teachers still need help on how to maintain a balance between these new strategies and standardized testing.

An important factor in the assessment of young children is when and how they should be measured. This is a controversial issue. The strengths and weaknesses of each type of assessment presented are discussed, as is research on the problems surrounding testing and evaluation in early childhood. Because many sources in the literature and other textbooks do not include the limitations as well as the merits of assessment techniques, this text provides an objective perspective on issues surrounding the efficacy and effectiveness of assessment strategies.

ORGANIZATION

The book is divided into four parts. Part I provides an introduction to assessment in early childhood in chapters 1 and 2. Part II is devoted to standardized tests and how they are designed, used, and reported in chapters 3 and 4. Informal assessments are discussed in part III. Observation, checklists, rating scales, and rubrics are covered in chapters 5 and 6, while teacher-designed strategies and performance-based strategies are described in chapters 7 and 8. Finally, part IV is devoted to the use of assessment systems and how all the strategies discussed in the chapters leading to part IV can be incorporated into an assessment system or comprehensive assessment plan.

Acknowledgments

I would like to thank the reviewers who provided valuable suggestions and feedback for this fourth edition. Their comments were perceptive and their suggestions, constructive. Those who reviewed the text before this edition was developed are Erin Anderson, University of Florida; Martha Baiyee, Eastern Michigan University; Barbara Foulks Boyd, Radford University; Janice Fletcher, University of Idaho; and Wenju Shen, Valdosta State University.

It is also important to thank the staff at Merrill/Prentice Hall, who helped in the conceptualization of important revisions as well as in the production process. These include Sheryl Langner, Production Editor; Linda Zuk, Production Coordinator; and, especially, Jeff Johnston, Vice President and Publisher, who has supported my work for *many* years.

Educator Learning Center:
An Invaluable Online Resource

Merrill Education and the Association for Supervision and Curriculum Development (ASCD) invite you to take advantage of a new online resource, one that provides access to the top research and proven strategies associated with ASCD and Merrill—the Educator Learning Center. At **www.EducatorLearningCenter.com** you will find resources that will enhance your students' understanding of course topics and of current educational issues, in addition to being invaluable for further research.

HOW THE EDUCATOR LEARNING CENTER WILL HELP YOUR STUDENTS BECOME BETTER TEACHERS

With the combined resources of Merrill Education and ASCD, you and your students will find a wealth of tools and materials to better prepare them for the classroom.

RESEARCH

- More than 600 articles from the ASCD journal *Educational Leadership* discuss everyday issues faced by practicing teachers.
- A direct link on the site to Research Navigator™ gives students access to many of the leading education journals, as well as extensive content detailing the research process.
- Excerpts from Merrill Education texts give your students insights on important topics of instructional methods, diverse populations, assessment, classroom management, technology, and refining classroom practice.

CLASSROOM PRACTICE

- Hundreds of lesson plans and teaching strategies are categorized by content area and age range.
- Case studies and classroom video footage provide virtual field experience for student reflection.
- Computer simulations and other electronic tools keep your students abreast of today's classrooms and current technologies.

LOOK INTO THE VALUE OF EDUCATOR LEARNING CENTER YOURSELF

A 4-month subscription to the Educator Learning Center is $25 but is FREE when used in conjunction with this text. To obtain free passcodes for your students, contact your Merill/Prentice Hall sales representative, and your representative will give you a special ISBN to give your bookstore when ordering your textbooks. To preview the value of this website to you and your student, please go to **www.EducatorLearningCenter.com** and click on "Demo."

Discover the Companion Website
Accompanying This Book

THE PRENTICE HALL COMPANION WEBSITE:
A VIRTUAL LEARNING ENVIRONMENT

Technology is a constantly growing and changing aspect of our field that is creating a need for content and resources. To address this emerging need, Prentice Hall has developed an online learning environment for students and professors alike—Companion Websites—to support our textbooks.

In creating a Companion Website, our goal is to build on and enhance what the textbook already offers. For this reason, the content for each user-friendly website is organized by topic and provides the professor and student with a variety of meaningful resources. Common features of a Companion Website include:

FOR THE PROFESSOR—

Every Companion Website integrates **Syllabus Manager™**, an online syllabus creation and management utility.

- **Syllabus Manager™** provides you, the instructor, with an easy, step-by-step process to create and revise syllabi, with direct links into Companion Website and other online content without having to learn HTML.
- Students may logon to your syllabus during any study session. All they need to know is the web address for the Companion Website and the password you've assigned to your syllabus.
- After you have created a syllabus using **Syllabus Manager™**, students may enter the syllabus for their course section from any point in the Companion Website.
- Clicking on a date, the student is shown the list of activities for the assignment. The activities for each assignment are linked directly to actual content, saving time for students.
- Adding assignments consists of clicking on the desired due date, then filling in the details of the assignment—name of the assignment, instructions, and whether or not it is a one-time or repeating assignment.
- In addition, links to other activities can be created easily. If the activity is online, a URL can be entered in the space provided, and it will be linked automatically in the final syllabus.
- Your completed syllabus is hosted on our servers, allowing convenient updates from any computer on the Internet. Changes you make to your syllabus are immediately available to your students at their next logon.

- **Introduction**—General information about the topic and how it will be covered in the website.
- **Web Links**—A variety of websites related to topic areas.
- **Timely Articles**—Links to online articles that enable you to become more aware of important issues in early childhood.
- **Learn by Doing**—Put concepts into action, participate in activities, examine strategies, and more.
- **Visit a School**—Visit a school's website to see concepts, theories, and strategies in action.
- **For Teachers/Practitioners**—Access information you will need to know as an educator, including information on materials, activities, and lessons.
- **Observation Tools**—A collection of checklists and forms to print and use when observing and assessing children's development.
- **Current Policies and Standards**—Find out the latest early childhood policies from the govenrment and various organizations, and view state, federal, and curriculum standards.
- **Resources and Organizations**—Discover tools to help you plan your classroom or center and organizations to provide current information and standards for each topic.
- **Electronic Bluebook**—Paperless method of completing homework or essays assigned by a professor. Finished work can be sent to the professor via email.
- **Message Board**—Virtual bulletin board to post and respond to questions and comments from a national audience.

To take advantage of these and other resources, please visit the *Assessment in Early Childhood Education*, Fourth Edition, Companion Website at

www.prenhall.com/wortham

Brief Contents

Contents

Part II   Standardized Tests

Part III   Informal Assessments

8   Informal Assessments: Performance-Based Strategies   180

Part IV   Using Assessment Systems

9   Assessment Systems: Portfolio Assessment   202

10   Assessment Systems: Communicating with Parents   227

NOTE: Every effort has been made to provide accurate and current Internet information in this book. However, the Internet and information posted on it are constantly changing, it is inevitable that some of the Internet addresses in this textbook will change.

CHAPTER 1

An Overview of Assessment in Early Childhood

Chapter Objectives

As a result of reading this chapter, you will be able to

1. Understand the purposes of assessment in early childhood
2. Understand different meanings of the term *assessment*
3. Understand the history of tests and measurement in early childhood
4. Develop an awareness of issues in testing young children

UNDERSTANDING ASSESSMENT IN INFANCY AND EARLY CHILDHOOD

Throughout elementary and high school, children take many different kinds of tests. Some tests determine their grades for each reporting period; some are achievement tests, IQ tests, or tests for admission to a college or university. Assessment, however, is more than the testing that is familiar to us. Furthermore, we may be unaware of the role that assessment plays with children in the years from birth to age 8.

What is assessment? Why do we need to test or evaluate children in the early childhood years? We live in a world in which we are interested not only in knowing more about how infants and young children grow and develop, but also in having access to tools to help us with problems in a child's development and learning. How is a book on assessment of young children different from a textbook prepared for a course in educational psychology? Most textbooks in testing and measurement focus primarily on the psychological and educational testing of school-age children and adults, with some attention to younger individuals. The tests and teacher assessments described usually assume some facility in reading and writing.

Assessment can mean many things. Goodwin and Goodwin (1982) describe assessment or measurement as "the process of determining, through observation or testing, an individual's traits or behaviors, a program's characteristics, or the properties of some other entity, and then assigning a number, rating, or score to that determination" (p. 523). The study of individuals for measurement purposes begins before birth, with assessment of fetal growth and development. At birth and throughout infancy and early childhood, various methods of measurement are used to evaluate the individual's traits or behaviors. Before a child is able to take a written test, he or she is measured through medical examinations and observation of developmental milestones by parents and other family members and is perhaps screened or evaluated for an early childhood program or service.

Assessment of children from birth through the preschool years is different from assessment of older people. Not only can young children not write or read, but the young developing child presents different challenges that influence the choice of measurement strategy. Assessment strategies must be matched with the level of mental, social, and physical development at each stage. Developmental change in young children is rapid, and there is a need to assess whether development is progressing normally. If development is not normal, the measurement and evaluation procedures used are important in making decisions regarding appropriate intervention services during infancy and the preschool years.

Assessment is used for various purposes. We may want to learn about individual children. We may conduct an evaluation to assess a young child's development in language or mathematics. When we need to learn more, we may assess the child to describe what he or she has achieved. For example, a first-grade teacher may use measurement techniques to determine what reading skills have been mastered and what weaknesses exist that indicate a need for additional instruction.

Assessment strategies may be used for diagnosis. Just as a medical doctor conducts a physical examination of a child to diagnose an illness, psychologists, teachers, and other adults who work with children can conduct an informal or formal assessment to diagnose a developmental delay or identify causes for poor performance in learning.

If medical problems, birth defects, or developmental delays in motor, language, cognitive, or social development are discovered during the early, critical periods of development, steps can be taken to correct, minimize, or remediate them before the child enters school. For many developmental deficits or differences, the earlier they are detected and the earlier intervention is planned, the more likely the child will be able to overcome them or compensate for them. For example, if a serious hearing deficit is identified early, the child can learn other methods of communicating and acquiring information.

Assessment of young children is also used to place them in infant or early childhood programs or to provide special services. To ensure that a child receives the best services, careful screening and more extensive testing may be conducted before selecting the combination of intervention programs and other services that will best serve the child.

Program planning is another purpose of assessment. After children have been identified and evaluated for an intervention program or service, assessment results can be used in planning the programs that will serve them. These programs, in turn, can be evaluated to determine their effectiveness.

Besides identifying and correcting developmental problems, assessment of very young children is conducted for other purposes. One purpose is research. Researchers study young children to better understand their behavior or to measure the appropriateness of the experiences that are provided for them.

How were these assessment strategies developed? In the next section, I describe how certain movements or factors, especially during this century, have affected the development of testing instruments, procedures, and other measurement techniques that are used with infants and young children.

EARLY INTERVENTION FOR A CHILD WITH HEARING IMPAIRMENT

Julio, who is 2 years old, was born prematurely. He did not have regular checkups during his first year, but he was taken by his mother to a community clinic when he had a cold and fever at about 9 months of age. When the doctor noticed that Julio did not react to normal sounds in the examining room, she stood behind him and clapped her hands near each ear. Because Julio did not turn toward the clapping sounds, the doctor suspected that he had a hearing loss. She arranged for Julio to be examined by an audiologist at an eye, ear, nose, and throat clinic.

Julio was found to have a significant hearing loss in both ears. He was fitted with hearing aids and is attending a special program twice a week for children with hearing deficits. Therapists in the program are teaching Julio to speak. They are also teaching his mother how to make Julio aware of his surroundings and help him to develop a vocabulary. Had Julio not received intervention services at an early age, he might have entered school with severe cognitive and learning deficits that would have put him at a higher risk for learning.

Interest in studying young children to understand their growth and development dates back to the initial recognition of childhood as a separate period in the life cycle. Johann Pestalozzi, a pioneer in developing educational programs specifically for children, wrote about the development of his 3½-year-old son in 1774 (Irwin & Bushnell, 1980). Early publications also reflected concern for the proper upbringing and education of young children. *Some Thoughts Concerning Education* by John Locke (1699), *Emile* (Rousseau, 1911/1762), and Frederick Froebel's *Education of Man* (1896) were influential in focusing attention on the characteristics and needs of children in the 18th and 19th centuries. Rousseau believed that human nature was essentially good and that education must allow that goodness to unfold. He stated that more attention should be given to studying the child so that education could be adapted to meet individual needs (Weber, 1984). The study of children, as advocated by Rousseau, did not begin until the late 19th and early 20th centuries.

Scientists throughout the world used observation to measure human behaviors. Ivan Pavlov proposed a theory of conditioning to change behaviors. Alfred Binet developed the concept of a normal mental age by studying memory, attention, and intelligence in children. Binet and Theophile Simon developed an intelligence scale to determine mental age that made it possible to differentiate the abilities of individual children (Weber, 1984). American psychologists expanded these early efforts, developing instruments for various types of measurement.

The study and measurement of young children today has evolved from the child study movement, the development of standardized tests, Head Start and other federal programs first funded in the 1960s, and the passage of Public Law 94–142, the Individuals with Disabilities Education Act, and Public Law 99–457. Currently, there is a movement toward more meaningful learning or authentic achievement and assessment (Newmann, 1996; Wiggins, 1993). At the same time, continuing progress is being made in identifying, diagnosing, and providing more appropriate intervention for infants and young children with disabilities (Meisels & Fenichel, 1996).

THE CHILD STUDY MOVEMENT

G. Stanley Hall, Charles Darwin, and Lawrence Frank were leaders in the development of the child study movement that emerged after the turn of the century. Darwin, in suggesting that by studying the development of the infant one could glimpse the development of the human species, initiated the scientific study of the child (Kessen, 1965). Hall developed and extended methods of studying children. After he became president of Clark University in Worcester, Massachusetts, he established a major center for child study. Hall's students— John Dewey, Arnold Gesell, and Lewis Terman—all made major contributions to the study and measurement of children. Dewey advocated educational reform that affected the development of educational programs for young children. Gesell first described the behaviors that emerged in children at each chronological age. Terman became a leader in the development of mental tests (Irwin & Bushnell, 1980; Wortham, 2002).

Research in child rearing and child care was furthered by the establishment of the Laura Spelman Rockefeller Memorial child development grants. Under the leadership of Lawrence

Frank, institutes for child development were funded by the Rockefeller grants at Columbia University Teacher's College (New York), the University of Minnesota, the University of California at Berkeley, Arnold Gesell's Clinic of Child Development at Yale University, the Iowa Child Welfare Station, and other locations.

With the establishment of child study at academic centers, preschool children could be observed in group settings, rather than as individuals in the home. With the development of laboratory schools and nursery schools in the home economics departments of colleges and universities, child study research could also include the family in broadening the understanding of child development. Researchers from many disciplines joined in an ongoing child study movement that originated strategies for observing and measuring development. The results of their research led to an abundant literature. Between the 1890s and the 1950s, hundreds of children were studied in academic settings throughout the United States (Weber, 1984). Thus, the child study movement has taught us to use observation and other strategies to assess the child. Investigators today continue to add new knowledge about child development and learning that aids parents, preschool teachers and staff members, and professionals in institutions and agencies that provide services to children and families. In the last decade of the 20th century and the 21st century, brain research has opened up a whole new perspective of the nature of cognitive development and the importance of the early years for optimum development and later learning (Begley, 1997; Shore, 1997). These new findings have caused early childhood educators to reflect on the factors that affect early development and the implications for programming for children in infancy and early childhood.

STANDARDIZED TESTS

Standardized testing also began around 1900. When colleges and universities in the East sought applicants from other areas of the nation in the 1920s, they found the high school transcripts of these students difficult to evaluate. The *Scholastic Aptitude Test* (SAT) was established to permit fairer comparisons of applicants seeking admission (Cronbach, 1990).

As public schools expanded to offer 12 years of education, a similar phenomenon occurred. To determine the level and pace of instruction and the grouping of students without regard for socioeconomic class, objective tests were developed (Gardner, 1961). These tests grew out of the need to sort, select, or otherwise make decisions about both children and adults.

The first efforts to design tests were informal. When a psychologist, researcher, or physician needed a method to observe a behavior, he or she developed a procedure to meet those needs. The procedure was often adopted by others with the same needs. When many people wanted to use a particular measurement strategy or test, the developer prepared printed copies for sale. As the demand for tests grew, textbook publishers and firms specializing in test development and production also began to create and/or sell tests (Cronbach, 1990).

American psychologists built on the work of Binet and Simon in developing the intelligence measures described earlier. Binet's instrument, revised by Terman at Stanford University, came to be known as the *Stanford–Binet Intelligence Scale*. Other Americans, particularly educators, welcomed the opportunity to use precise measurements to evaluate learning. Edward Thorndike and his students designed measures to evaluate achievement in reading, mathematics, spelling, and language ability (Weber, 1984). Due to the work of Terman and Thorndike, testing soon became a science (Scherer, 1999). By 1918, more than 100 standardized tests had been designed to measure school achievement (Monroe, 1918).

After World War II, the demand for dependable and technically refined tests grew, and people of all ages came to be tested. As individuals and institutions selected and developed their own tests, the use of testing became more centralized. Statewide tests were administered in schools, and tests were increasingly used at the national level.

The expanded use of tests resulted in the establishment of giant corporations that could assemble the resources to develop, publish, score, and report the results of testing to a large clientele. Centralization improved the quality of tests and the establishment of standards for test design. As individual researchers and teams of psychologists continue to design instruments to meet current needs, the high quality of these newer tests can be attributed to the improvements and refinements made over the years and to the increased knowledge of test design and validation (Cronbach, 1990).

HEAD START AND THE WAR ON POVERTY

Prior to the 1960s, tests for preschool children were developed for use by medical doctors, psychologists, and other professionals serving children. Developmental measures, IQ tests, and specialized tests to measure developmental deficits were generally used for noneducational purposes. Child study researchers tended to use observational or unobtrusive methods to study the individual child or groups of children. School-age children were tested to measure school achievement, but this type of test was rarely used with preschool children.

After the federal government decided to improve the academic performance of children from low-income homes and those from non-English-speaking backgrounds, test developers moved quickly to design new measurement and evaluation instruments for these preschool and school-age populations.

In the late 1950s, there was concern about the consistently low academic performance of children from poor homes. As researchers investigated the problem, national interest in improving education led to massive funding for many programs designed to reduce the disparity in achievement between poor and middle-class children. The major program that involved preschool children was Head Start. Models of early childhood programs ranging from highly structured academic, child-centered developmental to more traditional nursery school models were designed and implemented throughout the United States (White, 1973; Zigler & Valentine, 1979).

All programs funded by the federal government had to be evaluated for effectiveness. As a result, new measures were developed to assess individual progress and the programs' effectiveness (Laosa, 1982). The quality of these measures was uneven, as was comparative research designed to compare the overall effectiveness of Head Start. Nevertheless, the measures and strategies developed for use with Head Start projects added valuable resources for the assessment and evaluation of young children (Hoepfner, Stern, & Nummedal, 1971).

Other federally funded programs developed in the 1960s, such as bilingual programs, Title I, the Emergency School Aid Act, Follow Through, and Home Start, were similar in effect to Head Start. The need for measurement strategies and tests to evaluate these programs led to the improvement of existing tests and the development of new tests to evaluate their success accurately.

LEGISLATION FOR YOUNG CHILDREN WITH DISABILITIES

PL 94–142. Perhaps the most significant law affecting the measurement of children was Public Law (PL) 94–142, the Education for All Handicapped Children Act, passed in 1975. This law, later amended and renamed the Individuals with Disabilities Education Act, guaranteed all children with disabilities the right to an appropriate education in a free public school and placement in the least restrictive learning environment. The law further required the use of nondiscriminatory testing and evaluation of these children (McCollum & Maude, 1993).

The implications of the law were far-reaching. Testing, identification, and placement of students with mental retardation and those with other disabilities were difficult. Existing tests no longer were considered adequate for children with special needs. Classroom teachers had to learn the techniques used to identify students with disabilities and determine how to meet their educational needs (Kaplan & Saccuzzo, 1989).

ONE FAMILY'S EXPERIENCE WITH HEAD START

Rosa is a graduate of the Head Start program. For 2 years, she participated in a class housed in the James Brown School, a former inner-city school that had been closed and remodeled for other community services. Two Head Start classrooms were in the building, which was shared with several other community agencies serving low-income families. In addition to learning at James Brown School, Rosa went on many field trips, including the zoo, the botanical garden, the public library, and a nearby McDonald's.

This year Rosa is a kindergarten student at West Oaks Elementary School with her older brothers, who also attended Head Start. Next year Rosa's younger sister, Luisa, will begin the program. Luisa looks forward to Head Start. She has good memories of the things she observed Rosa doing in the Head Start classroom while visiting the school with her mother.

Luisa's parents are also happy that she will be attending the Head Start program. Luisa's older brothers are good students, which they attribute to the background they received in Head Start. From her work in kindergarten, it appears that Rosa will also do well when she enters first grade.

The law required that a team of teachers, parents, diagnosticians, school psychologists, medical personnel, and perhaps social workers or representatives of government agencies or institutions be used to identify and place students with disabilities. When appropriate, the child must also be included in the decision-making process. The team screens, tests, and develops an individual educational plan (IEP) for each child. Not all team members are involved in every step of the process, but they can influence the decisions made.

The term **mainstreaming** came to define the requirement that the child be placed in the least restrictive environment. This meant that as often as possible the child would be placed with children developing normally, rather than in a segregated classroom for students in special education. How much mainstreaming was beneficial for the individual student? The question was difficult. In addition, the ability of teachers to meet the needs of students with and without disabilities simultaneously in the same classroom is still debated. Nevertheless, classroom teachers were expected to develop and monitor the educational program prescribed for students with disabilities (Clark, 1976).

The identification and diagnosis of students with disabilities is the most complex aspect of PL 94–142. Many types of children need special education, including students with mental retardation, physical and visual disabilities, speech impairments, auditory disabilities, learning disabilities, emotional disturbances, and students who are gifted. Children may have a combination of disabilities. The identification and comprehensive testing of children to determine what types of disabilities they have and how best to educate them requires a vast array of assessment techniques and instruments. Teachers, school nurses, and other staff members can be involved in initial screening and referral, but the extensive testing used for diagnosis and prescription requires professionals who have been trained to administer psychological tests (Mehrens & Lehmann, 1991).

Under PL 94–142, all children with disabilities between the ages of 3 and 21 are entitled to free public education. This means that preschool programs must also be provided for children under age 6. Public schools have implemented early childhood programs for children with disabilities, and Head Start programs are required to include them (Guralnick, 1982; Spodek & Saracho, 1994). Other institutions and agencies also provide programs for children with and without disabilities.

PL 99–457. Many of the shortcomings of PL 94–142 were addressed in PL 99–457 (Education of the Handicapped Act Amendments), passed in 1986. The newer law authorized two new programs: the Federal Preschool Program and the Early Intervention Program. Under PL 94–142, the state could choose whether to provide services to children with disabilities between the ages of 3 and 5. Under PL 99–457, states must prove that they are meeting the needs of all these children if they wish to receive federal funds under PL 94–142. The Federal Preschool Program extends the right of children with disabilities under PL 94–142 to all children with disabilities between the ages of 3 and 5.

The Early Intervention Program established early intervention services for all children between birth and age 2 who are developmentally delayed. All participating states must now provide intervention services for all infants and toddlers with disabilities (McCollum & Maude, 1993; Meisels & Shonkoff, 1990).

How to measure and evaluate young children with disabilities and the programs that serve them is a continuing challenge (Cicchetti & Wagner, 1990). The design of measures to screen, identify, and place preschool children in intervention programs began with the passage of PL 94–142 and was extended under PL 99–457. Many of these instruments and strategies, particularly those dealing with developmental delay, were also used with preschool programs serving children developing normally, as well as those with developmental delays or disabilities.

As children with disabilities were served in a larger variety of settings, such as preschools, Head Start programs, child-care settings, infant intervention programs, and hospitals, early childhood educators from diverse backgrounds were involved in the determination of whether infants and young children were eligible for services for special needs. Early childhood educators and other practitioners in the field were challenged to be knowledgeable in measurement and evaluation strategies for effective identification, placement, and assessment of young children in integrated early childhood settings (Goodwin & Goodwin, 1993).

Many questions were raised about appropriately serving young children with diverse abilities. Meeting the developmental and educational needs of infants and preschool children with disabilities and at the same time providing mainstreaming was a complex task. How should these children be grouped for the best intervention services? When children with and without disabilities were grouped together, what were the effects when all of them were progressing through critical periods of development? Not only was identification of young children with disabilities more complex, but evaluation of the infant and preschool programs providing intervention services was also difficult.

PL 101–576. The Americans with Disabilities Act (ADA), passed in 1990 (Stein, 1993), and the amendments to PL 94–142, the Individuals with Disabilities Education Act (IDEA), have had an additional impact on the education of young children with disabilities. Under the ADA, all early childhood programs must be prepared to serve children with special needs. Facilities and accommodations for young children, including outdoor play environments, must be designed, constructed, and altered appropriately to meet the needs of young children with disabilities. The PL 94–142 amendments, passed in 1991, require that the individual educational needs of young children with disabilities must be met in all early childhood programs (Deiner, 1993; McCollum & Maude, 1993; Wolery, Strain, & Bailey, 1992). These laws advance the civil rights of young children and have resulted in the inclusion of young children in preschool and school-age programs. As a result, the concept of mainstreaming is being replaced by **integration** or **inclusion,** whereby all young children learn together with the goal that the individual needs of all children will be met (Krick, 1992; Wolery & Wilbers, 1994). The efforts of these programs and their services must be assessed and evaluated to determine whether the needs of children are being met effectively.

CURRENT ISSUES AND TRENDS IN ASSESSMENT IN EARLY CHILDHOOD EDUCATION

The 1980s brought a new reform movement in education, accompanied by a new emphasis on testing. The effort to improve education at all levels included the use of standardized tests to provide accountability for what students are learning. Minimum competency tests, achievement tests, and screening instruments were used to ensure that students from preschool through college reached the desired educational goals and achieved the minimum standards of education that were established locally or by the state education agency. As we continue in a new century, these concerns have increased.

TRENDS IN A NEW CENTURY

In the 1990s many schools were able to improve the learning environment and achievement for all children; nevertheless, a large percentage of schools were still low performing in 2000 and 2001. Inadequate funding, teacher shortages, teachers with inadequate training, aging schools, and poor leadership were factors that affected quality education (Wortham, 2002).

During the 2000 presidential campaign, candidate George W. Bush named quality education as one of the goals of his presidency. After his election, President Bush worked for legislation that would improve education for all children. After months of dialogue and debate, Congress passed a new education act in December 2001. The No Child Left Behind Act

(NCLB), signed into law on January 8, 2002, had an impact on testing required by individual states. In addition to other provisions, all states were required to administer tests developed by the state and to set and monitor adequate yearly progress (Moscosco, 2001; National Governors Association Center for Best Practices, 2002; Wortham, 2002).

President Bush was also committed to strengthening early childhood programs. In 2002, several projects were conducted to support early childhood programs. Under the Sunshine Schools program, the Department of Education focused on what is working in early childhood education and gave attention to highly effective state, district, city, county, and campus programs (Grissom, 2002).

Another Bush initiative, Good Start, Grow Smart, was intended to strengthen Head Start and improve the quality of experiences for children. The initiative provided:

- Training for nearly 50,000 Head Start teachers in the best techniques
- Assurance that preschool programs are more closely coordinated with K to 12 educational programs
- A research effort to identify effective early literacy programs and practices (Grissom, 2002).

In July 2001, the White House hosted the White House Summit on Early Childhood Cognitive Development. The Early Childhood–Head Start Task Force formed following the summit published a new guide, *Teaching Our Youngest* (Grissom, 2002).

The early childhood education projects initiated by the Bush administration to improve education stressed the importance of improving early childhood programs; nevertheless, there is no doubt that mandates for the increased testing that is standards-based will continue in the future in spite of concerns of their relevancy, especially for young children. Fortunately, child-outcome standards have also been developed by professional organizations in addition to state education agencies. The National Council for the Social Studies issued *Curriculum Standards for the Social Studies* (National Council for the Social Studies, 2001). Improved Head Start Performance Standards published in 1996 included children from birth to 5 (Early Head Start, 2000). These standards and others provide guidelines for early childhood educators as they strive to improve programs and experiences for young children.

THE NO CHILD LEFT BEHIND ACT OF 2001

The act requires states to:

- Provide public school choice and supplemental services for students in failing schools as early as fall, 2002.
- Integrate scientifically based reading research into comprehensive instruction for young children.
- Set and monitor adequate yearly progress, based on baseline 2001–2002 data.
- Issue annual report cards on school performance and statewide test results by 2002–2003.
- Implement annual, standards-based assessments in reading and math for grades 3 to 8 by 2005–2006.
- Assure that all classes are taught by a qualified teacher by 2005–2006 (National Governors Association Center for Best Practices, 2002).

CONCERNS ABOUT TESTING YOUNG CHILDREN IN PUBLIC SCHOOL SETTINGS

The increased use of testing at all levels has been an issue in American education, but the testing of young children is of particular concern. Standardized tests and other assessment measures are now being used in preschool, kindergarten, and primary grades to determine whether children will be admitted to preschool programs, promoted to the next grade, or retained. During the late 1980s and early 1990s, tests were used to determine if students should be promoted from kindergarten to first grade or placed in a "transitional" first grade. Although this practice is now less popular, it persists in some school districts and states (Smith, 1999). In 2000, the National Association of Early Childhood Specialists in State Departments of Education was concerned about the continuing trend to deny children entry to kindergarten and first grade. They issued a position statement, "Still! Unacceptable Trends in Kindergarten Entry and Placement" (National Association of Early Childhood Specialists in State Departments of Education, 2000). This continuing effort to advocate appropriate assessment of very young children was endorsed by the Governing Board of the National Association for the Education of Young Children (2001).

The announcement by President Bush in 2003 that all Head Start students would be given a national standardized test assessment raised new concerns. At issue were validity and reliability of tests for preschool children (Nagle, 2000) and whether such "high-stakes" testing should be used to evaluate the quality of Head Start programs (Shepard, Kagan, Lynn, & Wurtz, 1998). Policymakers had to address these and other concerns about appropriate assessment of young children in their decisions about how to evaluate preschool programs that receive federal funding (McMaken, 2003).

CONCERNS ABOUT TESTING YOUNG CHILDREN WITH CULTURAL AND LANGUAGE DIFFERENCES

A concurrent concern related to current trends and practices in the assessment of young children is the question of how appropriate our tests and assessment strategies are in the terms of the diversity of young children attending early childhood programs. Socioeconomic groups are changing dramatically and rapidly in our society, with an expansion of the poorer class and a corresponding shrinking of the middle class (Raymond & McIntosh, 1992). At the same time, an increase in minority citizens has occurred as the result of the continuing influx of people from other countries, especially Southeast Asia and Central and South America. Assessment of the developmental progress of children from these groups is particularly important if their learning needs are to be identified and addressed.

There is evidence that standardized test scores have had a high correlation to parents' occupations, level of education, the location of the student's elementary school, and the family's income bracket. Moreover, students from limited English backgrounds tend to score lower on reading and language fluency tests in English. They typically perform better on computational portions of mathematics tests (Wesson, 2001). The fairness of existing tests for children who are school disadvantaged and linguistically and culturally diverse serves as an indicator of the need for alternative assessment strategies for young children (Goodwin & Goodwin, 1993, 1997). Appropriate measurement and evaluation strategies that will

Assessments can be conducted while young children engage in independent work.

enhance, rather than diminish, the potential for achievement in minority children is a major issue in the 21st century.

The history of assessment of minorities who are bilingual students or learning English as a second language is one of potential bias. Children have been tested in their nondominant language or with instruments that were validated on an Anglo, middle-class sample of children.

The issue of appropriate assessment of these children has been addressed in court cases such as *Diana* vs. *The California State Board of Education* in 1968 and *Lau* vs. *Nichols* in 1974. More current authentic measures combined with multiple measurement procedures are recommended; nevertheless, there are few data on timeliness, interrater reliability, and standardization of norms on this population of children, which is also problematic (Rivas, no date).

Assessment of young children who are from families that are culturally and linguistically different must include many dimensions of diversity. It is not useful to proceed with assessment that is culturally fair for Hispanic or Asian populations generally. The many variations within communities and cultures must be considered, among them the educational background of the parents and the culture of the immediate community of the family. Congruence between the individual cultural perceptions of the assessors and the children being assessed, even when both are from the same culture or language population, must also be considered (Barrera, 1996). Many types of information, including the child's background and the use of assessments, must be combined to determine a picture of the child that is reflective of individual, group, and family cultural characteristics.

CONCERNS ABOUT TESTING YOUNG CHILDREN WITH DISABILITIES

The use of testing for infants and young children with disabilities cannot be avoided. Indeed, Meisels, Steele, and Quinn-Leering (1993) reflected that not all tests used are bad. Nevertheless, Greenspan and Meisels et al. (1996) believe assessments used with infants and young children have been borrowed from assessment methodology used with older children and do not represent meaningful information about their developmental achievements and capacities. Misleading test scores are being used for decisions about services, educational placements, and intervention programs. These developmental psychologists propose that assessment should be based on current understanding of development and use structured tests as one part of an integrated approach that includes observation of the child's interactions with trusted caregivers. Assessment should be based on multiple sources of information that will reflect the child's capacities and competencies and better indicate what learning environments will best provide intervention services for the child's optimal development.

Play-based assessment is one major source of information among the multiple sources recommended. Play assessment is nonthreatening and can be done unobtrusively. Moreover, during play, children can demonstrate skills and abilities that might not be apparent in other forms of assessment. Children's ability to initiate and carry out play schemes and use play materials can add significant information (Fewell & Rich, 1987; Segal & Webber, 1996).

AUTHENTIC AND PERFORMANCE ASSESSMENT

Assessment is in a period of transition. Teachers of young children are moving from more traditional strategies of assessing for knowledge and facts to assessing the students' ability to reason and solve problems.

A broader view of assessment has incorporated a multidimensional approach to measurement, as described earlier under concerns for assessment of children from diverse populations and children with disabilities. It is now felt that too much attention has been given to the use of standardized tests, rather than a multidimensional approach that uses many sources of information. The more inclusive practice of assessment, which includes work samples, observation results, and teaching report forms, is called **alternative assessment.** These alternatives to standardized tests measure how students can apply the knowledge they have learned (Blum & Arter, 1996; Maeroff, 1991). Within this evolution in the purposes for assessment and interpretation of assessments is the move to authentic and performance assessments. **Authentic assessments** must have some connection to the real world; that is, they must have a meaningful context. They are contextual in that they emerge from the child's accomplishments. **Performance assessments** permit the child to demonstrate what is understood through the performance of a task or activity (Wortham, 1998).

Performance assessment as applied through the use of portfolios provides a multifaceted view of what the young child can understand and use. Performance assessment is used because teachers in early childhood programs are seeking information about the child's development and accomplishments in all domains. Performance assessment combined with other assessments provides a longitudinal record of change in development, rather than an assessment of a limited range of skills at a particular time. It is appropriately used with infants, young children, school-age children, children from diverse populations, and children with disabilities (Barrera, 1996; Meisels, 1996; Wortham, 1998).

This broader view of assessment in early childhood programs is echoed by the organizations that endorsed and supported the Guidelines for Appropriate Curriculum Content and Assessment in Programs Serving Children Ages 3 Through 8, a position statement of the National Association for the Education of Young Children and the National Association of Early Childhood Specialists in State Departments of Education adopted in 1990 (1992). These guidelines proposed that the purpose of assessment is to benefit individual children and to improve early childhood programs. Appropriate assessment should help to enhance curriculum choices, help teachers to collaborate with parents, and help to ensure that the needs of children are addressed appropriately. Rather than being narrowly defined as testing, assessment should link curriculum and instruction with program objectives for young children (Hills, 1992). Authentic and performance assessments provide dynamic assessment approaches that benefit the child, parents, and caregivers and teachers.

AN OVERVIEW OF TOPICS COVERED IN THIS BOOK

This text has been organized into four parts. In part I, Introduction to Assessment in Early Childhood, which consists of chapters 1 and 2, the reader is introduced to background information on the measurement process. This includes the history of measurement and evaluation and issues and trends in the assessment of young children discussed in this chapter.

Chapter 2, How Infants and Young Children Should Be Assessed, begins with what assessment should do for young children. Consideration of how assessment is used appropriately with young children is followed by a description of a comprehensive assessment system. The components of a comprehensive assessment system are the assessment strategies that are described in the following chapters of the text.

In the chapters that follow, assessment is discussed in terms of how it is applied to infants and young children. Basic information is provided about each topic in general, and then the application of the information to young children is explained. Issues regarding each topic are also explored. Thus, the background information needed to understand a facet of assessment is presented, as well as the pertinence of the assessment approach when used with young children. Standardized tests are discussed in part II, chapters 3 and 4, and informal assessments are explained in part III, chapters 5 through 8. In part IV, the focus is on assessment systems. Portfolio assessment is discussed in chapter 9. Finally, chapter 10 focuses on parents and how the child's progress and achievements should be exchanged and communicated. More information on each chapter follows.

Chapter 3, Standardized Tests: How They Are Used, Designed, and Selected, describes how standardized tests are used with children of different ages in the early childhood years and how they are designed. People who use these tests must know how they should be constructed and pilot tested before they are made available to the public. Administration of tests and interpretation of test scores are also covered. Many issues surround the use of standardized tests, particularly with young children. These issues are explained in a discussion of the advantages and disadvantages of using such tests with young children. Also provided are suggestions on how standardized tests should be evaluated and selected. The reader is directed to strategies for determining the quality of these tests by studying the test manual and reading reviews of the test in test review resources.

Standardized tests can be classified as having norm-referenced results, criterion-referenced results, or both. Chapter 4, Standardized Tests: Using and Reporting Standardized Test Results, discusses the distinctions between the two types of tests and how each is used with young children. An important part of test administration and interpretation is knowing how to share the information about test results. Teachers must know how to report a child's performance to parents, while school district personnel must report school and district results to school staff, administrators, and the board of education. Also discussed are the advantages and disadvantages of using criterion-referenced and norm-referenced results.

In chapter 5, Informal Assessments: Observation, the focus shifts from standardized tests to informal means of assessment. The meaning of informal measures is described, followed by purposes for using observation. The role of observation in understanding specific areas of development is explained to include physical, social and emotional, cognitive, and language development. Many strengths and weaknesses are inherent in the use of observation; these are discussed, and guidelines for observation are suggested.

Checklists, rating scales, and rubrics are instruments that can be used for evaluation purposes. Chapter 6, Informal Assessments: Checklists, Rating Scales, and Rubrics, describes appropriate uses for these measures. The chapter includes how to develop these assessments and how they are used appropriately with young children at different stages of development in the early childhood years. Advantages and disadvantages of using each measure are discussed, as well as how to design quality assessments.

Another type of informal measure is discussed in chapter 7, Informal Assessments: Teacher-Designed Strategies. Teacher-conducted assessments designed for preschool children must be task oriented, rather than pencil-and-paper activities; various measures are discussed separately. Constructed response and selected response tests are developed as children transition into literacy. Designing a teacher-conducted assessment includes designing test objectives, constructing a table of specifications, organizing the instrument or tasks, and providing for instruction and extensions and correctives.

Chapter 8, Informal Assessments: Performance-Based Strategies, expands the concept of informal assessment to include performance assessments in which the children's progress is evaluated through an activity that permits the child to demonstrate understanding or accomplishment. Sometimes called authentic assessments, performance assessments include teacher-directed activities such as interviews with the child or child-initiated activities in which the child's natural interactions with materials or play activity allow the teacher to observe progress.

Chapter 9, Assessment Systems: Portfolio Assessment, first discusses purposes for portfolio assessments, followed by different types of portfolios. Steps in setting up portfolios are described, as well as examples of portfolio design used with young children.

Chapter 10, Assessment Systems: Communicating with Parents, discusses how to synthesize children's progress through narrative reports. Examples of assessment and reporting systems are discussed, as well as how to communicate student progress to parents. Planning and conducting parent conferences is part of the reporting process, as is involving parents in the evaluation and reporting process.

 ## SUMMARY

The measurement and assessment of children begins very early in the life-span. Newborns are tested for their neonatal status, and infant tests designed to assess development begin the trend for testing and assessment in the early childhood years. Assessments in the early childhood years have many purposes; some are beneficial for young children, while others are detrimental.

The advent of measures to assess and evaluate young children's development and learning began at the turn of the century. As the decades passed, significant trends in the study of young children and services and programs implemented for young children have driven the need to develop standardized tests and other measures to evaluate children's progress and program effectiveness.

There are issues surrounding the testing of young children. One may question the validity and reliability of standardized tests used with young children, as well as the purposes for administering tests to children who are culturally and linguistically diverse. At the same time, the value of using tests to identify and provide services for children with disabilities continues as a positive purpose for individual testing and evaluation.

REVIEW QUESTIONS

1. Why are very young children measured in infancy and the preschool years? Give examples.
2. Explain developmental deficits. How are developmental deficits identified and treated?
3. Why is research conducted on the development of very young children? How can such research be used?
4. How were Pestalozzi and Rousseau pivotal in the origins of understanding and measuring young children?
5. Why has the child study movement been the major resource for understanding child development?
6. How does the history of standardized testing include testing with infants and young children? What kinds of standardized tests are beneficial for children under age 6?
7. Why were standardized tests developed for Head Start? How were they used?
8. Why were standardized tests developed as a result of legislation for young children with disabilities? How are they used?
9. Why is it difficult to develop assessments for children who are culturally and linguistically different? What factors must be addressed in their assessment?
10. What are some of the weaknesses in assessments of young children with disabilities? How can these difficulties be overcome?
11. How is authentic assessment different from assessment using standardized tests?

SUGGESTED ACTIVITY

Review a recent journal article on a topic related to current issues in the testing and assessment of young children. The article should have been published within the last 5 years. Describe the major points in the article and your response. Be prepared to share in small groups.

KEY TERMS

alternative assessment
authentic assessment
inclusion

integration
mainstreaming
performance assessment

REFERENCES

Barrera, I. (1996). Thoughts on the assessment of young children whose sociocultural background is unfamiliar to the assessor. In S. J. Meisels & E. Fenichel (Eds.), *New visions for the developmental assessment of infants and young children* (pp. 69–84). Washington, DC: ZERO TO THREE: National Center for Infants, Toddlers, and Families.

Begley, S. (1997, Spring/Summer). How to build a baby's brain. *Newsweek Special Edition,* 28–32.

Blum, R. E., & Arter, J. A. (1996). Setting the stage. In R. E. Blum & J. A. Arter (Eds.), *A handbook for student performance assessment in an era of restructuring* (pp. 1:1–1:2). Alexandria, VA: Association for Supervision and Curriculum Development.

Cicchetti, D., & Wagner, S. (1990). Alternative assessment strategies for the evaluation of infants and toddlers: An organizational perspective. In S. J. Meisels & J. P. Shonkoff (Eds.), *Handbook of early childhood intervention* (pp. 246–277). New York: Cambridge University Press.

Clark, E. A. (1976). Teacher attitudes toward integration of children with handicaps. *Education and Training of the Mentally Retarded, 11,* 333–335.

Cronbach, L. J. (1990). *Essentials of psychological testing* (5th ed.). New York: Harper & Row.

Deiner, P. L. (1993). *Resources for teaching children with diverse abilities.* Fort Worth, TX: Harcourt Brace Jovanovich.

Early Head Start. (2000, December). What is Early Head Start? [online]. Available: www.chnrc.org/chs.htm

Fewell, R. R., & Rich, J. (1987). Play assessment as a procedure for examining cognitive, communication and social skills in multihandicapped children. *Journal of Psychoeducational Assessment, 2,* 107–118.

Froebel, F. (1896). *Education of man.* New York: Appleton.

Gardner, J. W. (1961). *Excellence: Can we be equal and excellent too?* New York: Harper & Row.

Goodwin, W. L., & Goodwin, L. D. (1982). Measuring young children. In B. Spodek (Ed.), *Handbook of research in early childhood education* (pp. 523–563). New York: Free Press.

Goodwin, W. L., & Goodwin, L. D. (1993). Young children and measurement: Standardized and nonstandardized instruments in early childhood education. In B. Spodek (Ed.), *Handbook of research on the education of young children* (pp. 441–463). New York: Macmillan.

Goodwin, W. L., & Goodwin, L. D. (1997). Using standardized measures for evaluating young children's learning. In B. Spodek & O. N. Saracho (Eds.), *Issues in early childhood educational assessment and evaluation* (pp. 92–107). New York: Teachers College Press.

Greenspan, S. I., Meisels, S. J., & the ZERO TO THREE Work Group on Developmental Assessment. (1996). Toward a new vision for the developmental assessment of infants and young children. In S. J. Meisels & E. Fenichel (Eds.), *New visions for the developmental assessment of infants and young children* (pp. 11–26). Washington, DC: ZERO TO THREE: National Center for Infants, Toddlers, and Families.

Grissom, S. (2002, April 4). The message from the Early Childhood Institute. E-mail message.

Guralnick, M. J. (1982). Mainstreaming young handicapped children: A public policy and ecological systems analysis. In B. Spodek (Ed.), *Handbook of research on the education of young children* (pp. 456–500). New York: Free Press.

Hills, T. W. (1992). Reaching potentials through appropriate assessment. In S. Bredekamp & T. Rosegrant (Eds.), *Reaching potentials: Appropriate curriculum and assessment for young children* (pp. 43–64). Washington, DC: National Association for the Education of Young Children.

Hoepfner, R., Stern, C., & Nummedal, S. (Eds.). (1971). *CSE-ECRC preschool/kindergarten test evaluations.* Los

Angeles: University of California, Graduate School of Education.

Irwin, D. M., & Bushnell, M. M. (1980). *Observational strategies for child study*. New York: Holt, Rinehart & Winston.

Kaplan, R. M., & Saccuzzo, D. P. (1989). *Psychological testing principles: Applications and issues* (2nd ed.). Belmont, CA: Brooks/Cole.

Kessen, W. (1965). *The child*. New York: Wiley.

Krick, J. C. (1992). All children are special. In B. Neugebauer (Ed.), *Alike and different: Exploring our humanity with young children* (Rev. ed., pp. 152–158). Washington, DC: National Association for the Education of Young Children.

Laosa, L. M. (1982). The sociocultural context of evaluation. In B. Spodek (Ed.), *Handbook of research in early childhood education* (pp. 501–520). New York: Free Press.

Locke, J. (1699). *Some thoughts concerning education* (4th ed.). London: A & J Churchill.

Maeroff, G. I. (1991, December). Assessing alternative assessment. *Phi Delta Kappan, 272–281.*

McCollum, J. A., & Maude, S. P. (1993). Portrait of a changing field: Policy and practice in early childhood special education. In B. Spodek (Ed.), *Handbook of research on the education of young children* (pp. 352–371). New York: Macmillan.

Mc Maken, J. (2000, March). *Early childhood assessment*. Denver, CO: Education Commission of the States. Available: www.ecs.org

Mehrens, W. A., & Lehmann, L. J. (1991). *Measurement and evaluation in education and psychology* (4th ed.). New York: Harcourt Brace.

Meisels, S. J. (1996). Charting the continuum of assessment and intervention. In S. J. Meisels & E. Fenichel (Eds.), *New visions for the developmental assessment of infants and young children* (pp. 27–52). Washington, DC: ZERO TO THREE: National Center for Infants, Toddlers, and Families.

Meisels, S. J., & Fenichel, E. (Eds.). (1996). *New visions for the developmental assessment of infants and young children*. Washington, DC: ZERO TO THREE: National Center for Infants, Toddlers, and Families.

Meisels, S. J., & Shonkoff, J. P. (Eds.). (1990). *Handbook of early childhood intervention*. New York: Cambridge University Press.

Meisels, S. J., Steele, D. M., & Quinn-Leering, K. (1993). Testing, tracking, and retaining young children: An analysis of research and social policy. In B. Spodek (Ed.), *Handbook of research on the education of young children* (pp. 279–292). New York: Macmillan.

Monroe, W. S. (1918). Existing tests and standards. In G. W. Whipple (Ed.), *The measurement of educational products. 14th yearbook of the National Society for the Study of Education, Part II* (pp. 71–104). Bloomington, IL: Public School Publishing.

Moscoso, E. (2001, December, 14). New federal education law passes. *Austin American Statesman*, A4.

Nagle, R. J. (2000). Issues in preschool assessment. In B. Bracken (ed.), *Principles and recommendations for early childhood assessments*. Washington, DC: National Goals Panel.

National Association for the Education of Young Children and the National Association of Early Childhood Specialists in State Departments of Education. (1992). Guidelines for appropriate curriculum content and assessment in programs serving children ages 3 through 8. In S. Bredekamp & T. Rosegrant (Eds.), *Reaching potentials: Appropriate curriculum and assessment for young children* (pp. 9–27). Washington, DC: Authors.

National Association for the Education of Young Children (2001). Still! Unacceptable trends for kindergarten entry and placement. *Young Children, 56,* 59–61.

National Association of Early Childhood Specialists in State Departments of Education (2000). *Still! Unacceptable trends in kindergarten entry and placement*. Washington, DC: Author.

National Council for the Social Studies (2001). *Curriculum standards for social studies*. [Online]. Available: www.ncss.org/standards/1.1.html.

National Governors Association Center for Best Practices (2002). No Child Left Behind Act. [Online]. Available: www.nga.org/center/topics.

Newmann, F. M. (1996). Introduction: The school restructuring study. In F. M. Newmann & Associates, *Authentic achievement: Restructuring schools for intellectual quality* (pp. 1–16). San Francisco: Jossey-Bass.

Raymond, G., & McIntosh, D. K. (1992). The impact of current changes in social structure on early childhood education programs. In B. Neugebauer (Ed.), *Alike and different: Exploring our humanity with young children* (Rev. ed., pp. 116–126). Washington, DC: National Association for the Education of Young Children.

Rivas, G. A. *Bilingual assessment*. (No date). [Online]. Available: www.hieducation.org.

Rousseau, J. J. (1911). *Emile or on education* (B. Foxley, Trans.). London: Dent. (Original work published in 1762.)

Scherer, M. (1999). Perspectives/measures and mismeasures. *Educational Leadership, 56,* 5.

Segal, M., & Webber, N. T. (1996). Nonstructured play observations: Guidelines, benefits, and caveats. In S. J. Meisels & E. Fenichel (Eds.), *New visions for the developmental assessment of infants and young children* (pp. 207–230). Washington, DC: ZERO TO THREE: National Center for Infants, Toddlers, and Families.

Shepard, L., Kagan, S. L., Lynn, S., & Wurtz, E. (1998). *Principles and recommendations for early childhood assessments*. Washington, DC: National Goals Panel.

Shore, R. (1997). *Rethinking the brain*. New York: Families and Work Institute.

Smith, S. S. (1999). Reforming the kindergarten round-up. *Educational Leadership, 56,* 39–44.

Spodek, B., & Saracho, O. N. (1994). *Dealing with individual differences in the early childhood classroom*. New York: Longman.

Stein, J. U. (1993). Critical issues: Mismanagement, informed consent, and participant safety. In S. J. Grosse, & D. Thompson (Eds.), *Leisure opportunities for individuals with disabilities: Legal issues* (pp. 37–54). Reston, VA: American Alliance for Health, Physical Education, Recreation, and Dance.

Weber, E. (1984). *Ideas influencing early childhood education. A theoretical analysis*. New York: Teachers College Press.

Wesson, K. A. (2001). "The Volvo effect"—Questioning standardized tests. *Young Children, 56,* 16–18.

White, S. H. (1973). *Federal programs for young children: Review and recommendations* (Vol. 13). Washington, DC: Government Printing Office.

Wiggins, G. P. (1993). *Assessing student performance*. San Francisco: Jossey-Bass.

Wolery, M., Strain, P. S., & Bailey, D. B. (1992). Reaching potentials of children with special needs. In S. Bredekamp & T. Rosegrant (Eds.), *Reaching potentials: Appropriate curriculum and assessment for young children* (pp. 92–112). Washington, DC: National Association for the Education of Young Children.

Wolery, M., & Wilbers, J. S. (Eds.). (1994). *Including children with special needs in early childhood programs*. Washington, DC: National Association for the Education of Young Children.

Wortham, S. C. (1998). Introduction. In S. C. Wortham, A. Barbour, & B. Desjean-Perrotta, *Portfolio assessment: A handbook for preschool and elementary educators* (pp. 7–13). Olney, MD: Association for Childhood Education International.

Wortham, S. C. (2002). *Childhood 1892–2002*. (2nd ed.). Olney, MD: Association for Childhood Education International.

Zigler, E., & Valentine, J. (Eds.). (1979). *Project Head Start: A legacy of the War on Poverty*. New York: Free Press.

CHAPTER 2

How Infants and Young Children Should Be Assessed

Chapter Objectives

As a result of reading this chapter, you will be able to

1. Discuss how assessment should be improved for the 21st century
2. Describe how assessment should be used in early childhood
3. Describe how measurement and evaluation are used with infants, preschoolers, and school-age children
4. Understand the differences between formal and informal assessments
5. Describe different types of informal assessments
6. Explain how performance assessments reflect authentic learning

T he topic of assessing young children was introduced in chapter 1. The fact that infants and preschool children are measured differently from older children and adults was discussed, as was the evolution of testing and assessment in the United States. Also discussed were issues and trends in assessment as we enter a new century in early childhood education.

In this chapter, methods of assessing infants and children will be described. The focus will be on the future and what assessment should do, as well as how assessment should specifically serve children in the early childhood years. The components of a comprehensive assessment system will be described, followed by how assessment results are used in preschool and school settings.

WHAT ASSESSMENT SHOULD DO

The history of assessment is cumulative. This means that each era in the history of measuring children has provided methods for assessment that are still in use today. Although there are issues as to when and how some of the methods are used, as discussed in chapter 1, all contributions are still relevant in some context to learn about children's development and learning. The goal of the discussion in this part of the chapter is to address the concerns and issues raised about testing and evaluation of young children and to set criteria for higher goals for the process. The objective is not to eliminate established methods and replace them with new ones, but to formulate how to use each most effectively to serve the needs of the child. First, criteria for optimal approaches to assessment will be described generally, followed by how assessment should be used for the benefit of young children specifically.

PRINCIPLES FOR ASSESSMENT

ASSESSMENT SHOULD USE MULTIPLE SOURCES OF INFORMATION. No matter what strategy is used for assessment, a single application for evaluation is insufficient (Greenspan & Meisels, 1996). Each assessment strategy has strengths and limitations; moreover, a single method provides only one portion of what needs to be known about a child. A variety of strategies provides a comprehensive picture of the child's development and learning from different perspectives (Feld & Bergan, 2002). For infants and toddlers, several observations are better than a single observation, and other inputs into development, such as parents and caregivers' views of the child, provide a more complete picture of the child's progress. For older children who have entered school, achievement of learning becomes important. The kindergarten and school-age child should be able to demonstrate learning in more than one way and on more than one occasion. Use of a variety of measures of learning ensures an accurate view of the child's accomplishments (Greenspan & Meisels et al., 1996; National Education Association, 1994; Shepard, 1989; Wiggins, 1993).

ASSESSMENT SHOULD BENEFIT THE CHILD AND IMPROVE LEARNING. When infants and toddlers are evaluated, the purpose is generally to determine if the child is developing normally or exhibits delay and needs assistance or intervention. The purposes of assessment are to benefit the child. When young children enter school, however, assessments can have negative purposes that are not related to the needs and interests of the child.

As is discussed elsewhere in this text, tests are sometimes administered to young children to determine if they can be admitted to a preschool program or promoted in grade. In the primary grades, tests are administered to determine the child's achievement during a school year. When such tests are given to determine the child's progress and to plan appropriate instruction based on what the child has accomplished, the purpose will benefit the child and improve learning. On the other hand, when such tests are used merely for evaluation of the school program and have no implications for how the child will be served, they are not beneficial to the child and should not be used. Whatever assessment strategies are used, the information should be used to guide the child and enhance learning (Wiggins, 1993, 1998).

ASSESSMENT SHOULD INVOLVE THE CHILD AND FAMILY. Infants and toddlers are unable to understand their developmental progress; however, their parents and caregivers are primary sources of information. Although tests can be administered to measure development, a parent's knowledge about the child is essential for a true understanding of the child's developmental characteristics (Popper, 1996; Rocco, 1996).

Preschool, kindergarten, and primary school children are more able to understand what they know and what they are able to do. This ability increases with the child's age and maturity. However, parental input is still very important. By the time the child is in the primary grades, self-assessment improves. Students can evaluate their progress and have a voice in how they can best succeed in mastering learning objectives. Assessment is not just administered to students, but accomplished with active participation by the student.

ASSESSMENT SHOULD BE FAIR FOR ALL CHILDREN. In chapter 1, it was pointed out that many tests are inappropriate for children who are culturally or linguistically different. In addition, there must be concern that children with disabilities are evaluated accurately and fairly. Because tests may not reflect a child's culture or language, other methods must be employed that are more effective. As was mentioned earlier, a variety of strategies can overcome the limitations of a single method or test. The person administering the evaluation must be alert to limitations and have other strategies to acquire the needed information. This is especially important in the case of children who are culturally and linguistically different or whose abilities are outside normal developmental ranges (Barrera, 1996; Goodwin & Goodwin, 1993).

ASSESSMENT SHOULD BE AUTHENTIC. Each assessment strategy provides information using a different method. Until recent decades, the type of information focused on what children have learned. While infants, toddlers, and children under age 6 demonstrated what they could do developmentally, measurement in school-age children focused on the child's achievement in the content areas. With the advent of authentic assessment, another dimension has been included. The assessment should be meaningful to the child's experiences and reflect how the child can apply knowledge in a real context. This broadens the purposes of assessment for young children. It is child centered and pertinent to the child's background. Authentic assessment is used to accurately measure the learning outcomes used to plan the child's learning program, which is grounded in the child's interests and what the child has experienced (Winograd & Perkins, 1996).

PRINCIPLES FOR EARLY CHILDHOOD ASSESSMENTS

In 1990, then President George Bush and the nation's governors established national education goals that were to be accomplished by the year 2000. Goal 1 was stated as follows: "By the year 2000, all children in America will start school ready to learn." Concerns about how this goal was to be measured, and the unique challenges of measuring children in the early childhood years, led to the establishment of the National Early Childhood Assessments Resource Group to establish principles and recommendations. The following principles were developed by this group (National Education Goals Panel, 1998, pp. 4–5):

Assessment should bring about benefits for children.   Gathering accurate information from young children is difficult and potentially stressful. Formal assessments may also be costly and take resources that could otherwise be spent directly on programs and services for young children. To warrant conducting assessments, there must be a clear benefit—either in direct services to the child or in improved quality of educational programs.

Assessments should be tailored to a specific purpose and should be reliable, valid, and fair for that purpose.   Assessments designed for one purpose are not necessarily valid if used for other purposes. In the past, many of the abuses of testing with young children have occurred because of misuse. The recommendations in the sections that follow are tailored to specific purposes.

Assessment policies should be designed recognizing that reliability and validity of assessments increase with children's age.   The younger the child, the more difficult it is to obtain reliable and valid assessment data. It is particularly difficult to assess children's cognitive abilities accurately before age 6. Because of problems with reliability and validity, some types of assessment should be postponed until children are older, while other types of assessment can be pursued, but only with necessary safeguards.

Assessments should be age appropriate in both content and the method of data collection.   Assessments of young children should address the full range of early learning and development, including physical well-being and motor development; social and emotional development; approaches toward learning; language development; and cognition and general knowledge. Methods of assessment should recognize that children need familiar contexts in order to be able to demonstrate their abilities. Abstract paper-and-pencil tasks may make it especially difficult for young children to show what they know.

Assessments should be linguistically appropriate, recognizing that to some extent all assessments are measures of language.   Regardless of whether an assessment is intended to measure early reading skills, knowledge of color names, or learning potential, assessment results are easily confounded by language proficiency, especially for children who come from home backgrounds with limited exposure to English, for whom the assessment would essentially be an assessment of their English proficiency. Each child's first- and second-language development should be taken into account when determining appropriate assessment methods and in interpreting the meaning of assessment results.

Parents should be a valued source of assessment information, as well as an audience for assessment results.   Because of the fallibility of direct measures of young children, assessments should include multiple sources of evidence, especially reports from parents and teachers. Assessment results should be shared with parents as part of an ongoing process that involves parents in their child's education.

The National Early Childhood Assessment Resource Group further describes appropriate uses of assessment that should be used in the early childhood years as follows: (1) assessments to support learning, (2) assessments for identification of special needs, (3) assessments for program evaluation and monitoring needs, and (4) assessments for high-stakes accountability. Figure 2.1 describes these four purposes and how they change across the early childhood years.

FIGURE 2–1 Purposes for early childhood assessments.

Appropriate Uses and Technical Accuracy of Assessments Change Across

Birth	1	2	3	4

Purpose 1: Assessing to promote children's learning and development

Parents and caregivers observe and respond as children develop language and physical skills.	Parents, caregivers, and preschool teachers use direct measures, including observations of what children are learning to decide what to teach next.

Purpose 2: Identifying children for health and special services

All children should be screened regularly for health needs, including hearing and vision checks, as part of routine health care services.	Children entering Head Start and other preschool programs should be screened for health needs, including hearing and vision checks.
Many serious cognitive and physical disabilities are evident at birth or soon thereafter. As soon as developmental delays or potential disabilities are suspected, parents and physicians should seek in-depth assessments.	Individual children with possible developmental delays should be referred for in-depth assessment.

Purpose 3: Monitoring trends and evaluating programs and services

Because direct measures of children's language and cognitive functioning are difficult to aggregate accurately for ages from birth to 2, state reporting systems should focus on living and social conditions that affect learning and the adequacy of services.	Assessments, including direct and indirect measures of children's physical, social, emotional, and cognitive development, could be constructed and used to evaluate prekindergarten programs, but such measures would not be accurate enough to make high-stakes decisions about individual children.

Purpose 4: Assessing academic achievement to hold individual students,

---

Source: Shepard, L., Kagan, S. L., & Wurtz, E. (Eds.). (1998). *Principles and recommendations for early childhood assessments.* Washington, DC: *Report to the National Education Goals Panel,* pp. 20–21. Washington, DC: US Government Printing Office.

the Early Childhood Age Continuum (Birth to Age 8).

Kindergarten	1st grade	2nd grade	3rd grade	
5	6	7	8 years	Beyond age 8

Teachers use both formal and informal assessments to plan and guide instruction.

All children should be screened at school entry for vision and hearing needs and checked for immunizations.

Some mild disabilities may only become apparent in the school context. Districts and states must by law have sound teacher and parent referral policies so that children with potential disabilities are referred for in-depth assessment.

Beginning at age 5, it is possible to use direct measures, including measures of children's early learning, as part of a comprehensive early childhood assessment for monitoring trends. Matrix sampling should be used to ensure technical accuracy and to provide safeguards for individual children. Because of the cost of such an assessment, states or the nation should pick one grade level for monitoring trends in early childhood, most likely kindergarten or first grade.

teachers, and school accountable

Before age 8, standardized achievement measures are not sufficiently accurate to be used for high-stakes decisions about individual children and schools. Therefore, high-stakes assessments intended for accountability purposes should be delayed until the end of third grade (or preferably fourth grade).

HOW INFANTS AND YOUNG CHILDREN ARE ASSESSED

As exemplified in the *Principles and Recommendations for Early Childhood Assessments* (National Education Goals Panel, 1998) just discussed, there are many reasons for measuring and evaluating young children, and various methods are available to accomplish our goals. Sometimes we measure the child informally. We might look for characteristics by watching the child's behaviors at play or in a setting arranged for that purpose. A pediatrician may watch a baby walk during an examination to determine whether he or she is progressing normally. In a similar fashion, a teacher may observe a child playing to determine how he or she is using language. A second-grade teacher who constructs a set of subtraction problems to evaluate whether his students have mastered a mathematics objective is also using an **informal test.**

Formal methods, or standardized instruments, are also used for measurement and evaluation. These are more extensive and proven measures for evaluation. Specialists in tests and measurements design and then try out, with a large number of children, instruments that evaluate the characteristics that have been targeted. This process ensures that they can use the information gained each time the test is given to another child or group of children. This type of test is called a **standardized test** because a standard has been set from the results achieved by using the test with children who are representative of the population.

Why do we measure infants and young children? The most common purpose is to assess development. Soon after a child's birth, the **obstetrician** or **pediatrician** evaluates the newborn by using the *Apgar Scale* (Apgar, 1975) to determine whether he or she is in good health. Thereafter, at regular intervals, parents, doctors, and teachers follow the baby's development by using tests and informal evaluation strategies (Greenspan & Meisels et al., 1996; Wodrich, 1984). The screening test for phenylketonuria (PKU) may also be administered to detect the presence of the enzyme phenylalanine, which can cause mental retardation if not managed through diet. In addition, there are newborn screening tests for cystic fibrosis and congenital hypothyroidism (Widerstrom, Mowder, & Sandall, 1991).

But what if development is not progressing normally? How can evaluation measures be used to help the young child? In recent years, researchers, medical specialists, and educators have learned how to work with children at increasingly younger ages to minimize the effects of delays in growth or other problems that retard the child's developmental progress. Various strategies and instruments are now available. A **neonatologist** conducts a comprehensive evaluation on a premature baby to determine what therapy should be initiated to improve the infant's chances for survival and optimal development. A young child can be tested for hearing loss or mental retardation. The child who does not speak normally or who is late in speaking is referred to a speech pathologist, who assesses the child's language and prescribes activities to facilitate improved language development.

During a child's infancy and toddler years, child development specialists follow the child's progress and initiate therapy when development is not normal (Meisels, 1996). During the preschool years, this effort includes evaluating and predicting whether the child is likely to experience difficulties in learning. Tests and other measures are used to help to determine whether the child will develop a **learning disability** and how that disability will affect his or her success in school. Again, when problems are detected, plans are made to work with the child in a timely manner to help him or her to overcome as much of the disability as possible before entering school. The child may have a vision problem, difficulty in hearing, or a disability that may interfere with learning to read. The evaluation measures used will assist in identifying the exact nature of the problem. In addition, test results will be used to help determine what kind of intervention will be most successful (Greenspan & Meisels et al., 1996; Wodrich, 1984).

ASSESSMENT FOR RISK IN DEVELOPMENTAL STATUS

When Sarah was 6 months old, her teenage mother gave her up for adoption. Because Sarah's father could not be located to agree to release her for adoption, Sarah was placed temporarily in a foster home.

Prior to placement with the foster family, Sarah had lived with her mother in her maternal grandparents' home. In addition to Sarah's mother, six other children were in the family. Both grandparents were employed. Sarah's primary caregiver had been an aunt with mental retardation who was 12 years old.

For the first few days after Sarah was placed in the foster home, she cried when the foster parents tried to feed her. She sat for long periods of time and stared vacantly without reacting to toys or people. She had no established patterns for sleeping and usually fretted off and on during the night.

When Sarah was examined by a pediatrician, she was found to be malnourished, with sores in her mouth from vitamin deficiencies. As determined by the *Denver Developmental Screening Test,* she was developing much more slowly than normal.

A special diet and multivitamins were prescribed for Sarah. Members of the foster family patiently taught her to enjoy eating a varied diet beyond the chocolate milk and cereal that she had been fed previously. Regular times for sleeping at night gradually replaced her erratic sleeping habits. Her foster family spent many hours playing with her, talking with her, and introducing her to various toys.

By the age of 11 months, Sarah had improved greatly. She was alert, ate well, began to walk, and said a few words. Her development was within the normal range, and she was ready for adoption.

Sarah had benefited from being placed in a home where she received good nutrition, guidance in living patterns, and stimulation for cognitive, physical, and social development. Without early intervention, Sarah's delay in development might have become more serious over time. Adaptability to an adoptive home might have been difficult for her and her adoptive parents. If she had been unable to adjust successfully with an adoptive family, she might have spent her childhood years in a series of foster homes, rather than with her adoptive family. She also would have been at risk for learning, beginning in the first years of schooling.

During the preschool period or even earlier, a different kind of developmental difference may emerge. Parents or other adults who deal with the child may observe that the child demonstrates a learning ability or potential that is much higher than the normal range. A more formal evaluation using a standardized test may confirm these informal observations.

Plans then can be made to facilitate the child's development to help him or her to achieve full potential for learning.

COMBATING LIMITATIONS IN VOCABULARY AND CONCEPT DEVELOPMENT

Micah, who is 4 years old, is the sixth child in a family of seven children. Both of his parents work, and he and his younger brother are cared for by a grandmother during the day. Although Micah's parents are warm and loving, their combined income is barely enough to provide the basic necessities for the family. They are unable to buy books and toys that will enhance Micah's development. Because the family rarely travels outside the immediate neighborhood, Micah has had few experiences that would broaden his knowledge of the larger community.

Fortunately, Micah's family lives in a state that provides a program for 4-year-old children who can benefit from a prekindergarten class that stresses language and cognitive development. The program serves all children who come from low-income homes or who exhibit language or cognitive delay.

In response to a letter sent by the school district, Micah's grandmother took him to the school to be tested for the program. Micah's performance on the test showed that he uses a limited expressive vocabulary and lacks many basic concepts. When school begins in late August, Micah will start school with his older brothers and sisters and will be enrolled in the prekindergarten class.

Micah will have the opportunity to play with puzzles, construction toys, and other manipulative objects that will facilitate his cognitive development. Stories will be read and discussed each day, and Micah will be able to look at a variety of books. Micah's teacher will introduce learning experiences that will allow Micah to learn about shapes, colors, numbers, and many other concepts that will provide a foundation for learning in the elementary school grades.

Micah will also travel with his classmates to visit places that will help him to learn about the community. They may visit a furniture or grocery store or a bread factory. Visitors to the classroom will add to the students' knowledge about occupations and cultures represented in the community. The children will have opportunities to paint, participate in cooking experiences, and talk about the new things they are learning. They will dictate stories about their experiences and learn many songs and games. When Micah enters kindergarten the following year, he will use the knowledge and language he learned in prekindergarten to help him to learn successfully along with his 5-year-old peers.

Although potential for learning may be assessed at a very early age in the child who is gifted or talented, learning aptitude may also be evaluated in the general population during the preschool and primary school years. Educators wish to determine children's learning abilities and needs, as well as the types of programs that will be most beneficial for them. Informal strategies and formal tests are used with individual children and groups of children to assess what and how much they have already learned and to evaluate weak areas that can be given special attention. Informal and formal strategies are also used to evaluate the success of programs that serve children, as well as provide indicators for how programs can be improved.

DEVELOPING A COMPREHENSIVE SYSTEM OF ASSESSMENT

If measurement and evaluation of infants and young children is to follow the criteria for assessment in a new century, a system for assessment should be developed. The combination of measurement methods used will depend on the uses for the system, but, overall, many of the components to be described will be included in any plan for evaluation.

COMPONENTS OF AN ASSESSMENT SYSTEM

STANDARDIZED TESTS. Standardized tests are designed to measure individual characteristics. The test may be administered to an individual or to a group. The purpose of standardized tests is to measure abilities, achievements, aptitudes, interests, attitudes, values, and personality characteristics. The results can be used to plan instruction, to study differences between individuals and groups, and for counseling and guidance.

INFORMAL ASSESSMENT STRATEGIES. Standardized tests are not the only tools available for evaluation and assessment. Various types of informal instruments and strategies to determine development and learning are available as well.

School districts often use informal tests or evaluation strategies developed by local teachers or staff members. In early childhood programs, an informal screening test may be administered to preschool children at registration to determine their instructional needs. Likewise, the speech teacher may use a simple screening instrument to evaluate the child's language development or possible speech difficulties.

Observation. One of the most valuable ways to become aware of the individual characteristics of young children is through observation. Developmental indicators in early childhood are more likely to be noted from children's behavior in natural circumstances than

Teachers can use a variety of informal strategies to assess learning.

from a designed assessment or instrument. Adults who observe children as they play and work in individual or group activities are able to determine progress in all categories of development (Segal & Webber, 1996). The child who shows evidence of emerging prosocial skills by playing successfully in the playground is demonstrating significant growth in social development. Children who struggle to balance materials on both sides of a balance scale demonstrate visible signs of cognitive growth. Physical development can be evaluated by the observation of children using playground equipment. Because young children learn best through active involvement with their environment, evaluation of learning may be assessed most appropriately by observation of the child during periods of activity. Observation records can be used to plan instruction, to report progress in various areas of development, and to keep track of progress in mastery of preschool curriculum objectives.

Teacher-Designed Measures. Teachers have always used tests that they have devised to measure the level of learning after instruction. Early childhood teachers are more likely to use concrete tasks or oral questions for informal assessment with young children. Teachers frequently incorporate evaluation with instruction or learning experiences. Activities and games can be used both to teach and to evaluate what the child has learned. Evaluation can also be conducted through learning centers or as part of a teacher-directed lesson. Although pencil-and-paper tests are also a teacher-designed measure, they should not be used until children are comfortable with reading and writing.

Checklists. **Developmental checklists** or other forms of learning objective sequences are used at all levels of preschool, elementary, and secondary schools. Often referred to as a **scope** or **sequence of skills**, a checklist is a list of the learning objectives established for areas of learning and development at a particular age, grade level, or content area. Many checklists are standardized, while others are locally developed by a teacher or school district and are not standardized.

Skills continuums are available from many sources. The teacher may construct one, or a school district may distribute checklists for each grade level. Educational textbook publishers frequently include a skills continuum for teachers to use as an instructional guide with the textbook they have selected. State education agencies now publish objectives to be used by all school districts in the state.

Rating Scales. **Rating scales** are similar to checklists. They contain criteria for measurement that can be based on learning objectives or other factors. The major difference between checklists and rating scales is that rating scales provide for measurement on a continuum. Checklist items are rated with a negative or positive response. Rating scales can be used for many purposes when a range of criteria is needed to acquire accurate information.

Rubrics. **Rubrics** have been developed to evaluate authentic and performance assessments. They include a range of criteria like rating scales, but have indicators that can be used to determine quality of performance or to assign a grade. Rubrics are used most frequently with portfolio assessment, but are appropriate for performance assessment that is not part of a portfolio.

Performance and Portfolio Assessments. Additional forms of informal assessments focus on more meaningful types of evaluation of student learning. Sometimes called **performance assessments** or **authentic assessments** (Goodwin & Goodwin, 1993; Wiggins, 1993), these evaluation measures use strategies that permit the child to demonstrate his or her understanding of a concept or mastery of a skill. The evaluation might take the form of a teacher-directed **interview** in which a dialogue with the child would reveal the child's thinking and understanding. Other procedures might include games, **directed assignments,** or activities related to a project.

Processes for reporting student progress related to outcome-based or authentic assessments are also intended to communicate learning and development from a meaningful perspective. Traditional report cards and standardized test results do not necessarily reflect accurately the student's progress. **Portfolios** with samples of student work are one type of reporting of progress that is compatible with outcome-based assessment. A detailed narrative or **narrative report** of the student's progress developed by the teacher is another process that enables the teacher to describe the nature of the child's activities that have resulted in achievement and learning.

Technology-Based Assessments.   Early childhood educators in the 21st century have access to computers and assessments that are available through technology. One source of technological assessment is **assessment software.** Assessments from computer software can be an adaptation of paper-based assessments, such as reading or mathematics checklists, or assessments that are linked to a specific curriculum. Other software can be acquired that permits the design of activities and lesson plans or continuous revision of assessment tools.

Assessment resources are also available on the Internet. **Electronic management of learning (EML)** makes it possible to collect, analyze, and report progress in children's learning that can then be used to document learning outcomes and plan for subsequent learning objectives and activities. This type of assessment management utilizes Web pages. Through EML it is possible for parents, teachers, and administrators to access information about children's learning and assessment-based curriculum planning (Feld & Bergan, 2002).

USING ASSESSMENT RESULTS

Earlier in the chapter, we discussed the kinds of assessments that are needed for a new century. Components of a comprehensive system of evaluation were described. Now, how and when the system of assessment should be used can be summarized. The discussion will relate to preschool and primary-grade children rather than infants and toddlers. In keeping with the premise that assessment should benefit the child and improve learning, three primary purposes for comprehensive assessment can be reviewed: assessments can be used to plan for instruction, to report progress, and to evaluate the instructional program.

Assessment occurs throughout the year. The teacher employs assessment strategies to plan for instruction, to determine and report progress, and to evaluate the effectiveness of instruction continuously from the beginning until the end of the school term.

USING ASSESSMENT RESULTS TO PLAN FOR INSTRUCTION

If assessments should benefit the child, then assessments in preschool and primary-grade settings should be linked to learning experiences and instruction. If they are to be fair for all children and authentic, they will include all types of strategies that will provide a comprehensive picture of each child's progress and needs. The teacher will select the assessment methods that are relevant to the information needed and use the results in planning for curriculum and instruction. This assumes that the teacher will be concerned with individual rates of development and learning and will be prepared to address individual differences. The learning activities that are available in the classroom and through teacher instruction reflect not only curriculum goals established by the school, but also how each child can best achieve these goals.

USING ASSESSMENT RESULTS TO REPORT PROGRESS

The limitations of report cards were discussed earlier in relationship to the broader information provided by performance assessments. Just as we need multiple assessment strategies to assess young children, these assessment strategies should be used to report how the child has developed and what has been learned. If the assessment system is comprehensive, the method to report the child's progress should also be comprehensive and provide many examples of how the child demonstrated growth and achievement. Parents receive limited information from reports that rate a child average, above average, or below average in preschool settings. Likewise, a report that indicates that the child's progress is satisfactory or unsatisfactory tells little about the child's learning experiences and accomplishments. Rather than a snapshot of progress, a comprehensive picture of the child should be conveyed in the progress report, regardless of whether the child is in preschool or the primary grades.

USING ASSESSMENT RESULTS TO EVALUATE THE INSTRUCTIONAL PROGRAM

The assessment process includes evaluation of the effectiveness of the teacher's instruction and the activities and materials used with children. The teacher uses assessment information to determine if instructional strategies were successful for children to learn new concepts and skills or if new approaches are needed. The teacher might ask the following questions about the success of instruction. Were the children interested and engaged in the materials or activities? Did the children demonstrate a deeper understanding of concepts as a result of an instructional activity? Was the activity the right length of time? Too short? Too long? What changes might be made to improve the effectiveness of the activity?

With this type of evaluative reflection, the teacher demonstrates that assessment should not focus on student achievement, but rather on how well students are progressing and the role that the quality of instruction has on this progress. If some students need additional opportunities to learn information and skills, the teacher considers how more varied activities might accomplish the goal. Should the concepts be incorporated into different types of activities, or should they become a part of a continuum that includes a new direction in focus? Young children need many opportunities to learn new skills, and encountering concepts in new contexts provides meaningful routes to understanding and the ability to use what is being learned.

ASSESSMENT OF YOUNG CHILDREN: THE PROCESS

It was proposed earlier that assessment occurs throughout the school year. In this section, we will describe how a process of assessment proceeds from the beginning of the school year until the final evaluation at the end of the year. Assessment that is ongoing is complemented by periodic assessment for reporting periods.

ASSESSMENT AT THE BEGINNING OF THE YEAR: PREASSESSMENT

Each year, when a teacher receives a new group of students, the first task is to learn about individual differences and determine each child's current developmental level. Young children have uneven rates of development. Each domain in development—physical, social, cognitive, and language—develops differently within and between children. Development occurs in spurts and may lag for a period of time. The teacher might use observation, checklists, and discussions with the child and parents to determine each child's current status. This initial evaluation provides the teacher with a starting place for planning learning experiences and activities. This step in the assessment process is also called **preassessment,** because the teacher is conducting assessment prior to planning curriculum based on individual needs.

ONGOING ASSESSMENT

Ongoing assessment is conducted almost continuously throughout the year. In the course of group lessons, activities in learning centers, and observation of play, the teacher notes the child's progress or difficulties that might be impeding progress. Notation of this information is made in anecdotal records or some other type of record-keeping system so that the information can be utilized for planning.

ASSESSMENT AT THE END OF REPORTING PERIODS

Generally, at the end of a period of several weeks, teachers are asked to evaluate a child's progress and accomplishments. At this time, the teacher might need to record the child's progress for the period of time, as well as plans for the child in the next reporting period. Since some type of report, either oral or written, is made to parents at the end of the reporting period, the teacher might include documentation of the child's work and/or a written summary of progress. In addition to observation of the child, the teacher might use specific tasks to document acquisition of a concept or skill. The teacher might interview the child to determine how the child perceives and uses information introduced in classroom activities. In addition, the child might have the opportunity to self-evaluate, and parents can provide input on their observations of the child's progress.

ASSESSMENT AT THE END OF THE SCHOOL YEAR

The most complete assessment and reporting of progress occurs at the end of the school year. At this time, the teacher needs to summarize the child's progress for all the reporting periods. In some settings, this summarization occurs at a midpoint in the year, as well as at the end of the year. A variety of strategies might be used to determine progress, including teacher-designed assessments in different content areas, standardized achievement tests, student self-evaluation, and a written narrative of the student's accomplishments. As will be discussed in later chapters, a variety of possibilities exists to document what the student has accomplished during the year. In many school districts, this summative information is passed on to the next teacher to help in the initial assessment at the beginning of the next school year.

WORKING WITH YOUNG CHILDREN IN AN ASSESSMENT SETTING

When teachers and other professionals conduct assessments with infants and young children, they need to be sensitive to the special requirements of working with very young children. Young children have very short attention spans and are easily distracted. Administrators of assessment instruments and other strategies will benefit from the following guidelines:

1. Have all materials ready prior to the assessment session and review procedures for administering the assessment before the child arrives.

2. If at all possible, be sure that the child is familiar with the environment when conducting an assessment. For very young children, the session might need to be conducted in the home. For assessments administered to children entering a group setting, results will be more accurate if the child has been given time to adjust to the school setting. The test administrator should also be familiar to the child.

3. Before beginning the assessment session, develop rapport with the child. Engage the child in a conversation and/or introduce a toy before the session begins. Once the child seems comfortable, the first assessment tasks can begin.

4. Be alert to signs of fatigue or behaviors that indicate that the child is no longer responding to assessment tasks. Take a brief break or remind the child how to respond to tasks before resuming the session.

5. Use assessment time efficiently. The child should not be hurried, but assessment tasks should be administered with little lag in time while the child is alert and attentive.

6. Consider adaptations that might be needed for children with disabilities. Be knowledgeable about how tasks might be adapted within requirements for how standardized tests should be administered. If alternative procedures can be used, permit the child to respond differently to a test item. Caution must be used, however, not to change the intent of the item or the type of response that is appropriate as well as correct.

ASSESSING AGGIE'S KNOWLEDGE OF CONCEPTS

Aggie is 6 years old and entering first grade in an inclusion class. All the children are administered a test of basic concepts that requires the child to mark the correct answer for three pictures given to identify the concept asked for by the teacher. Because Aggie's physical limitations have affected her fine motor development, she is unable to hold a pencil or crayon or to make a mark on the test. Instead, her teacher conducts the test orally and asks Aggie to indicate which of the three pictures is the correct answer. Aggie can point with some difficulty, so the teacher exposes only one row of pictures at a time and asks Aggie to point to the picture that matches the concept she has described.

SUMMARY

We need to be able to evaluate the growth and development of young children for various purposes. Specialists who work with children from various perspectives have devised formal and informal assessments that can be used with newborns, as well as later in the early childhood years. Members of the medical profession, psychologists, educators, and parents all have an interest and concern for knowing that the young child is developing at a normal rate. If development deviates from acceptable progress in some way, tests and other evaluation strategies are available to study the child and to help in devising early intervention measures that can minimize or eliminate the developmental problem.

As we enter a new century, we need to consider how the assessment methods that are available to us are best used. In view of the many concerns and issues about testing young children, assessment should now focus on meeting the child's developmental and learning needs. We should take advantage of the many assessment strategies available but, at the same time, be sure that we understand the purposes, strengths, and limitations of each type when including them in a system for comprehensive evaluation and reporting. All assessments should have a meaningful purpose and method and be related to the child's development and learning. The assessments used to report progress should also be meaningful to parents and other adults who need to understand the child's profile of progress and learning needs. The assessment process should include the child and the child's parents if the process is to be the most comprehensive and informative.

In the next eight chapters, each component of a comprehensive evaluation system will be discussed, beginning with standardized tests. Informal methods will then be discussed, with portfolio assessment serving as a model for the desired comprehensive assessment plan that will best benefit the young child.

REVIEW QUESTIONS

1. What should be the purposes for assessing young children?
2. Who are the professionals who test young children?
3. How can a young child's development be atypical? Give examples.
4. Why are infant neonatal scales administered? Infant development scales?
5. What is the purpose of preschool intelligence tests?
6. How are adaptive scales used? Give examples.
7. Why do schools administer tests to preschool children? Describe the purposes.
8. How do schools use group achievement tests? State education agencies? National agencies?
9. How are informal measures different from psychological or standardized tests?
10. Why is observation an important evaluation method to use with young children?
11. How do performance assessments differ from other types of informal assessment? What should performance assessments reflect?
12. What is a comprehensive assessment system? How is it used for instruction and reporting progress?
13. Why is a comprehensive assessment system better than more traditional reporting methods?
14. How is assessment used throughout the school year? Describe different purposes for assessment at the beginning of the school year, at the end of reporting periods, and at the end of the school year.

SUGGESTED ACTIVITIES

1. Examine a test for infants and a test for primary-grade children discussed in this chapter. Describe the similarities and differences between the two measures.

2. Conduct an interview with a preschool teacher and a primary-grade teacher. Find out what kinds of standardized tests are administered in the classroom and what types of informal assessment strategies are used by the teacher.

KEY TERMS

assessment software
authentic assessment
developmental checklist
directed assignment
electronic management of learning (EML)
informal test
interview
learning disability
narrative report
neonatologist

obstetrician
pediatrician
performance assessment
portfolio
preassessment
rating scale
rubric
scope (sequence of skills)
standardized test

REFERENCES

Apgar, V. (1975). A proposal for a new method of evaluation of a newborn infant. *Anesthesia and Analgesia, 32,* 260–267.

Barrera, I. (1996). Thoughts on the assessment of young children whose sociocultural background is unfamiliar to the assessor. In S. J. Meisels & E. Fenichel (Eds.), *New visions for the developmental assessment of infants and young children* (pp. 69–84). Washington, DC: ZERO TO THREE: National Center for Infants, Toddlers, and Families.

Feld, J. K., Bergan, K. S. (2002). Assessment tools in the 21st century. *Child Care Information Exchange, 146,* 62–66.

Goodwin, W. L., & Goodwin, L. D. (1993). Young children and measurement: Standardized and nonstandardized instruments in early childhood education. In B. Spodek (Ed.), *Handbook of research on the education of young children* (pp. 441–463). New York: Macmillan.

Greenspan, S. I., Meisels, S. J., & the ZERO TO THREE Work Group on Developmental Assessment. (1996). To-

ward a new vision for the developmental assessment of infants and young children. In S. J. Meisels & E. Fenichel (Eds.), *New visions for the developmental assessment of infants and young children* (pp. 11–26). Washington, DC: ZERO TO THREE: National Center for Infants, Toddlers, and Families.

Meisels, S. J. (1996). Charting the continuum of assessment and intervention. In S. J. Meisels & E. Fenichel (Eds.), *New visions for the developmental assessment of infants and young children* (pp. 27–52). Washington, DC: ZERO TO THREE: National Center for Infants, Toddlers, and Families.

National Education Association. (1994). *Assessing learning in the classroom*. Washington, DC: Author.

National Education Goals Panel. (1998). *Principles and recommendations for early childhood assessments*. Washington, DC: Author.

Popper, B. K. (1996). Achieving change in assessment practices: A parent's perspective. In S. J. Meisels & E. Fenichel

(Eds.), *New visions for the developmental assessment of infants and young children* (pp. 59–66). Washington, DC: ZERO TO THREE: National Center for Infants, Toddlers, and Families.

Rocco, S. (1996). Toward shared commitment and shared responsibility: A parent's vision of developmental assessment. In S. J. Meisels & E. Fenichel (Eds.), *New visions for the developmental assessment of infants and young children* (pp. 55–58). Washington, DC: ZERO TO THREE: National Center for Infants, Toddlers, and Families.

Segal, M., & Webber, N. T. (1996). Nonstructured play observations: Guidelines, benefits, and caveats. In S. J. Meisels & E. Fenichel (Eds.), *New visions for the developmental assessment of infants and young children* (pp. 207–230). Washington, DC: ZERO TO THREE: National Center for Infants, Toddlers, and Families.

Shepard, L. A. (1989). Why we need better assessments. *Educational Leadership, 46,* 4–9.

Widerstrom, A. H., Mowder, B. A., & Sandall, S. R. (1991). *At-risk and handicapped newborns and infants.* Upper Saddle River, NJ: Prentice Hall.

Wiggins, G. P. (1993). *Assessing student performance.* San Francisco: Jossey-Bass.

Wiggins, G. P. (1998). *Educative assessment.* San Francisco: Jossey-Bass.

Wodrich, D. (1984). *Children's psychological testing.* Baltimore: Paul H. Brookes.

Winograd, P., & Perkins, F. D. (1996). Authentic assessment in the classroom: Principles and practices. In R. E. Blum & J. A. Arter (Eds.), *A handbook for student performance assessment in an era of restructuring* (pp. 1–8:1 to 1–8:11). Alexandria, VA: Association for Supervision and Curriculum Development.

Standardized Tests

How They Are Used, Designed, and Selected

CHAPTER 3

Chapter Objectives

As a result of reading this chapter, you will be able to

1. **Understand how standardized tests are used with infants and young children**
2. **Understand the process of standardized test design**
3. **Understand the differences between test validity and test reliability**
4. **Use resources and strategies for selecting and evaluating standardized tests**
5. **Understand issues in selecting and using standardized tests**

V arious methods and purposes for measuring and evaluating infants and young children were discussed in chapter 2. We differentiated between formal measures and informal measures of measurement. Psychological tests and some educational tests are considered formal instruments because they have been standardized.

In this chapter, we will look at some ways that standardized tests are used with infants and young children. Specific examples of tests and their purposes will be discussed.

How are standardized tests different from other kinds of measures? We will discuss how standardized tests are designed and tested to measure the desired characteristics. Test validity and reliability are explained, as well as their effects on the dependability of the test.

People who use standardized tests with young children must be able to interpret the results. Teachers especially need to be able to interpret test results and communicate them in a meaningful way to parents. To understand more clearly how scores on a test are translated into meaningful information, raw scores and standard scores are described. The normal curve and its role in interpreting test scores are also explained.

HOW STANDARDIZED TESTS ARE USED WITH INFANTS AND YOUNG CHILDREN

TYPES OF STANDARDIZED TESTS

Many types of standardized tests are available for use with infants and young children. All are psychological tests, whether they measure abilities, achievements, aptitudes, interests, attitudes, values, or personality characteristics. In the following sections, we will discuss each of these types of tests.

Ability refers to the current level of knowledge or skill in a particular area. Three types of psychological tests—**intelligence tests, achievement tests,** and **aptitude tests**—are categorized as ability tests because they measure facets of ability. Young children are often measured to determine the progress of their development. A measure used with such children may assess ability in motor, language, social, or cognitive skills. *McCarthy's Scales of Children's Abilities* (McCarthy, 1983), for example, has indexes for verbal, perceptual–performance, quantitative, cognitive, memory, and motor abilities.

Achievement is related to the extent to which a person has acquired certain information or has mastered identified skills. An achievement test measures ability in that it evaluates the child's achievement related to specific prior instruction. The *Peabody Individual Achievement Test—Revised* (American Guidance Service, 1997) is a measure of achievement in mathematics, reading recognition, reading comprehension, spelling, and general information.

Aptitude is the potential to learn or develop proficiency in some area, provided that certain conditions or training is available. An individual may have a high aptitude for music or art. Like achievement tests, aptitude tests also measure learned abilities. An aptitude test measures the results of both general and incidental learning and predicts future learning.

Intelligence tests are ability tests in that they assess overall intellectual functioning. They are also aptitude tests because they assess aptitude for learning and problem solving. The *Stanford–Binet Intelligence Scale—Fourth Edition* (Thorndike, Hagen, & Sattler, 1986) is an example of an intelligence scale that also measures individual aptitude.

Personality tests measure a person's tendency to behave in a particular way. Such tests are used to diagnose children's emotional problems. Because an inventory is used to assess personality characteristics, the test is quite lengthy, usually containing several hundred items in a true–false format. Test items are answered by the parent or child or by both together and are analyzed to determine whether the child has certain personality traits.

Interest inventories are used to determine a person's interest in a certain area or vocation and are not used with very young children. A school-age child may be given a reading interest inventory to provide the teacher with information that will serve as a guide when helping the child to select reading material.

Attitudes are also measured in older children and adults, rather than in young children. An **attitude measure** determines how a person is predisposed to think about or behave toward an object, event, institution, type of behavior, or person or group of people. Politicians frequently use such measures to determine the attitudes of voters on controversial issues.

TESTS FOR INFANTS.   Various psychological tests have been constructed for infants and young children. Such tests are challenging because of the child's developmental limitations. Babies are particularly difficult to evaluate because of their short attention span. Their periods of alertness are brief, and they have their own schedules of opportune moments for testing. In addition, developmental changes occur rapidly, making test results unreliable for more than a short time. Generally, because of these limitations, the validity and reliability of infant scales are questionable. The tests are difficult to administer and interpret. Nevertheless, they are useful in evaluating the status of newborns and infants (Wodrich, 1997).

The status of a newborn can be determined by various measures. The *Apgar Scale* (Apgar, 1975), administered 1 minute and 5 minutes after birth, assesses the health of the newborn by evaluating the heart rate, respiratory effort, muscle tone, body color, and reflex irritability. Each characteristic is scored on a scale of 0 to 2. A score of 7 to 10 indicates the infant is in good condition; a score of 5 may indicate developmental difficulties. A score of 3 or below is very serious and indicates an emergency concerning the infant's survival. The *Brazelton Neonatal Behavioral Assessment Scale,* another neonatal measure (Als, Tronick, Lester, & Brazelton, 1979), measures temperamental differences, nervous system functions, and the capacity of the neonate to interact. Its purpose is to locate mild neurological dysfunctions and variations in temperament. A newer scale, the *Neonatal Behavioral Assessment Scale* (NBAS) (Brazelton, 1984, 1996), is used with newborns from the first day of life through the end of the first month. In this test, the infant's competence is measured through behavioral items. In addition to identifying the infant's performance, if administered with the parents present, it can be used to help parents to understand their infant's signals and skills. This knowledge of child development generally and their baby's competence specifically can facilitate improvement in parenting skills (Widerstrom, Mowder, & Sandall, 1991).

An adaptation of the NBAS to assess preterm infants came through the design of the *Assessment of Preterm Infants' Behavior* (APIB) (Als, Lester, Tronick, & Brazelton, 1982). It includes many of the items in the NBAS, but refined them to be able to observe the preterm infant's functioning (Als, 1986).

Infant development scales go beyond measuring neonatal status to focusing on development from 1 month to 2 years. The *Gesell Developmental Schedules* (Yang, 1979) were the first scales devised to measure infant development. Gesell designed them to detect infants who were delayed in development and might need special services. The *Bayley Scales of Infant Development* (BSID—II) (Bayley, 1993) were designed to learn about the infant's intelligence, rather than overall development, while the *Communication and Symbolic Behavior Scales* (Wetherley & Prizant, 1993) are used to assess communicative and symbolic development, including symbolic play and constructive play. The Gesell and Bayley instruments are difficult to administer because of their length; however, they are supposed to provide diagnostic information. The *Denver II* (Frankenburg et al.1990) is a simple screening instrument designed to identify children who are likely to have significant delays and need early identification and intervention, while the *Adaptive Behavior Assessment System—Infant and Preschool* (Oakland, 2002) assesses strengths and weaknesses in adaptive skills. Figure 3–1 presents information about some neonatal and infant tests; Figure 3–2 provides examples of categories included in screening tests.

TESTS FOR PRESCHOOL CHILDREN. Psychologists have designed a variety of tests to evaluate development and to detect developmental problems during the preschool years. Just as the testing of infants and toddlers presents challenges to test administrators because of the children's developmental limitations, the evaluation of preschool children under age 6 must also be conducted with their developmental characteristics in mind. Instruments that assess characteristics used to identify developmental delays or to diagnose sources of disabilities that put the young child at risk for learning are administered to one child at a time. Test items are concrete tasks or activities that match the child's ability to respond, nevertheless, validity and reliability are affected by such factors as the child's limited attention span and willingness to attempt to respond to the examiner.

Preschool intelligence tests and adaptive behavior scales are used to diagnose mental retardation. Although intelligence measures during the preschool years are generally unreliable because children's IQs can change enormously between early childhood and adolescence, they are used with young children to measure learning potential.

The *Stanford–Binet Intelligence Scale—Fourth Edition* (Thorndike et al., 1986), the original IQ test, was designed to assess general thinking or problem-solving ability. It is valuable in answering questions about developmental delay and retardation. Conversely, *McCarthy's Scales of Children's Abilities* (McCarthy, 1983) is useful in identifying mild retardation and learning disabilities. Another instrument, the *Wechsler Preschool and Primary Scale of Intelligence* (WPPSI—III) (Wechsler, 2002), is useful in identifying signs of uneven development.

Measures of adaptive behavior assess possible developmental problems related to learning disabilities. Adaptive behavior instruments attempt to measure how well the young child has mastered everyday living tasks such as toileting and feeding.

FIGURE 3-1   Neonatal and infant tests

NAME	LEVEL	TYPE	PURPOSE
Apgar Scale	Neonate	Birth status	Assess health of the newborn infant
Brazelton Neonatal Behavioral Assessment Scale	Neonate	Neonatal status	Locate mild neurological dysfunctions and variations in temperament
Neonatal Behavioral Assessment Scale	First month		Identify the infant's ability to modulate its behavioral systems in response to external stimuli
Adaptive Behavior Assessment System™ Infant and Preschool	Infant and Preschool	Adaptive skills	Assess strengths and weakness in adaptive skills
Assessment of Preterm Infants' Behavior (APIB)	Preterm infants	Preterm development	Identify current status and intervention targets
Bayley Scales of Infant Development	Infant	Intelligence	Diagnose developmental delays in infants
Gesell Developmental Schedules	Infant	Development	Detect developmental delays
Denver II	1 month to 6 years	Developmental screening	Identify significant developmental delays
Communication and Symbolic Behavior Scales (CSBS)	Infants, toddlers, preschoolers	Language development	Assess communication and symbolic development

The *Vineland Adaptive Behavior Scale* (Sparrow, Balla, & Cicchetti, 1984) assesses the everyday behavior of the child that indicates the level of development. The scale determines areas of weakness and strength in communication, daily living, socialization, and motor skills. A newer instrument, *First Step: Screening Test for Evaluating Preschoolers* (First Step) (Miller, 1993) assesses five developmental areas to identify preschoolers at risk for developmental delay. The *Developmental Indicators for the Assessment of Learning* (DIAL III) (Mardell-Czundowski & Goldenberg, 1998) and *AGS Early Screening Profiles* (Harrison et al., 1990) can be used to screen a child for overall developmental delay, and the AAMR (American Association on Mental Retardation) *Adaptive Behavior Scale—School Edition—S:2* (Nihira & Lambert, 1993) assesses adaptive behavior in 16 domains for social competence and independence. The

FIGURE 3–2 Examples of items on screening tests

Motor Skills
Gross Motor
 jumping, skipping, hopping, catching, walking a straight line
Fine Motor
 building with cubes, cutting, copying forms, writing name and copying words,
 drawing shapes
Cognitive Development
 pointing to body parts
 rote counting
 counting objects
 sorting and classifying pictures
 identifying and naming colors and shapes
 answering simple questions about concepts
Language Development
 identifying correct item in an array of pictures
 answering personal questions
 identifying objects and pictures
 placing object using positional words (under, over, in, etc.)

FIGURE 3–3 Some categories assessed in adaptive behaviors

Independent Living Categories
Physical development
Language development
Independent functioning

Social Behavior Categories
Social engagement
Conformity
Trustworthiness
Disturbing interpersonal behavior
Hyperactive behavior
Self abusive behavior
Stereotyped behavior

Preschool Language Scale, Fourth Edition (PLS-4) (Zimmerman, Steiner, & Pond, 2002) measures children's receptive and expressive language. Figure 3–3 provides some categories of adaptive behaviors. Figure 3–4 presents the characteristics of preschool tests.

TESTS FOR SCHOOL-AGE CHILDREN.   For the child old enough to attend preschool and elementary school, many tests are available for use by teachers, school psychologists, program evaluators, and other personnel with responsibilities for students and the early childhood curriculum. In addition to preschool programs for children with disabilities, many states conduct programs for 4-year-old and kindergarten children as well. Although individual tests are available for some purposes in these programs, group testing is also used. Group tests require the child to use paper and pencil; therefore, test results may be affected by the child's ability to respond in this manner. Test validity and reliability may be affected by the

FIGURE 3–4 Preschool tests

NAME	LEVEL	TYPE	PURPOSE
Stanford-Binet Intelligence Scale—Fourth Edition	Ages 2 to adult	Global intelligence	Detects delays and mental retardation
McCarthy's Scales of Children's Abilities	Ages 2½ to 8	Intelligence	Identifies and diagnoses delays in cognitive and noncognitive areas through subtests
Wechsler Preschool and Primary Scale of Intelligence	Ages 4 to 6	Intelligence	Identifies signs of uneven development; detects overall delay
Vineland Adaptive Behavior Scale	Ages 1 to 25	Adaptive behavior	Assesses whether the child has mastered living skills expected for the age level in terms of everyday behavior
AAMR Adaptive Behavior Scale-School, Second Edition	Ages 3 to 16	Adaptive behavior	Assesses adaptive behavior in terms of personal independence and development; can be compared to norms for children developing normally, with retardation, and with severe retardation
Preschool Language Scale—Fourth Edition (PLS-4)	Birth to 6.11 years	Language	Measures receptive and expressive language
First Step™: Screening Test for Evaluating Preschoolers	2.9 to 6.2 years	Developmental	Assesses five developmental domains to identify preschoolers at risk for developmental delay
AGS Early Screening Profiles	Ages 2 to 6	Developmental	Measures cognitive, language, motor, self-help and social, articulation, and health development
Developmental Indicators for the Assessment of Learning (DIAL III)	Ages 2 to 5	Developmental	Assesses motor, language, and cognitive development

child's ability both to respond in a group setting and to use a pencil to find and mark responses on the test. As students move into the primary grades, these factors become less important.

Many preschool programs are designed for children at high risk for learning disabilities. Available are bilingual programs for children whose first language is not English, intervention programs for children with a physical or mental disability, and preschool programs for children from low-income homes who lack the early childhood experiences that predict successful learning. These programs may include a screening instrument to determine which children are eligible. Thus, the *Bilingual Syntax Measure* (Burt, Dulay, & Hernandez, 1976) is a standardized test that can be used to screen children for language ability and dominance; the *Wechsler Intelligence Scale for Children—Revised* (WISC-III) (Wechsler, 1991) and the *Bender Visual Motor Gestalt Test* (Bender & Clawson, 1962) may be administered to a preschool or school-age child with disabilities by a school psychologist or school diagnostician to determine whether the child needs educational services in a program for early childhood children with disabilities. Poor performance on the *Bender Visual Motor Gestalt Test* by a school-age child indicates the need for further study of the child (Cronbach, 1990). A similar test is the *Test of Visual Motor Integration* (Hamill, Pearson, & Voress, 1996). The *Peabody Picture Vocabulary Test—3rd ed.* (Dunn & Dunn, 1997) provides information on a child's language ability, which can help to determine whether a child will benefit from a language enrichment program.

Achievement tests are useful when making decisions about instruction. If a child is exhibiting learning difficulties, a psychologist might administer the *Peabody Individual Achievement Test—Revised* (American Guidance Service, 1997) or the *Wide Range Achievement Test 3* (WRAT 3) (Stone, Jastak, & Wilkinson, 1995) to gain information about specific learning disabilities. The *Early School Inventory* (Nurss & McGauvran, 1976), the *Boehm Test of Basic Concepts—Third Edition* (Boehm, 2000), or the *Bracken Basic Concept Scale—Revised* (Bracken, 1998), might be administered by the teacher to young children to determine their need for instruction in basic concepts or to assess successful learning of concepts previously taught.

Primary grade teachers also may need specific information about a child having difficulties in the classroom. Diagnostic tests such as the *Brigance Screens* (Brigance, 1998), the *Diagnostic Reading Skills* (Spache, 1981), or the *Battelle Developmental Inventory* (Newborg, Stork, Wnek, Guidubaldi, & Svinicki, 1988) can be administered by classroom teachers to pinpoint skills in which students need additional instruction. The *Child Observation Record* (COR) developed by the High/Scope Educational Research Foundation (2003) can be used in preschools in six developmental domains, including social development. Figure 3–5 includes examples of initiative items relating to adults, other children, and social problem solving. The checklists can also be used in Head Start programs, day-care centers, and with children who speak English as a second language. Figure 3–6 presents information about tests used with school-age children.

Group achievement tests are used to evaluate individual achievement, group achievement, and program effectiveness. A school district may administer achievement tests every year to determine each student's progress, as well as to gain diagnostic information on the child's need for future instruction. The same test results can be used at the district level to give information on student progress between and within schools and to determine the effectiveness of the district's instructional program.

Instructional effectiveness may also be evaluated at the state or national level. A state agency may administer statewide achievement tests to work toward establishing a standard

FIGURE 3–5   Examples from the Preschool Child Observation Record

I. Initiative

A. Making choices and plans
1. Child indicates a choice by pointing or some other action.
2. Child expresses a choice in one or two words.
3. Child expresses a choice with a short sentence.
4. Child makes a plan with one or two details.
5. Child makes a plan with three or more details.

B. Solving problems with materials
1. Child expresses frustration when encountering a problem with materials.
2. Child identifies a problem with materials and asks for help.
3. Child tries one way to solve a problem with materials.
4. Child tries two ways to solve a problem with materials.
5. Child tries three or more ways to solve a problem with materials.

C. Initiating play
1. Child engages in exploratory play.
2. Child makes something with materials.
3. Child engages in pretend play.
4. During play with other children, child adds an idea that modifies the play.
5. Child joins with other children in playing a game with rules.

D. Taking care of personal needs
1. Child observes as others do a self-care activity.
2. Child accomplishes some parts of a self-care activity.
3. Child accomplishes all parts of a self-care activity.
4. Child identifies the need for a tool and uses it independently to accomplish a personal goal.
5. Child helps another child in a self-care activity or program routine.

II. Social Relations

E. Relating to adults
1. Child participates in a conversation initiated by a familiar adult.
2. Child participates in a conversation initiated by an unfamiliar adult.
3. Child initiates an interaction with an adult.
4. Child sustains an interaction with an adult.
5. Child involves an adult in an activity and sustains the involvement.

F. Relating to other children
1. Child responds when another child initiates an interaction.
2. Child initiates an interaction with another child.
3. Child sustains an interaction with another child.
4. Child invites another child to play.
5. Child shows loyalty to another child.

G. Resolving interpersonal conflict
1. In a conflict with another child, child responds with yelling or physical action.
2. Child requests adult help in resolving a conflict with another child.
3. Child identifies the problem in a conflict with another child.
4. With adult help, child offers a solution to a conflict.
5. Child negotiates the resolution of a conflict with another child.

H. Understanding and expressing feelings
1. Child expresses an emotion.
2. Child comforts another child.
3. Child talks about an emotion.
4. Child represents an emotion through pretend play or art.
5. Child identifies an emotion and gives a reason for it.

Source: Preschool Child Observation Record (COR) (2003). Ypsilanti, MI: High/Scope Educational Research Foundation, 2003. Used with permission.

FIGURE 3–6 School-age tests

NAME	LEVEL	TYPE	PURPOSE
Bilingual Syntax Measure	Kindergarten to Grade 2	Language	To determine language dominance
Wechsler Intelligence Scale for Children—Revised	Ages 6½ to 16½	Intelligence	To diagnose mental retardation and learning disability; includes verbal and performance subscales
Bender Visual Motor Gestalt Test	Ages 4 to 10	Visual motor functioning	To assess perceptual skills and hand-eye coordination, identify learning disabilities
Test of Visual Motor Integration	Ages 4 to 17	Visual motor functioning	To assess visual–motor ability
Peabody Picture Vocabulary Test—III	Ages 2½ to 18	Vocabulary	To measure receptive vocabulary for standard American English
Peabody Individual Achievement Test—Revised	Kindergarten to Grade 12	Individual achievement	To assess achievement in mathematics, reading, spelling, and general information
Early School Inventory	Kindergarten	Development	To assess physical cognitive, language, and social-emotional development
Boehm Test of Basic Concepts—Third Edition	Kindergarten to Grade 2	Cognitive ability	To screen for beginning school concepts
Bracken Basic Concept Scale—Revised	Ages 2.5 to 7.11	Basic concept development	To identify quickly or diagnose comprehensively basic concept development
Brigance Diagnostic Inventory of Basic Skills	Kindergarten to Grade 6	Academic achievement	To assess academic skills and diagnose learning difficulties in language, math, and reading
Spache Diagnostic Reading Skills	Grades 1 to 8 reading levels	Diagnostic reading test	To locate reading problems and plan remedial instruction
Battelle Developmental Inventory	Birth to 8 years	Comprehensive developmental assessment	To identify child's strengths and weaknesses and plan for intervention or instruction

of instructional effectiveness in all schools within the state. Test results can identify school districts that both exceed and fall below the set standard. Indicators of poor instructional areas in many school districts will pinpoint weaknesses in the state's instructional program and facilitate specific types of improvement. As was discussed in chapter 1, the No Child Left Behind Act passed in 2001 required all states to develop and administer tests to measure achievement in public schools. For the first time, effectiveness of student achievement would be compared on a national basis across states to ensure higher standards for education. National assessments are made periodically to pinpoint strengths and weaknesses in the educational progress of U.S. children in different subject areas. These findings are frequently compared with achievement results of students in other countries.

In this section, we discussed how standardized tests are used. Although the tests described include various types with different purposes, the process used for their development is essentially the same. The next part of the chapter will focus on how standardized tests are designed, that is, the steps followed in the development of all standardized tests.

 # STEPS IN STANDARDIZED TEST DESIGN

Test designers follow a series of steps when constructing a new test. These steps ensure that the test achieves its goals and purposes. In planning a test, the developers first specify the purpose of the test. Next, they determine the test format. As actual test design begins, they formulate objectives; write, try out, and analyze test items; and assemble the final test form. After the final test form is administered, the developers establish norms and determine the validity and reliability of the test. As a final step, they develop a test manual containing procedures for administering the test and statistical information on standardization results.

SPECIFYING THE PURPOSE OF THE TEST

Every standardized test should have a clearly defined purpose. The description of the test's purpose is the framework for the construction of the test. It also allows evaluation of the instrument when design and construction steps are completed. The *Standards for Educational and Psychological Testing* (American Psychological Association [APA], 1995) has established standards for including the test's purpose in the test manual. The standards are as follows:

> B2. The test manual should state explicitly the purpose and applications for which the test is recommended.
>
> B3. The test manual should describe clearly the psychological, educational and other reasoning underlying the test and the nature of the characteristic it is intended to measure. (p. 15)

Test designers should be able to explain what construct or characteristics the test will measure, how the test results will be used, and who will take the test or to whom it will be administered.

The population for whom the test is intended is a major factor in test design. Tests constructed for infants and young children are very different from tests designed for adults. As test developers consider the composition and characteristics of the children for whom they are designing the test, they must include variables such as age, intellectual or educational level, socioeconomic background, cultural background, and whether the young child is able to read.

DETERMINING TEST FORMAT

Test format decisions are based on determinations made about the purpose of the test and the characteristics of the test takers. The test format results from the developer's decision on how test items will be presented and how the test taker will respond (Brown, 1983). One consideration is whether the test will be verbal or written. Although adults are most familiar with written tests, infants and young children are unable to read or write. Tests designed for very young children are usually presented orally by a test administrator. An alternative is to use a psychomotor response; the child is given an object to manipulate or is asked to perform a physical task.

For older children, high school students, and adults, other test formats are possible. Test takers may respond to an alternative-choice written test such as one with true–false, **multiple-choice**, or matching items. The test may be given as a **group test**, rather than administered as an **individual test** to one person at a time. Short-answer and essay items are also possibilities.

After the test designers have selected the format most appropriate for the test's purpose and for the group to be tested, actual test construction begins. Experimental test forms are assembled after defining test objectives and writing test items for each objective.

PURPOSE OF AND RATIONALE FOR SELECTED TESTS

The test developers of the *Kaufman Assessment Battery for Children* (K–ABC) (Kaufman & Kaufman, 1983) state the test's purpose as follows:

> The K–ABC is intended for psychological and clinical assessment, evaluation of learning-disabled and other exceptional children, educational planning and placement, minority group assessment, preschool assessment, neuropsychological assessment, and research. (p. 2)

Information about the expected uses of the *Peabody Picture Vocabulary Test— (3rd ed.)* (Dunn & Dunn, 1997) includes school, clinical, vocational, and research uses. Part of the school use description follows:

> Since the PPVT–R is a reasonably good measure of scholastic aptitude for subjects where the language of the home is Standard English, it should also be useful as an initial *screening device* in scanning for bright, low ability, and language impaired children who may need special attention. Too, it should be helpful in identifying underachievers, when used in conjunction with a measure of school achievement. (p. 3)

The *Bracken Basic Concept Scale Revised* (Bracken, 1998) measures concepts in the early childhood years. A partial description follows:

> Divided into two separate instruments for quick identification or comprehensive diagnosis of basic concept development in children, the diagnostic full-scale instrument measures 258 concepts and is appropriate for use with children from ages 2.5 years through 7 years 11 months. The 30-item screening tests (forms A and B) are used to screen small groups of children to determine if further diagnosis is necessary. The screening tests are intended for children in kindergarten and grade 1.

DEVELOPING EXPERIMENTAL FORMS

In preparing preliminary test forms, developers use the test purpose description as their guide. Test content is then delimited. If an achievement test for schoolchildren is to be written, for example, curriculum is analyzed to ensure that the test will reflect the instructional program. If the achievement test is to be designed for national use, then textbook series, syllabi, and curricular materials are studied to check that test objectives will accurately reflect curriculum trends. Teachers and curriculum experts will be consulted to review the content outlines and behavioral objectives that serve as reference points for test items.

The process of developing good test items involves writing, editing, trying out, and rewriting or revising test items. Before being tried out, each item for an achievement test may be reviewed and rewritten by test writers, teachers, and other experts in the field. Many more items than will be used are written because many will be eliminated in the editing and rewriting stages (Burrill, 1980).

A preliminary test is assembled so that the selected test items can be tried out with a sample of students. The experimental test forms resemble the final form. Instructions are written for administering the test. The test may have more questions than will be used in the final form because many questions will be revised or eliminated after the tryout. The sample of people selected to take the preliminary test is similar to the population that will take the final form of the test.

The tryout of the preliminary test form is described as *item tryout and analysis*. **Item analysis** involves studying three characteristics of each test question: difficulty level, discrimination, and grade progression in difficulty. The *difficulty level* of a question refers to how many test takers in the tryout group answered the question correctly. *Discrimination* of each question involves the extent to which the question distinguishes between test takers who did well or poorly on the test. Test takers who did well should have been more successful in responding to an item than test takers who did poorly. The item differentiates between people who have more or less knowledge or ability. The *grade progression of difficulty* refers to tests that are taken by students in different grades in school. If a test question has good grade progression of difficulty, a greater percentage of students should answer it correctly in each successively higher grade (Burrill, 1980).

ASSEMBLING THE TEST

After item analysis is completed, the final form of the test is assembled. As a result of item analysis, test items have been reexamined, rewritten, or eliminated. Test questions or required behaviors to measure each test objective are selected for the test. If more than one test form is to be used, developers must ensure that alternative forms are **equivalent** in content and difficulty. Test directions are made final with instructions for both test takers and test administrators. In addition, information for test administrators includes details about the testing environment and testing procedures.

STANDARDIZING THE TEST

Although test construction is complete when the final form is assembled and printed, the test has not yet been standardized. The final test form must be administered to another, larger sample of test takers to acquire norm data. **Norms** provide the tool whereby children's test performance can be compared with the performance of a reference group.

A reference group that represents the children for whom the test has been designed is selected to take the test for the purpose of establishing norms. The performance of the reference or sample group on the final test form during the standardization process will be used to evaluate the test scores of individuals and/or groups who take the test in the future.

The norming group is chosen to reflect the makeup of the population for whom the test is designed. If a national school achievement test is being developed, the standardization sample will consist of children from all sections of the country to include such variables as gender, age, community size, geographic area, and socioeconomic and ethnic factors. For other types of tests, different characteristics may be used to match the norming sample with future populations to be tested.

Various kinds of norms can be established during the standardization process. Raw scores of sample test takers are converted into derived scores or standard scores for purposes of comparison. Standard scores are achieved by calculating the **raw score,** or the number of items answered correctly, into a score that can be used to establish a norm. Various types of standard scores can be used to compare the people selected to standardize the test with future populations who will be given the test. Each type of **grade norm** allows test users to interpret a child's test scores in comparison with the scores of children used to norm the test (Burrill, 1980). For example, an age score is established by determining the norms for age groups when the test is given to the norming sample. The age norms describe the average performance of children of various ages. Likewise, grade norms or grade-equivalent norms are established by determining the average scores made by children at different grade levels in the norming group (Brown, 1983).

DEVELOPING THE TEST MANUAL

The final step in test design is development of the test manual. The test developer describes the purpose of the test, the development of the test, and the standardization procedures. Information on test validity and reliability is also included to give test users information on the dependability of the test. When explaining standardization information in the users' manual, test developers will describe the method used to select the norming group. The number of individuals included in standardizing the test is reported, as well as the geographic areas, types of communities, socioeconomic groups, and ethnic groups that they represent.

VALIDITY AND RELIABILITY

Norm information is important for establishing confidence in analyzing and interpreting the significance of test scores. Test users also need information demonstrating that the test will be valuable for the intended purposes. Therefore, the test manual must provide information on validity and reliability. Both types of dependability indicators are equally important in determining the quality of the test. **Validity** is the degree to which the test serves the purpose for which it will be used; **reliability** is the extent to which a test is stable or consistent. Test validity can be determined through content validity, criterion-related validity, or construct validity.

When first designing a test, the developers describe its purpose. Test objectives or the test outlines provide the framework for the content of the test. When a manual provides information on **content validity,** the test developers are defining the degree to which the test items measured the test objectives and fulfilled the purpose of the test. Thus, for example, on an achievement test, content validity is the extent to which the content of the test represents an adequate sampling of the instructional program it is intended to cover.

Criterion-related validity is concerned with the validity of an aptitude test. Rather than analyzing course content, test items focus on skills or tasks that predict future success in some area. The estimates of predictive validity are concerned with stability over time. For example, an **intelligence quotient (IQ)** test might be predictive of school achievement. Likewise, the *Scholastic Aptitude Test* scores may predict whether high school students will be successful in college. Validity is predictive because the criteria for success are the future grades the student will earn in college or the student's future grade-point average.

Criterion-related validity may be **concurrent validity,** rather than predictive validity. Instead of using a future measure to determine validity, current measures are used. The outside criterion is assessed when the test is standardized. The developer of an intelligence test may cite an existing intelligence test as the criterion to measure validity. The developer administers both intelligence tests to the sample group. If the new test scores correlate highly with scores on the existing test, they may be used to establish concurrent validity.

If a test measures an abstract psychological trait, the users' manual will describe how the sample group was tested to establish construct validity. **Construct validity** is the extent to which a test measures a relatively abstract psychological trait such as personality, verbal ability, or mechanical aptitude. Rather than examine test items developed from test objectives, one examines construct validity by comparing test results with the variables that explain the behaviors. For example, suppose the construct is believed to include certain behavioral characteristics, such as sociability or honesty. An instrument's construct validity can be checked by analyzing how the trait is affected by changing conditions. Alternatively, an instrument may measure level of anxiety; its construct validity is determined by creating experiments to find out what conditions affect anxiety (Linn & Gronlund, 2000).

Construct validity is necessary when measuring creativity. To have construct validity, the test designed to measure creativity must differentiate the behavior of creative people from that of uncreative people (Mehrens & Lehmann, 1991).

The validity of a test is the extent to which the test measures what it is designed to measure. Test users, however, are also interested in a test's dependability or stability in measuring behaviors. Test developers, therefore, also establish and report on the reliability of the instrument as part of the standardization process.

Test reliability is related to test item discrimination. When test items are analyzed after the initial item tryout, they are examined for discrimination power. After the final test form is administered to a norming sample, the items are analyzed again to ensure that the instrument is fairly reliable. The whole test is analyzed, rather than individual test items. The test manual will report the test's reliability as determined by using alternative-form, split-half, or test–retest reliability measures. A test's reliability coefficient describes the degree to which a test is free from error of measurement. If **alternative-form reliability** strategies are used, test developers construct two equivalent forms of the final test. Both forms are administered to the norming group within a short period. The correlation between the results on the two different forms measures the coefficient of reliability.

If a **split-half reliability** coefficient is used to establish reliability, the norming group is administered a single test, and scores on one-half of the test are correlated with scores on the other half of the test. Split-half reliability is determined from the contents of a single test. A test with split-half reliability is also considered to have **internal consistency**; that is, the items on each half of the test are positively correlated in measuring the same characteristics.

Test–retest reliability is also derived from the administration of a single test form. In this case, however, the test is administered to the norming group and then is administered again after a short interval. The two sets of scores are compared to determine whether they were consistent in measuring the test objectives.

FACTORS THAT AFFECT VALIDITY AND RELIABILITY

Despite the measures and procedures that are used to ensure the validity and reliability in standardized tests, there are other factors that can affect test outcomes. Some common factors are reading ability, the physical condition of the testing room, memory, and the physical condition of the individual taking the test. Thus, if the testing room is uncomfortably warm or a student had inadequate rest the night before the test, scores will be affected.

Lack of adherence to time limits and lack of consistency in test instructions affect test scores. Other factors are inconsistency in the rating of essays from individual to individual and student guessing of test answers (Payne, 1997).

Validity is affected by such factors as unclear directions, difficulty of reading vocabulary on the test, and test items that are not appropriate for the test objectives (Linn & Gronlund, 2000). Reliability is affected by the number of test items or the length of the test, lack of interrater reliability, and extraneous events that affect the testing situation (Linn & Gronlund, 2000; McMillan, 1997).

These and other factors affect the possible errors on a test and the quality of the test. This variation in testing quality is accounted for in the **standard error of measurement** that is discussed next.

STANDARD ERROR OF MEASUREMENT

No matter how well designed, no test is completely free from error. Although there is a hypothetical **true score**, in reality it does not exist. The reliability of the test depends on how large the standard error of measurement is after analysis of the chosen method of determining reliability. If the reliability correlations are poor, the standard error of measurement will be large. The larger the standard error of measurement, the less reliable the test. Standard error of measurement is the estimate of the amount of variation that can be expected in test scores as a result of reliability correlations.

Several variables that are present during standardization affect test reliability as discussed earlier. First is the size of the population sample. Generally, the larger the population sample, the more reliable the test will be. Second is the length of the test. Longer tests are usually more reliable than shorter tests. Longer tests have more test items, resulting in a better sample of behaviors. The more items that measure a behavior, the better the estimate of the true score and the greater the reliability. Strict adherence to test directions by test administrators contributes to higher reliability, whereas variations in test instructions or coaching students can distort the reliability of test results.

The third variable that can affect standard error of measurement is the range of test scores obtained from the norming group. The wider the spread of scores, the more reliably the test can distinguish among them. Thus, the range of scores demonstrates how well the test discriminates between good and poor students (Gronlund, 1990). The spread of test scores can be related to the number of students taking the test. The larger the testing sample, the more likely there will be a wider spread of test scores.

CONSIDERATIONS IN CHOOSING AND EVALUATING TESTS

Whenever a private school, public school district, preschool, or child-care center decides to use a test to evaluate children, one must decide how to select the best test for that purpose. Those charged with the responsibility for selecting the test must determine the relevant questions to ask about the test. Brown (1983) identifies various factors that must be considered by test users: (1) the purpose of the testing, (2) the characteristics to be measured, (3) how the test results will be used, (4) the qualifications of the people who will interpret the scores and use the results, and (5) any practical constraints (pp. 449–450). All these factors are important in selecting tests for young children. Because of the developmental limitations of young test takers, test formats must be compatible with their ability to respond. Developmental limitations include short attention span, undeveloped fine-motor skills, inability to use reading skills for test responses, and poor performance on group tests. Limitations in training and experience in those who administer the test are also factors in test selection.

Other relevant concerns, particularly in selecting tests for young children, are the costs involved, testing time, and ease of scoring and using test results (Cronbach, 1990). The test must be reasonable in cost, and the time needed to administer the test should be suitable for young children.

A major issue is whether the test has quality. Is it a good test to use with the children? The person searching for an appropriate test will want to examine the test manual for indications of how well the test was designed and normed. The test manual should include information on the following:

1. *Purpose of the test.* The statement of purpose should include the rationale for the test, the characteristics the test is designed to measure, and the uses for the test.

2. *Test design.* The procedures and rationale for selecting test items and the development and trial of test forms should be explained.

3. *Establishment of validity and reliability.* The description should describe the procedures used to establish validity and reliability to include sufficient data on validity, reliability, and norms.

4. *Test administration and scoring.* Specific information should be given on how to administer and score the test and to interpret test results. Information should be adequate for users to determine whether the test is practical and suitable for their purposes. Potential problems should be pointed out that can be encountered when administering and scoring the test (Kaplan & Saccuzzo, 1989). See Figure 3–7 for

FIGURE 3–7 Questions about test manuals

Checklist of questions that should be answered in the test manual

Standardization Sample
1. How many subjects were used to establish the reliability, validity, and norms for the test?
2. What were the demographic and personal characteristics of these subjects? Are they similar to those of the group you will give the test to?

Reliability
1. What methods were used to estimate the reliability of the test?
2. Is the reliability high enough for your purposes (usually .90 or above for tests used to make decisions about individuals and .70 or above for research purposes)?

Validity
1. Is there evidence that the test is meaningful for your purposes?
2. What specific criteria was the test validated against?

Scoring
1. Are scoring keys available?
2. If the test can be scored by machine, how much does it cost and what sort of report is offered?

Practical Considerations
1. How long does it take to administer the test?
2. Does the test require reading? If so, is it at the right level for the people you will test?
3. How much training is required for the test administrator? How can the training be obtained?

Source: Psychological testing: Principles, applications, and issues, 2nd edition by Kaplan & Saccuzzo © 1989. Reprinted with permission of Wadsworth, a division of Thomson Learning: www.thomsonrights.com. Fax 800-730-2215.

questions that should be answered in a test manual, including an acceptable coefficient of reliability.

Test users need extensive training in tests and measurements to interpret a test manual adequately. For many users, the explanations and data reported in test manuals are complex and difficult to understand. A reader may have difficulty in deciding whether the reliability coefficient is adequate, whether the size and demographic characteristics of the norming population are appropriate, or whether test content and format are suitable for the intended uses. To obtain additional help in understanding the suitability of the test, test users will want to consult resources for test standards and reviews. The *Standards for Educational and Psychological Testing* (APA, 1995) includes standards for tests, manuals, and reports. It also includes standards for reliability and validity, as well as information that should be included on the use of tests. A less technical, but dated resource is *Guidelines for Test Use: A Commentary on the Standards for Educational and Psychological Tests* (Brown, 1980).

Other sources identify, describe, and evaluate published tests. *Tests in Print V* (Buros, 1999) is a comprehensive bibliography of almost 2,500 tests. The tests are listed by type, and basic information is given about each test. The *Thirteenth Mental Measurements Yearbook* (Impara & Plake, 1998) includes test information and sources of information about test construction, validation, and use. Critical reviews of the tests are included. For example, the *Stanford–Binet Intelligence Scale* (Terman & Merrill, 1973) is the oldest and most highly regarded IQ test used in the United States. However, the fourth edition of the test (Thorndike et al., 1986) was found to be significantly different from the earlier editions. Reviewers pointed out that users are given poor information on the accuracy of reliability scores, the test is less gamelike and therefore likely to be less appealing to children, and it overrepresents parents from high occupational and educational levels in the sample of children used for norming (Anastasi, 1989; Cronbach, 1989). Educators charged with the responsibility of choosing a test need to be informed of the quality of the test being considered for selection.

A resource that is particularly helpful to persons without a background in test design at a technical level is *Test Critiques,* Volumes I–X (Keyser & Sweetland, 1984–1994). It includes information about test design and use, as well as a critique of the tests. Other resources for test evaluation and selection are particularly suitable for users of early childhood tests. Readers who desire more information on sourcebooks are directed to "Measuring Young Children" (Goodwin & Goodwin, 1982). Additional information on standardized tests used with young children is located in an appendix.

Brown (1983) summarized the steps in selecting and evaluating tests as follows:

1. Outline your general requirements: the purpose of testing, the characteristics to be measured, and the nature of the group to be tested. Consider also the qualifications of test users and practical considerations.
2. Identify what tests are available that appear to meet your needs. Here sources such as *Tests in Print,* the *Mental Measurement Yearbooks,* test publishers' catalogs, and test compilations will be most helpful.
3. Obtain further information about these tests from texts, journals, reference books, and consultation with people who have used this type of test.
4. Select the most promising tests. Obtain sample(specimen sets) of these tests.
5. Make a detailed evaluation of these tests, keeping in mind the unique requirements of your situation. On the basis of these evaluations, select the test(s) to be used.
6. If at all possible, conduct an experimental tryout of the test before putting it to use.
7. Use the test. Constantly monitor and evaluate its usefulness and effectiveness. (p. 463)

 SUMMARY

Standardized tests, despite their shortcomings, are useful for test users. Because they have been carefully developed through a series of steps that ensure their dependability, educational institutions, in particular, use them to measure students' characteristics. Good standardized tests are normed by using many individuals from various backgrounds who live in different parts of the United States. As a result, the tests also accurately measure the population to whom they are given.

Although the process of developing a standardized test may seem to be unnecessarily tedious, good test design requires careful planning and attention to each step. The ultimate validity and reliability of the test result from attention to design details, beginning with the definition of the test's purpose and ending with the description of technical data about the test's construction in the users' manual.

REVIEW QUESTIONS

1. What is a standardized test? Describe different types of standardized tests.
2. What is meant by quantifiable scores?
3. Describe norm referencing.
4. Why does a test need to have validity? Reliability? Can you have one without the other?
5. Why is the description of a test's purpose important? How does test purpose affect test design?
6. List some factors that test developers must consider before starting to develop a test.
7. What are the best test formats to use with preschool children?
8. How are experimental test forms used?

9. What is meant by item tryout and analysis? What is accomplished during this procedure?
10. Discuss three types of item analysis.
11. What kinds of information are acquired when a test is standardized?
12. How is a norming population selected?
13. Explain content validity, criterion-related validity, and construct validity.
14. Explain alternative-form reliability, split-half reliability, and test–retest reliability.
15. Why does every test have a standard error of measurement?

SUGGESTED ACTIVITIES

1. Interview a kindergarten teacher in a public school to determine whether standardized tests are administered to kindergarten children. If tests are used, find out what tests are given and the purpose for test results. If standardized tests are not administered, find out the school's position on the use of standardized tests with young children under age 8.
2. Learn how to administer a standardized test such as the *Peabody Picture Vocabulary Test—*

Revised and administer it to two preschool children. Be sure you use a test that is suitable to be given by teachers without extensive training. Evaluate the test results and write a report describing what you learned, including the following: (1) the process of test administration, (2) the similarities and differences between the two children tested, and (3) the difficulties you had in administering the test.

KEY TERMS

achievement tests
aptitude tests
alternative-form reliability
attitude measure
concurrent validity
construct validity
content validity
criterion-related validity
equivalent
grade norm
group test
individual test
intelligence quotient (IQ)
intelligence tests

interest inventories
internal consistency
item analysis
multiple choice
norms
personality tests
raw score
reliability
split-half reliability
standard error of measurement
test–retest reliability
true score
validity

REFERENCES

Als, H. (1986). Assessing the neurobehavioral development of the premature infant in the environment of the neonatal intensive care unit: A syntactive model of neonatal behavioral organization. *Physical and Occupational Therapy in Pediatrics, 5,* 3–53.

Als, H., Lester, B. M., Tronick, E., & Brazelton, T. B. (1982). Towards a research for the assessment of preterm infants' behavior (APIB). In H. E. Fitzgerald, B. M. Lester, & M. W. Yogman (Eds.), *Theory and research in behavioral pediatrics* (Vol. 1, pp. 1–35). New York: Plenum.

Als, H., Tronick, E., Lester, B. M., & Brazelton, T. B. (1979). Specific neonatal measures: The Brazelton Neonatal Behavioral Assessment Scale. In J. D. Osofsky (Ed.), *Handbook of infant development* (pp. 185–215). New York: Wiley.

American Guidance Service. (1997). *Peabody Individual Achievement Test—Revised.* Circle Pines, MN: Author.

American Psychological Association (APA). (1995). *Standards for educational and psychological testing.* Washington, DC: Author.

Anastasi, A. (1989). Review of the *Stanford–Binet Intelligence Scale—Fourth Edition.* In J. C. Conoley & J. J.

Kramer (Eds.), *The tenth mental measurement yearbook* (pp. 771–772). Lincoln, NE: University of Nebraska Press.

Apgar, V. (1975). A proposal for a new method of evaluation of a newborn infant. *Anesthesia and Analgesia, 32,* 260–267.

Bayley, N. (1993). *Bayley Scales of Infant Development (BSID—II) Second Edition.* San Antonio, TX: Psychological Corp.

Bender, L., & Clawson, A. (1962). *Bender Visual Motor Gestalt Test for Children.* Los Angeles: Western Psychological Services.

Boehm, A. E. (2000). *Boehm Test of Basic Concepts—Third edition.* San Antonio, TX: Psychological Corp.

Bracken, B. A. (1998). *Bracken Basic Concept Scale—Revised.* San Antonio, TX: Psychological Corp.

Brazelton, T. B. (1984). *Neonatal Behavioral Assessment Scale* (2nd ed.). Philadelphia: J. B. Lippincott.

Brazelton, T. B. (1996). A window on the newborn's world: More than two decades of experience with the Neonatal Behavioral Assessment Scale. In S. J. Meisels & E. Fenichel (Eds.), *New visions for the developmental assessment of infants and young children* (pp. 127–146). Washington, DC: ZERO TO THREE: National Center for Infants, Toddlers, and Families.

Brigance, A. H. (1998). *Brigance Screens.* Woburn, MA: Curriculum Associates.

Brown, E. G. (1980). *Guidelines for test use: A commentary on the standards for educational and psychological tests.* Washington, DC: National Council on Measurement in Education.

Brown, E. G. (1983). *Principles of educational and psychological testing* (3rd ed.). New York: CBS College Publishing.

Buros, O. K. (1999). *Tests in print V.* Lincoln, NE: University of Nebraska Press.

Burrill, L. E. (1980). *How a standardized achievement test is built.* Test Service Notebook 125. New York: Psychological Corp.

Burt, M. K., Dulay, H. C., & Hernandez, E. C. (1976). *Bilingual Syntax Measure.* Orlando, FL: Harcourt Brace Jovanovich.

Cronbach, L. J. (1989). Review of the *Stanford–Binet Intelligence Scale—Fourth Edition.* In J. C. Conoley & J. J. Kramer (Eds.), *The tenth mental measurement yearbook* (pp. 773–775). Lincoln, NE: University of Nebraska Press.

Cronbach, L. J. (1990). *Essentials of psychological testing* (5th ed.) New York: Harper & Row.

Dunn, L. M., & Dunn, L. (1997). *Peabody Picture Vocabulary Test* (3rd ed.). Circle Pines, MN: American Guidance Service.

Frankenburg, et al. (1990). *Denver II.* Denver, CO: Denver Developmental Materials.

Goodwin, W. L., & Goodwin, L. D. (1982). Measuring young children. In B. Spodek (Ed.), *Handbook of research in early childhood education* (pp. 523–563). New York: Free Press.

Gronlund, N. E. (1990). *Measurement and evaluation in teaching* (6th ed.). New York: Macmillan.

Hammill, D. D., Pearson, N. A., Voress, J. K. (1996). *Test of Visual Motor Integration.* Austin, TX: PRO-ED.

Harrison, P., et al. (1990). *AGS Early Screening Profiles* (ESP). Circle Pines, MN: American Guidance Service.

Kaplan, R. M., & Saccuzzo, D. P. (1989). *Psychological testing principles: Applications and issues* (2nd ed.). Belmont, CA: Brooks/Cole.

Kaufman, A., & Kaufman, N. (1983). *Kaufman Assessment Battery for Children (K—ABC): Sampler manual.* Circle Pines, MN: American Guidance Service.

Keyser, D. J., & Sweetland, R. C. (1984–1994). *Test critiques* (Vols. I–X). Kansas City, MO: Test Corporation of America.

Linn, R. L., & Gronlund, N. E. (2000). *Measurement and assessment in teaching* (8th ed.). Upper Saddle River, NJ: Merrill/Prentice Hall.

Mardell-Czundowski, C. D., & Goldenberg, D. S. (1998). *Developmental Indicators for the Assessment of Learning* (3rd ed.). Circle Pines, MN: American Guidance Service.

McCarthy, D. (1983). *McCarthy's Scales of Children's Abilities.* New York: Psychological Corp.

McMillan, J. H. (1997). *Classroom assessment.* Boston: Allyn and Bacon.

Mehrens, W. A., & Lehmann, L. J. (1991). *Measurement and evaluation in education and psychology* (4th ed.). New York: Harcourt Brace.

Miller, L. J. (1993). *First Step: Screening Test for Evaluating Preschoolers* (First Step). San Antonio, TX: Psychological Corp.

Newborg, J., Stork, J. R., Wnek, L., Guidubaldi, J., & Svinicki, J. (1988). *Battelle Developmental Inventory.* Allen, TX: Teaching Resources.

Nihira, K., & Lambert, N. (1993). *AAMR Adaptive Behavior Scale, S:2.* Washington DC: Amercian Association on Mental Retardation.

Nurss, J. R., & McGauvran, M. E. (1976). *Early School Inventory.* Orlando, FL: Harcourt Brace Jovanovich.

Oakland, T. (2002). *Adaptive Behavior Assessment System— Infant and Preschool.* San Antonio, TX: Psychological Corp.

Payne, D. A. (1997). *Applied educational assessment.* Belmont, CA: Wadsworth.

Spache, G. D. (1981). *Diagnostic Reading Scales: Examiner's manual.* Monterey, CA: CTB/McGraw-Hill.

Sparrow, S. S., Balla, D. A., & Cicchetti, D. V. (1984). *Vineland Adaptive Behavior Scale.* Circle Pines, MN: American Guidance Service.

Stone, M. H., Jastak, S., & Wilkinson, G. (1995). *Wide Range Achievement Test 3.* Wilmingon, DE: Jastak Assessment Systems.

Thorndike, R. L., Hagen, E. P., & Sattler, J. P. (1986). *Stanford–Binet Intelligence Scale: Fourth Edition.* Chicago: Riverside Publishing Company.

Wechsler, D. (1991). *Wechsler Intelligence Scale for Children (WISC-III).* San Antonio, TX: Psychological Corp.

Wechsler, D. (2002). *Wechsler Preschool and Primary Scale of Intelligence (WPPSI).* San Antonio, TX: Psychological Corp.

Wetherley, A. M., & Prizant, B. M. (1993). *Communication and Symbolic Behavior Scales (CSBS).* Baltimore: Paul H. Brookes.

Widerstrom, A. H., Mowder, B. A., & Sandall, S. R. (1991). *At-risk and handicapped newborns and infants.* Upper Saddle River, NJ: Prentice Hall.

Wodrich, D. (1997). *Children's psychological testing: A guide for nonpsychologists.* Baltimore: Paul H. Brookes.

Yang, R. K. (1979). Early infant assessment: An overview. In J. D. Osofsky (Ed.), *Handbook of infant development* (pp. 1–23). New York: Wiley.

Zimmerman, I. L., Steiner, V. G., & Pond, R. E. (2002). *Preschool Language Scale, Fourth Edition (PLS—4).* San Antonio, TX: Psychological Corp.

CHAPTER 4

Standardized Tests

Using and Reporting Standardized Test Results

Chapter Objectives

As a result of reading this chapter, you will be able to

1. Explain the difference between norm-referenced and criterion-referenced tests

2. List common characteristics of norm-referenced and criterion-referenced tests

3. Explain the advantages and disadvantages of using tests that have been standardized

4. Understand how test scores are interpreted and reported

5. Describe how individual and group test results are used to report student progress and program effectiveness

6. Discuss the advantages and disadvantages of using norm-referenced and criterion-referenced tests with young children

7. Understand the difficulties in using standardized tests with young children

Tests are administered to young children to acquire beneficial information about them. In chapter 3, we discussed how standardized tests are planned, designed, and standardized.

In this chapter, we discuss in more detail how to use information from children's test scores. In the process of standardizing a test, developers establish the norms that make test score interpretation useful. We not only take a more detailed look at norm-referenced tests, but also study how another type of standardized test, the criterion-referenced test, is used to meet the learning needs of young children. Group test scores can be used to analyze and improve curriculum and instruction at various levels within a school district; individual test scores can be used by the classroom teacher to organize appropriate learning experiences for individual students or the class as a whole.

We also discuss how individual and group test results are used to report student progress and program effectiveness. Test results are important to teachers, school district administrators, parents, and school boards. Results are reported to each in a context that provides meaningful interpretation of the test. Finally, we consider the disadvantages and advantages of using norm- and criterion-referenced tests with young children.

USES OF NORM-REFERENCED AND CRITERION-REFERENCED TESTS

DISTINCTIONS BETWEEN NORM-REFERENCED AND CRITERION-REFERENCED TESTS

Norm-referenced and criterion-referenced tests are both standardized instruments. Some standardized tests are designed for norm-referenced results and others for criterion-referenced results. The current trend is to design tests that are both norm and criterion referenced. The two types of tests have different purposes, and test items are used differently when measuring student learning or achievement. **Norm-referenced tests** provide information on how the performance of an individual compares with that of others. The individual's standing is compared with that of a known group. The person's percentile rank is obtained to determine the relative standing in a norm group by recording what percentage of the group obtained the same score or a lower score.

In contrast, **criterion-referenced tests** provide information on how the individual performed on some standard or objective. These test results allow users to interpret what an individual can do without considering the performance of others. Criterion-referenced tests are designed to measure the results of instruction; they determine the individual's performance on specific behavioral or instructional objectives (Wilson, 1980). Linn and

Gronlund (2000) describe the difference between the two types of tests as the ends of a continuum: "The criterion-referenced test emphasizes description of performance and the norm-referenced test emphasizes discrimination among individuals" (p. 44).

Regardless of whether tests are norm or criterion referenced, the process of their design and development is as described in chapter 3. They are constructed and standardized through all the steps that will result in validity and reliability. It is also possible that norm- and criterion-referenced tests have not been standardized; however, it is criterion-referenced tests that are more often nonstandardized (Goodwin & Goodwin, 1993). It is equally important that criterion-referenced tests have validity and reliability if they are to be used to make decisions about young children.

A case in point is the *Brigance K and I Screen for Kindergarten and First Grade* (Brigance, 1982), which was used to deny entry into kindergarten or to place children into a second year of kindergarten. The test was criticized because it had no empirical data to support its use (Gnezda & Bolig, 1988). Shepard and Graue (1993) proposed that norms and validity were essential if a test is used for placement purposes. Potential users were warned not to use the *Brigance* for placement purposes (Boehm, 1985). Norms and validity data were published in 1995 (Glascoe, 1995), and new forms of the *Brigance Screens* were published in 1998 (Brigance, 1998). The *Screens* that are now available in both English and Spanish meet requirements set by the Individuals with Disabilities Act (IDEA) for developmental delays.

Norm- and criterion-referenced tests have characteristics in common. Linn and Gronlund (2000) describe these as follows:

1. Both require a relevant and representative sample of test items.
2. Both require specification of the achievement domain to be measured.
3. Both use the same type of test items.
4. Both use the same rules for item writing (except for item difficulty).
5. Both are judged by the same qualities of goodness (validity and reliability).
6. Both are useful in educational measurement. (p. 14)

Both tests measure what students have learned; nevertheless, the objectives for measurement are different. The norm-referenced test is broad in content. Many aspects of the content are measured. Because the test is concerned with overall achievement, only a small sample of behaviors for each objective can be assessed. The criterion-referenced test focuses on mastery of objectives. Each objective has many test questions to determine whether the objective has been mastered.

Goodwin and Goodwin (1993) further clarify the differences between norm- and criterion-referenced measures. They describe norms as numerical descriptions of the test performance of the test takers. The raw scores of individual test takers are converted into derived scores so that they can be compared with the scores of other test takers. No goal or standard is involved. Criterion-referenced tests make no comparisons among test takers. Test scores are used to determine whether individual students have met a level of performance or absolute standard. If they have met the standard on an objective, they have "passed" or "mastered" the objective. The purpose of test results is to determine how many of the test objectives have been mastered.

An achievement test in mathematics provides a good example. The norm-referenced test for the first grade may have items on addition, subtraction, sets, and all other areas included in the mathematics curriculum. Test items are written to sample the student's overall performance in first-grade mathematics. The student's total raw score is then transformed to compare overall achievement with the test norms. On the criterion-referenced test, student performance on individual curriculum objectives is important. Test items are written to measure whether the child has mastered a particular learning objective in subtraction, addition, or other components of the mathematics curriculum (Goodwin & Goodwin, 1982).

Another difference between norm- and criterion-referenced tests also relates to differences in test items. In a norm-referenced instrument, test items must cover a wide range of difficulty. Because the test is intended to discriminate between the performance of students and groups of students, the difficulty of test items will range above the grade level for which the test is intended. Test items designed primarily for criterion-referenced purposes are written specifically for learning tasks. Easy items are not omitted, and the intent is to evaluate how well the student has learned the objectives for one grade level (Wilson, 1980).

New standardized tests have been developed with dual referencing; that is, they are designed for both norm- and criterion-referenced assessment. Although it is difficult to develop a single test that works equally well for both types of measurements, obtaining both kinds of performance results is helpful to educators. Compromises in test construction are offset by more effective use of the test (Linn & Gronlund, 2000). It should be noted that some criterion-referenced tests have not been standardized. This does not imply that they are not well designed and useful, but readers should be aware of this condition.

USES OF NORM-REFERENCED TESTS WITH PRESCHOOL CHILDREN

Norm-referenced test scores are used to measure individual achievement within a designated group. Norms are not standards to be reached; they are numerical descriptions of the test performance of a group of students. Norms can be established at a national or local level. Norm-referenced tests commonly are used to measure school achievement, intelligence, aptitude, and personality traits. Formal tests are administered at the preschool level to identify children who need or can benefit from special instruction, as well as to determine the success of an early childhood program.

Measures of intelligence such as the *Wechsler Preschool and Primary Scale of Intelligence* (WPPSI III) (Wechsler, 2002) and the *Wechsler Intelligence Scale for Children* (WISC III) (Wechsler, 1991) are norm-referenced instruments that allow test examiners to differentiate the knowledge skills of the students who are tested. Preschool intelligence tests may be used to identify students for a class for children with learning disabilities, as well as to qualify children for a preschool gifted program. They may be used with any children for whom an intelligence measure is deemed necessary.

Norm-referenced tests are used with preschool children to measure their present level of knowledge, skills, or performance. In federally funded programs such as Head Start, a norm-referenced measure may be used to evaluate the learning acquired by the children as a result of the program. The *Peabody Picture Vocabulary Test* (3rd ed.) (Dunn & Dunn, 1997) provides a measure for language development. The *Boehm Test of Basic Concepts, Third Edition* (Boehm, 2000) and the *Learning Accomplishments Profile—Revised* (Sanford & Zelman, 1995) assess the child's abilities and skills, including the acquisition of concepts.

USES OF NORM-REFERENCED TESTS WITH SCHOOL-AGE CHILDREN

After children enter primary school, achievement tests are the most frequently administered norm-referenced tests. Locally developed achievement tests, as well as state and national tests, can be given in order to measure and analyze individual and group performance resulting from the educational program. Children experiencing difficulties in school are evaluated with screening and diagnostic tests, but all students take achievement tests as early as kindergarten, more frequently beginning in first grade.

Norm-referenced test results are used for more general comparisons of group test results. One such use is to assess achievement level in subject areas. The achievement of a single class in a school, all classes of a certain grade level in the school, all schools at a grade level in a school district, and all schools within a state with that grade level can be studied to determine general progress in one or more subject areas. The results of batteries of tests can be analyzed for trends in achievement.

In a similar type of analysis, components of an instructional program can be studied by using group test scores. If a new instructional program is to be tried or if an existing method is to be evaluated to help in deciding whether changes are needed, an achievement test can be used to investigate the effectiveness of the program. Particular areas of weakness and strength can be pinpointed, and decisions and plans can be made to improve weak components in the curriculum.

USES OF CRITERION-REFERENCED TESTS WITH PRESCHOOL CHILDREN

Criterion-referenced test scores are used to describe individual performance on specific objectives. Criterion-referenced measures de-emphasize distinctions among individual performances; rather, they indicate whether the individual has mastered the objectives that were tested. Criterion-referenced tests are used for developmental screening, **diagnostic evaluation,** and instructional planning.

In the preschool years, developmental and diagnostic assessments are the criterion-referenced tests used most frequently. Although **developmental screening** is used primarily to identify children who might profit from early education intervention or from special services before kindergarten or first grade, it is also used as a checkpoint for children who are developing normally. Figure 4–1 is an example of a developmental scale to measure social development (Alpern, Boll, & Shearer, 1984).

Many screening tests have been developed as a result of Public Law 94–142, the Individuals with Disabilities Act, which required children with disabilities to be placed in the "least restrictive environment" possible. As described by Meisels (1994), "Early childhood developmental screening is a brief assessment procedure designed to identify children who, because of the risk of a possible learning problem or handicapping condition, should proceed to a more intensive level of diagnostic assessment" (p. 1). Thus, developmental surveys assess affective, cognitive, and psychomotor characteristics to determine whether further testing evaluation is needed to identify disabilities and strategies for remediation.

Various screening tests have been developed for the preschool child. The *Denver II* (Frankenburg, et al., 1990) is commonly used by pediatricians and other medical professionals.

TODDLER II: 2-1 to 2-6 years
(25–30 months)
Basal Credit 30 months

Does the child name his/her own sex or tell the sex of others? Child may pass by showing he/she knows that certain clothes, activities, or toys usually go with one sex or another.

Does the child like to help the parents around the house? Does the child enjoy such activities as picking things up from the floor, putting raked leaves in a basket, dusting, setting or clearing the table?

TODDLER III: 2-7 to 3-0 years
(31–36 months)
Basal Credit 36 months

Does the child follow the rules in group games run by an adult? Such rules might mean being able to sit in a circle, follow directions, imitate a leader, or do the same things as the rest of the group.

Is the child able to take turns? Although some help may be needed, the child understands the idea of waiting for someone else to go first *and* allows others to go first 75% of the time.

PRESCHOOLER I: 3-1 to 3-6 years
(37–42 months)
Basal Credit 42 months

Does the child play group games with other children such as tag, hide-and-seek, hopscotch, jump rope, or marbles without needing constant supervision by an adult?

Is the child able to keep "working" for at least *30 minutes* with a similar-age child on a *single task*, such as block building, sand or mud play, or playing store, school, or house?

PRESCHOOLER II: 3-7 to 4-6 years
(43–54 months)
Basal Credit 54 months

Does the child draw a person so that an adult could tell what was drawn? It need not be a whole person, but there should be a head *and* body, *or* a head *and* eyes, nose, or mouth that any adult could recognize.

Is the child allowed to play in his/her own neighborhood without being watched by an adult? This does not mean the child is allowed to cross the street alone.

FIGURE 4–2 Sample of a developmental screening instrument

ESI·K™

For detailed administration directions, consult the *ESI-R Examiner's Manual*

KINDERGARTEN
4½–6

Early Screening Inventory·Revised™ Meisels et al.
Score Sheet for Ages 4.6 to 6.0 Years

Child: _____ Male ☐ Female ☐

Examiner: _____

School: _____

Teacher: _____

Parent Questionnaire completed? Yes ☐ No ☐

Total Screening Score: _____
Refer ☐   Rescreen ☐   OK ☐

Date of Screening: _____ YEAR / MONTH / DAY

Date of Birth: _____ YEAR / MONTH / DAY

Current Age: _____ YEAR / MONTH / DAY

Rounded Age: _____ YEAR / MONTH

I VISUAL-MOTOR/ADAPTIVE	*Circle Points, or F, or R*			Comments
	Points	Fail	Refuse	
A Warm-Up With 10 Blocks/Block Building				
1 Tower				
Put 10 blocks on a piece of construction paper.				
Here are some blocks for us to play with. Let's build a tower.				
See how high you can make it go. Use all the blocks.				
Tower	0		R	
2 Gate from model (build gate <u>behind</u> a screen)				
Build on construction paper.				
Now I'm going to build a gate. When I finish I want you to make one just like mine.				
Make gate behind screen. Remove screen.				
Now you make one just like mine. *Give child 5 blocks.*				
When child seems finished: Is that just like the one I made?				
Gate from model	2	F	R	
or, if fails — Gate by imitation (build gate <u>without</u> a screen)				
Watch how I make this one. *Construct gate.*				
Now you make one just like mine. *Give child 5 blocks.*				
When child seems finished: Is that just like the one I made?				
or Gate by imitation	or 1	F	R	

(continued)

The *Early Screening Inventory—Revised* (Meisels, Marsden, Wiske, & Henderson, 1997) and *McCarthy's Scales of Children's Abilities* (McCarthy, 1978, 1983) are also used for screening purposes. Figure 4–2 shows some of the criterion-referenced screening items on the *Early Screening Inventory—Revised*.

When children have a developmental problem that should be investigated beyond screening procedures, diagnostic evaluation may be needed. The purposes of this assessment are to identify a child's strengths and weaknesses and, ultimately, to suggest strategies for remediation. An example of a diagnostic evaluation instrument that can be used with preschool children is the *Kaufman Assessment Battery for Children* (K—ABC) (Kaufman & Kaufman, 1983).

FIGURE 4–2 continued

II LANGUAGE AND COGNITION	Circle Points, or F, or R			
	Points	Fail	Refuse	Comments
A Number Concept				
1 10 Block Counting				
Count these blocks. Point to each one and count out loud so that I can hear you. *Place 10 blocks in random order on a piece of construction paper. Blocks should not touch each other. Child may rearrange blocks when counting.*				
10 Blocks (counting)	2	F	R	
If child passes, proceed promptly to All Together				
or, if child fails 10 Block Counting — 5 Block Counting				
Remove 5 blocks. Count these blocks. Point to each one and count out loud so that I can hear you.				
or 5 Blocks (counting)	or 1	F	R	
If child passes, proceed promptly to All Together				
or, if child fails both counting trials, go directly to Verbal Expression				
2 All Together				
If child passes either counting trial, promptly ask: How many are there all together?				
If child begins counting (again): Tell me without counting.				
10 Blocks *or* 5 Blocks (all together)	1	F	R	

ESI-K

3

USES OF CRITERION-REFERENCED TESTS WITH SCHOOL-AGE CHILDREN

Diagnostic evaluation measures are also used with school-aged children. Intelligence batteries and diagnostic tests in academic content areas are used with students who demonstrate learning difficulties. In addition, criterion-referenced results are used for instructional planning with children at all levels of learning needs and achievement.

Criterion-referenced scores on achievement tests are used to describe individual performance. Reports of individual performance are then used for instructional planning. Individual performance can also be used in teaching groups of children with the same instructional needs.

Mastery testing is a common criterion-referenced measure in which instructional objectives are assessed. After mastery on a test objective has been achieved, instruction proceeds with a new objective. In the case of an achievement test, performance results may be charted to show which objectives have been mastered by the test taker and which need further attention. This result can be used in planning instruction for a group of students. In a similar manner, individualized instruction can be initiated as a result of criterion-referenced test results. Figure 4–3 gives examples of criterion-referenced objectives in early achievement tests.

In **individualized instruction,** students are taught singly on the basis of personal needs, rather than in large groups. Instead of planning learning activities for the class as a whole, the teacher diversifies instruction on the basis of the progress of each student. Instructional groups of different sizes are formed, and the pace of instruction is differentiated on the basis of individual progress. Criterion-referenced tests are one source of information for individualized instruction.

Minimum-competency testing also uses criterion-referenced test results. In minimum-competency testing, a minimum standard is set regarding competence in achieving test objectives. Individual test scores are interpreted to screen for test takers who have reached or exceeded the established level of competency. Many states have instituted minimum-competency tests for students at the elementary school level whose results help to determine promotion or retention.

On a larger scale, criterion-referenced test scores are used for broad surveys of educational accomplishment. Group achievement on a local, state, or national level is assessed to better understand educational progress. The achievement of very large groups of children is analyzed to assess strengths and weaknesses in instruction beyond the level of an individual school district. For example, students tested on a national achievement test in reading were found to be stronger in word identification skills than in comprehension skills. More recently, the National Assessment of Educational Progress report on writing showed that in 11 states only 20% of the students scored at a proficient level or better in the national writing tests, and 31% scored at a proficient level or better in only 5 states (Heath,

FIGURE 4–3   Examples of objectives used in criterion-referenced tests

Criterion-referenced items in beginning reading
1.   Matches uppercase and lowercase letters
2.   Recognizes uppercase and lowercase letters
3.   Matches three-letter words
4.   Matches four-letter words
5.   Recognizes letters, words, and numbers
6.   Recognizes words in context
7.   Demonstrates skill in copying letters, numbers, and words

Criterion-referenced items in mathematics
1.   Counts to 10
2.   Recognizes numbers to 20
3.   Recognizes coins
4.   Matches number to numeral to 10
5.   Adds numbers to 10
6.   Subtracts numbers from 10
7.   Recognizes basic shapes

1999). After such information is acquired at a state or national level, curriculum resources and teaching practices can be investigated to correct the problem. In addition to the *California Achievement Test (5th Edition) (CAT/5)* (1992), another achievement test that includes criterion-referenced information is the *Comprehensive Tests of Basic Skills, Fourth Edition (CTBS)* (1989). In the preceding sections information was given on how tests are used for beneficial purposes with infants and young children, especially for identification of children with developmental delay.

It would be easy to assume that teachers don't have a need for standardized test results because other types of assessment are preferable for classroom use. Information in chapter 2 stressed that assessments should benefit the child and standardized tests should be used for instructional planning. Although the prevalent use of standardized tests is for accountability of effective instruction and standards-based evaluation of students, teachers, and schools, it should be remembered there is also valuable information in standardized test results that the teacher can use to understand student needs and accomplishments. In particular, criterion-referenced results provide a guide for general assessment and instructional planning.

Group testing can provide information that teachers can use for both individual and group instructional planning. Individual and class results yield a profile of level of achievement for criterion-referenced test objectives. If the test objectives are a good fit with the learning objectives designed for the classroom, the teacher has a start in determining how to plan instruction at the beginning of the year.

In chapter 2 it was recommended that all assessment be integrated with instruction. However, recent studies showed that teachers perceive standardized tests as separate from instruction. They did not understand that standardized tests could be helpful in planning for student needs. (Shepard, 2000). To the contrary, in spite of many concerns about standardized tests, they can be included as one of many tools for instructional planning when used appropriately and effectively by the classroom teacher.

INTERPRETING TEST SCORES

A child's performance on a standardized test is meaningless until it can be compared with other scores in a useful way. The raw score must be translated into a score that reports how well the child's performance compared with that of other children who took the same test. In describing the standardization process, we have discussed how norms are set for comparing individual or group test scores on the basis of the scores made by a norming sample. Although several different scoring systems have been established for translating and interpreting raw scores, the bell-shaped normal curve is the graph on which the distribution of scores is arranged by using some type of standard score.

THE NORMAL CURVE

The normal curve (Figure 4–4) represents the ideal **normal distribution** of test scores of groups of people, as well as the distribution of many other human characteristics. Physical and psychological traits are distributed in a bell-shaped frequency polygon, with most scores clustered toward the center of the curve. If, for example, we were to chart the heights

FIGURE 4–4 Normal curve

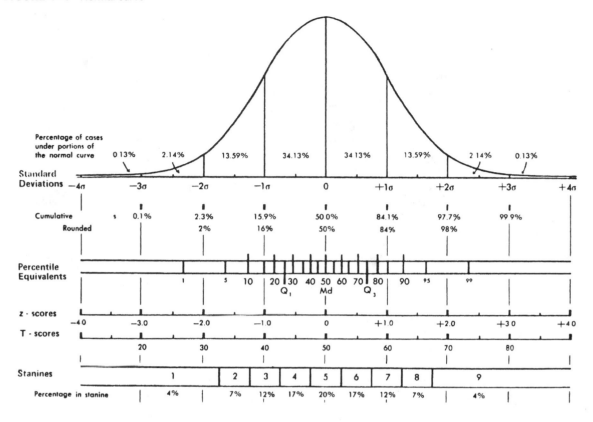

of all adult men in the United States, most heights would be grouped around a mean height, with fewer distributed toward very short and very tall heights.

Ideally, group test scores have a similar distribution, and the normal curve can be used as a reference for understanding individual test scores. Any numerical scale can be used with the normal curve to demonstrate the range of scores on a test instrument.

The midpoint of the curve is the **mean.** Because the curve represents the total number of scores in the distribution of scores on a test, the mean divides the curve into two halves. As many scores are distributed above the mean as below it. The normal curve is used to describe or pinpoint an individual's performance on a standardized test. Derived scores are used to specify where the individual score falls on the curve and how far above or below the mean the score falls (Cronbach, 1990).

STANDARD DEVIATIONS

The normal curve is divided further into eight equal sections called **standard deviations** (designated by a sigma, σ). Standard deviations are used to calculate how an individual scored, compared with the scores of the norming group on a standardized test. Standard deviations describe how test scores are dispersed around the mean. For example, an individual score that is one standard deviation above the mean indicates that the individual scored higher than the mean of test scores on the norming sample. Furthermore, the individual scored higher than about 84% of the individuals who normed the test. If we look at the percentage of scores in each standard deviation, we find that about 68% of the scores are found between one standard deviation below the mean and one standard deviation above the mean. The percentage of scores in each successive standard deviation above and below the mean decreases sharply beyond one standard deviation. When raw scores are transformed into percentiles, or standard scores, standard deviations further explain individual scores compared to the normal distribution of scores (Brown, 1983).

All scoring scales are drawn parallel to the baseline of the normal curve. Each uses the deviation from the mean as the reference to compare an individual score with the mean score of a group. In the next section, the transformation of raw scores into standard scores is explained in terms of percentile ranks, stanines, and Z scores and T scores, as illustrated in Figure 4–4.

PERCENTILE RANKS AND STANINES

After a test is standardized, percentile ranks and stanines may be used as the measures of comparison between the norming sample and individual test scores. Figure 4.4 shows how **percentile ranks** are arrived at by looking at cumulative percentages and percentile equivalents under the normal curve. We already understand that a percentage of the total distribution of scores is arranged within each standard deviation on the normal curve, with a smaller percentage located in each deviation as we move away from the mean. These percentages can also be understood in a cumulative fashion.

Beginning at the negative end of the curve, percentages in each standard deviation can be added together. At the mean, the cumulative percentage is 50%, while 99.9% is reached at three standard deviations above the mean.

Percentile equivalents are derived from the accumulated percentages. If the cumulative percentages represent the percentage of test scores falling into standard deviations along the normal curve, **percentiles** represent a point on the normal curve below which a percentage of test scores is distributed. A score at the 40th percentile equals or surpasses 40% of the scores on the test being used. A student's percentile rank on a test thus indicates the percentage of students who scored lower in the comparison group. If a student's percentile rank is 60%, the student scored better than 60% of the comparison group who took the test. Most important, the percentile rank is compared to scores of a particular group when the test was standardized and norms established.

After a percentile rank norm is established for a standardized test, the developers determine how the distribution of scores acquired from the norming sample is arranged on the normal curve. The distribution is calculated by standard deviations and percentiles. Future test users can then use these norms as measures of comparison to interpret individual or group scores in comparison with the scores of the original norming group.

Stanines provide another way to understand the distribution of scores. As shown in Figure 4–4, stanines divide the norm population represented by the normal scale into nine groups. Except for stanine 9, the top, and stanine 1, the bottom, each stanine represents one-half of a standard deviation. Stanines provide a helpful way to compare cumulative percentages and percentile ranks on the normal curve. One can look at the percentage of scores distributed in each stanine and understand how the percentile rank is correlated with the overall distribution. In reporting group test scores, the stanine rank of an individual score provides a measure of how the individual ranked within a group of test takers (Seashore, 1980). Thus, the stanines clustered at the center of the normal curve represent the highest percentage of scores, while the stanines one or more standard deviations above or below the mean reflect much lower percentages of scores.

Parents usually find stanine results the easiest to understand when looking at their child's performance on a standardized test. They can understand where the child's score falls when described as follows:

9 Very superior
8 Superior
7 Considerably above average
6 Slightly above average
5 Average
4 Slightly below average
3 Considerably below average
2 Poor
1 Very poor (Psychological Corporation, 1980, p. 4)

Z SCORES AND T SCORES

Some standardized test results are reported in terms of Z scores or T scores because they provide a simple way to locate an individual score along the normal curve. **Z scores** and **T scores** are called **standard scores** because they report how many standard deviations a person's transformed raw score is located above or below the mean on the normal curve.

Z scores are considered to be the most basic of all standard scores and the building blocks for other standard scores. They are used to determine how far above or below the mean a score is located in standard deviation units. Percentile ranks are understood by looking at where cumulative percentages fall on the normal curve. Z scores make a similar comparison; however, with Z scores the standard deviations are used as the criteria for determining where an individual score falls. Z scores are parallel to standard deviations in that the mean is at the center of the normal distribution; if a score falls within one standard deviation above the mean, the Z score will be +1. If the score falls two standard deviations below the mean, the Z score will be −2.

T scores also report scores that are parallel to standard deviations on the normal curve. Like percentiles, T scores are cumulative along the curve. T scores range from 0 to 100, with a range of 10 points from one standard deviation to the next. T scores are almost the same as Z scores; Z scores have a mean of 0 and a standard deviation on 1.0, while T scores have a mean of 50 and a standard deviation of 10 (Hopkins, 1997; Kubiszyn & Borich, 1996). Various standardized tests use T scores. *McCarthy's Scales of Children's Abilities* (McCarthy, 1983) report T scores, as do IQ tests such as the *Stanford–Binet Intelligence Scale* (Terman & Merrill, 1973).

REPORTING STANDARDIZED TEST RESULTS

After a standardized test has been administered and scored and individual and group scores have been interpreted, test users can use the information to report not only to professionals within the school district but also to parents of the students. Reporting originates with individual test results, which then are combined and recombined with the scores of other individuals to form class, school, and district reports.

INDIVIDUAL TEST RECORD

The individual test record in Figure 4–5 is from the *Stanford Achievement Test Series, Ninth Edition* (Harcourt Brace & Company, 1996). The hypothetical student is Amy Allen, who is in the first grade. The test was administered in April, the eighth month of the school year. In this form of the test report, only norm-referenced scores are reported. In Figure 4–5, the norm-referenced scores are listed on the left side of the page.

NORM-REFERENCED SCORES

The individual record includes the subtests or content areas of the test battery. Reading has three subtests, and mathematics has two subtests. The other content area is language. Within each test and subtest, the scaled score, national percentile rank and stanine, and the normal curve equivalent are reported. The scaled score is a continuous score measured over all grade levels. It indicates the student's progress on the continuum for each category.

To the right of Amy's scores is the National Grade Percentile Bands Report. In these bands the percentile score is reported as a possible range for the score that accounts for the standard error of measurement on the test. For example, Amy's total reading score was in the 23rd percentile; however, the percentile band ranged between about the 20th to the 30th percentile. Examination of Amy's scores demonstrate that her scores generally fall within the range that is below the mean. The exceptions are the procedures subtest in mathematics, which is in the 76th percentile, and the total mathematics score, which is in the 48th percentile and ranges from the 40th to slightly above the 50th percentile bands.

CLASS REPORTS

Figure 4–6 is a class report on the *Stanford Achievement Test* for fourth grade. The norm-referenced scores appear on the top left section of the page under the letter A. The information includes how many were tested (19 to 21), the mean raw score on each test and subtest, and the mean scaled score. This class report combines the percentile rank and stanine into one section and also includes the normal curve equivalent scores. The NCE Mean score on this test reflects the class average score on the normal curve for each test and subtest.

The National Grade Percentile Ranks appear on the top right of the page with the letter C. As a class, the percentile ranks were below average to average. A few categories were slightly above average. The weakest subtest was Procedures under Mathematics; the strongest achievement areas were reading vocabulary and the listening test.

Criterion-referenced scores are shown at the bottom of the page. Each subtest is represented by the categories or types of questions and the number of test items for each category. The teacher can determine strengths and weaknesses in the class by examining what percentage of the class was below average, average, or above average. The results can be compared with individual reports to determine students who would benefit from additional instruction and those who are ready to move to more advanced learning experiences. Note that the individual report for Amy Allen in Figure 4–5 did not include criterion-referenced scores; however, the information written at the bottom of the page summarized Amy's strengths and weaknesses and included suggestions on how to help her to progress in school.

FIGURE 4-5 Individual Student Report

SUBTESTS AND TOTALS	No. of Items	Raw Score	Scaled Score	National PR-S	National NCE		AAC Range
Total Reading	70	34	498	23-4	34.4		
Word Study Skills	20	11	517	29-4	38.3		
Word Reading	20	10	489	31-4	39.6		
Reading Comp.	30	13	485	19-3	31.5		
Total Mathematics	50	33	528	48-5	48.9		
Problem Solving	30	17	523	25-4	35.8		
Procedures	20	16	536	76-6	64.9		
Language	30	14	538	29-4	38.3		
Partial Battery	150	81	NA	34-4	41.4		

STANFORD — *ACHIEVEMENT TEST SERIES, NINTH EDITION* ABBREVIATED

TEACHER: COVARUBIAS
SCHOOL: NEWTOWN ELEM
DISTRICT: NEWTOWN
TEST TYPE: MULTIPLE CHOICE

GRADE: 01
TEST DATE: 04/96

STUDENT REPORT FOR AMY ALLEN
Age: 6 Yrs 11 Mos

NATIONAL GRADE PERCENTILE BANDS

Recently this student took the *Stanford Achievement Test*. This brief description of the scores presented above tells how the student did on the test, compared to the 1995 performance of students in the same grade from across the country. The Battery score is a global indication of how well the student performed on the test. The score for this student is in the low middle range for the grade, which means that performance on all subtests combined was somewhat below average.

In reading, the score is somewhat below average for the grade. Continued opportunities to read a variety of materials should be helpful.

In mathematics, the score is within the average range for the grade. Continued experiences in working with mathematics procedures and problem solving could be helpful to future learning in mathematics.

Performance on the Language subtest was somewhat below average for the grade. The student should be encouraged to reinforce these skills with many different kinds of listening and writing activities.

It is important to keep in mind that test scores give only one picture of how a student is doing in school and that many things can affect a student's test scores. Therefore, it is important to consider other kinds of information as well. The school has more detailed information about how the student is doing.

FIGURE 4-6 Group Test Report

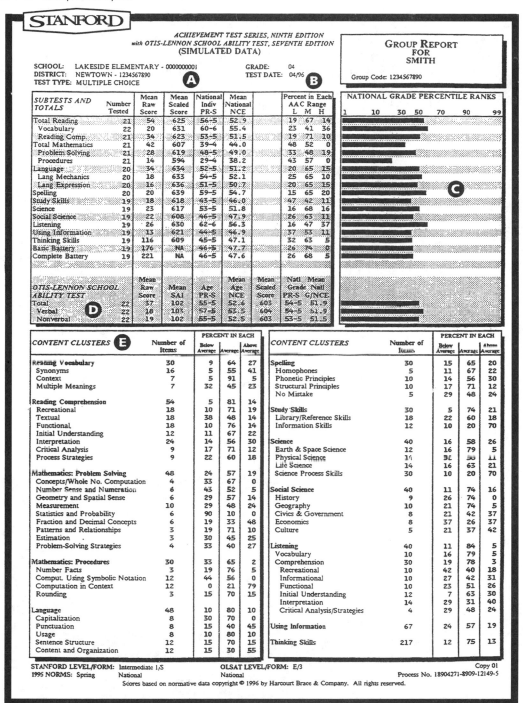

Source: *Stanford Achievement Test Series, Ninth Edition.* Reprinted by permission Harcourt Educational Measurement.
Copyright © 1996 by Harcourt Brace.

SCHOOL AND DISTRICT REPORTS

Summaries of class reports can be grouped to form school and district reports. Both norm- and criterion-referenced information can be organized in a useful form for building principals, school district evaluators, superintendents, and governing boards. Achievement reports can be studied by grade level, across a school, or among all the schools in the district serving a grade level. Instructional strengths and weaknesses can be analyzed by content areas, as well as by school and grade level. Achievement can be compared over several years to determine long-term improvement or decline in achievement. Each type of analysis must take into account the error of measurement on the test so that realistic conclusions are drawn from the study of test results.

REPORTING TEST RESULTS TO PARENTS

Parents have the right to know about their child's performance in school, and schools have the responsibility to keep parents informed. One method used to report student learning is the standardized achievement test. The school should report the test results in a manner that is helpful to the parents.

Statistical data that are part of standardized test reports can be confusing to parents. Because of the seeming complexity of test reports, it is important to give parents an opportunity to meet with the teacher for an explanation of their child's test results. Test results can be discussed in a parent–teacher conference.

The classroom teacher can have the major responsibility for explaining standardized test results to parents. The teacher not only knows the children from working with them every day, but also is aware of the kinds of information that individual parents will understand and want to acquire. It is helpful for the teachers to explain both the value and the limitations of the test scores. Parents may also benefit from knowing why the test was chosen and how the results will be used.

It may be helpful for parents to understand how the criterion-referenced test results may be used to plan appropriate learning experiences for their child. For example, the teacher may use test results to suggest activities that the parent can use at home to help the child, such as those suggested in Figure 4.5.

The teacher may also wish to discuss the comparison of test scores of various children, particularly siblings. Parents can be reassured that individual differences in test scores result from many variables. Comparing test scores made by different children is neither accurate nor useful.

Once children enter the primary grades, parents are eager to know how well their child is progressing and whether the child is achieving as well as he or she should be at that grade level. Analysis of the results of a standardized test can provide the information that parents need.

The *Stanford Diagnostic Reading Test,* Fourth Edition (Harcourt, Brace, and Company, 1995) shown in Figure 4–7 demonstrates how performance on specific objectives can be reported to parents. The test was administered in November to a child in the second grade. Phonetic Analysis, Vocabulary, and Comprehension were the subtests in reading that were included on the test. The norm-referenced scores are listed across the top of the page, with the

FIGURE 4-7 *Stanford Diagnostic Reading Test: Primary grade individual record*

SDRT — Stanford Diagnostic Reading Test, 4th Edition

INDIVIDUAL DIAGNOSTIC REPORT for _____

TEACHER: _____
SCHOOL: _____
DISTRICT: _____
TEST DATE: 11/95

GRADE: 02
1994 NORMS: FALL
LEVEL: ORANGE
FORM: J

Subtest and Total Scores

The scores below show the student's performance compared to that of students who took SDRT at the same time of year.

Subjects and Total	No. of Items	Raw Score	Scaled Score	Grade Equivalent	National NCE	Local PR	Local S	National PR	National S
Phonetic Analysis	30	23	619	2.5	59.3	61	6	67	6
Vocabulary	40	31	577	2.8	64.2	55	5	75	6
Comprehension	40	37	649	4.4	73.7	74	6	87	7
SDRT Total	110	91	611	3.1	70.9	61	6	84	7

NATIONAL PERCENTILE BANDS — 1 10 30 50 70 90 99

Skills Analysis

This analysis shows the number of questions the student answered correctly out of the number possible for each skill. A shaded oval indicates that the score is at or above the Progress Indicator cutoff score.

23/30 PHONETIC ANALYSIS

16/18 Consonants
5/6 Single Consonants
6/6 Consonant Blends
5/6 Consonant Digraphs

7/12 Vowels
3/6 Short Vowels
4/6 Long Vowels

NOTE: Progress Indicators are not available because the student tested out-of-level.

31/40 VOCABULARY

10/10 Listening Vocabulary
18/25 Synonyms
3/5 Classification

37/40 COMPREHENSION

8/8 Close
29/32 Paragraphs w/Questions

13/13 Recreational Reading
7/10 Textual Reading
9/9 Functional Reading

9/10 Initial Understanding
16/17 Interpretation
4/5 Critical Analysis & Process Strategies

Reading Strategies Survey

Date _____
Level _____
_____ % Correct

Reading Questionnaire

Date _____
Level _____
_____ % Correct

Story Retelling

Oral _____
Written _____

Date		Level			
Introduction	0	1	2	3	
Setting	0	1	2	3	
Character(s)	0	1	2	3	
Problem	0	1	2	3	
Plot/Events	0	1	2	3	
Resolution	0	1	2	3	
Theme	0	1	2	3	

Sequence	0	1	2	3
Literal Information	0	1	2	3
Inferences	0	1	2	3
Critical Analysis	0	1	2	3
Summarize/Generalizations	0	1	2	3
Prior Knowledge	0	1	2	3
Creativity/Expressiveness/Aud.	0	1	2	3

Performance Assessment

Instrument _____
Date _____
Level _____
Performance Level _____

Source: Stanford Diagnostic Reading Test, 4th Edition. Copyright © 1995 by Harcourt Educational Measurement, a Harcourt Assessment Company. Reproduced by permission. All rights reserved.

National Percentile Bands at the right of the page. Note that all the percentile bands are above the 50th percentile, indicating that the child's overall performance was well above average.

This test reports a score not seen in the other test examples, the **grade equivalent.** The grade equivalent is a method of comparing student achievement at particular grade levels. After a test is given at a particular grade level, it is compared with test results from one grade below and one grade above the grade. Some test publishers recommend that grade equivalents not be used to report to parents because these are the most easily misunderstood norm.

Parents can understand that a grade equivalent is the grade level reported, in years and months, of the average or mean score of the norming group. Parents can misunderstand that grade-equivalent scores are not an indicator of the grade-level work that the child is capable of doing. Rather, these scores indicate that the child made the same number of correct responses as the children in the norming group at the grade level in the grade-equivalent score. The test score indicates whether the child performed above or below average, but it does not show grade placement in school. The child reflected in the *Stanford Diagnostic Reading Test* was tested in November, the third month of school. All the grade-equivalent scores are higher than 2.3, but do not indicate that the child should be placed at a higher grade level.

The criterion-referenced scores at the bottom of the page are reported in a different format. Each skill is reported in the ovals as the number of correct responses compared to the total number. A shaded oval indicates that the score is at or above a progress indicator cut-off score indicating mastery. A note below the scores indicates that none of the ovals is shaded because the student's scores were higher than the level of the test. In other words, the student mastered all the skills at a high level for second grade.

ADVANTAGES AND DISADVANTAGES OF STANDARDIZED TESTS

Norm-referenced and criterion-referenced achievement tests can provide valuable information regarding the effectiveness of curriculum and instruction. At the beginning of the school year, such tests can show what children know in relation to an instructional program (Durkin, 1987). Likewise, achievement tests administered at the end of the school year can demonstrate how well children learned the content of a program. Teachers can use the test results to determine how to reteach or change program content and/or instructional methods. In other words, teachers can use test results to evaluate their program and to make changes to more effectively meet the instructional needs of their students. In the sections that follow, we continue the discussion of the advantages of using standardized tests. Then we discuss the disadvantages of using standardized tests, including concerns regarding their inappropriate use with young children.

ADVANTAGES OF STANDARDIZED TESTS

Standardized tests can be described as measuring instruments. Each test is constructed, administered, and scored to measure some human characteristic. An individual's responses to the test items provide samples of his or her behavior, which can be scored and evaluated according to an established standard. In contrast to informal strategies, standardized tests have unique qualities that are advantageous for measuring human behavior. Among these characteristics are uniformity in test administration, quantifiable scores, norm referencing, and validity and reliability.

UNIFORMITY IN TEST ADMINISTRATION.   Standardized tests have precise administration procedures. Because the results should be dependable, test designers must be sure that all persons who give the test to children will follow the instructions exactly. Whether the test is being given in Wisconsin or in Florida, the procedures are the same. Informal methods are less specific; the examiner uses personal strategies for assessment.

QUANTIFIABLE SCORES.   Standardized tests are quantifiable because they have numerical scores. The correct answers are totaled to determine the raw score. The raw score is then translated into a derived score so that the child's performance on the test can be compared with the performance of other test takers. The derived score can be interpreted to evaluate the child's performance when compared to the established standard.

NORM REFERENCING.   Norm referencing refers to the process of developing a standard for interpreting test scores on a standardized test. To compare a child's performance on a test with the performance of other children, a norm group is selected. The test is administered to that group to determine what normal performance is. The norm group's test responses will result in a range of scores with which a child's performance can be compared.

VALIDITY AND RELIABILITY.   Unlike informal evaluation and measurement strategies, standardized tests have established dependability through determination of validity and reliability. Reliability is the test's ability to measure the child's characteristics accurately under different conditions. If the child were given the test more than once, would the results be similar?

Validity establishes whether a test measures the characteristics it was designed to measure. If the test is designed to measure intelligence, does it actually yield results that show the child's level of intelligence?

Tests that have proven reliability and validity are dependable. They can be administered to many children, either individually or as a group, and children's scores can be interpreted with confidence that the results accurately reflect each child's behaviors or characteristics.

Validity, reliability, norm referencing, and other test characteristics that contribute to the effectiveness of the standardized test result from careful and thorough test design. Each step in test construction has the goal of producing a dependable test to measure a human characteristic accurately.

DISADVANTAGES OF STANDARDIZED TESTS

Although standardized tests are carefully designed and normed before they are used with children, they are not necessarily the best method of evaluation of young children. In chapters 1 and 2, this concern was discussed in terms of the fact that a variety of strategies should be used in assessing children. No matter how good a standardized test is, other methods of assessment should also be used. Other issues introduced in chapters 1 and 2 were the concerns about the increased use of standardized tests, the use of tests with children from a different culture or whose first language is not English, and the use of standardized tests to deny children entrance to school or retention in grade.

Concerns about the use of standardized tests was first introduced in the 1970s. Educators were particularly concerned about the poor performance of children from low-socioeconomic and minority populations (Wesson, 2001). Another early concern was the control that testing imposed on instruction, labeled by some as *measurement-driven instruction*. In the late 1990s, many of the concerns published in the 1970s persisted in spite of improvements in test design. New exams were matched to the curriculum, particularly in state achievement tests. In addition, essay questions and short-answer questions were added to the traditional multiple-choice questions (McGinn, 1999). However, on some tests, the results could be based on the answers to a few questions, and time limitations for achievement tests precluded adequate assessment of student achievement (Popham, 1999). Although standardized tests can give accurate information about students' relative strengths and weaknesses across content areas, most tests contain too few items to provide meaningful within-subject comparisons of strengths and weaknesses.

Despite these concerns about standardized tests, the long-term campaign to reduce their use has failed. Educational reforms responding to calls for excellence in education increased the reliance on standardized testing (McGinn, 1999; Popham, 2001). In the late 1990s, states had already raised new standards for what children should learn in each grade. Failure to pass the test could result in retention, mandatory attendance in summer school, or denial of a high school diploma. In some states, poor performing schools faced state takeover, and educators were fired or given a reduction in pay (McGinn, 1999).

As school districts are pressured to improve student achievement, administrators, in turn, raise their expectations of teachers in individual schools, which are reflected in achievement test scores at the end of the school year. Teachers then put pressure on their students in preparation to do well on the test. A third-grade teacher, Joseph Angaran (1999), summarized the issue for teachers:

> With increasing frequency assessments are now the focus of my students' lives. When I glance at my calendar, I hardly ever see a week when I am not either preparing to test or formally assessing my students. This is a significant change since I began my teaching career nearly 20 years ago. I question the usefulness and the implications of the data we gather, as well as the effect these tests have on my teaching and my students' learning. (p. 71)

The side effects of these practices are evident. In New York City, a scoring error led to thousands of students being forced to go to summer school. Those who chose not to attend summer school were kept back a grade. By the time the computational error was revealed, the students were well into a new school year and difficult decisions had to be made about grade placement (Check, 1999). In the same year, Austin Independent School District was in Travis County Court under 16 indictments of tampering with school achievement data on the Texas Assessment of Academic Skills (TAAS) in an effort to improve school and school district performance (Kurtz, 1999).

MISAPPLICATION OF TEST RESULTS

In chapter 1, the inappropriate use of standardized tests to prevent school entry or the placement of children in transitional classrooms in early childhood programs was discussed. Although there have been challenges to this practice and many states have dropped such policies, there is still evidence that it continues to be a problem (National Association of Early Childhood Specialists in State Departments of Education, 2000). It is appropriate at this point to further explain the concerns about the use of standardized tests for this purpose.

Early childhood specialists in the 1980s expressed concern about the use of individual intelligence tests, developmental screening measures, and school readiness tests for making decisions about school entry. They pointed out that developmental tests and IQ tests do not differentiate between limited intelligence and limited opportunities to learn. Like readiness tests, IQ tests and developmental tests should not be used to determine school entry (Shepard & Graue, 1993).

The use of developmental screening tests was recommended to predict quickly whether a child could profit from a special education placement if such tests have predictive validity, developmental content, and normative standardization (Meisels, 1987; Meisels, Steele, & Quinn-Leering, 1993). Nevertheless, Meisels stated that developmental screening tests should be used to identify children who need further evaluation. Decisions on such issues as enrollment, retention, and placement in special classes should never be based on a single test score. Other sources of information, including systematic observation and samples of children's work, should be a part of the evaluation process (Bredekamp & Copple, 1997; National Association for the Education of Young Children, 1988).

Another concern about misapplication of standardized test results surfaced in 2003. President Bush announced that in the fall of 2003, all Head Start students would be given a national standardized skills assessment test (McMaken, 2003). An immediate issue was whether preschool children should be given a standardized test and whether the test, the *National Reporting System*, had the desired reliability and validity (Raver & Zigler, 2004). Other issues related to the limitations of the test to measure only cognitive skills and omit measurement of children's competence, emotional development, and cultural diversity (Schumacher, Greenberg & Mezey, 2003). It was proposed that a narrow test of skills and literacy and math should not be used to measure the overall quality of the Head Start program (Meisels & Atkins-Burnett, 2004).

A new direction is being taken to overcome the limitations of standardized tests for identifying and diagnosing children with disabilities. **Play-based assessment,** which uses observation of children's play as the major assessment strategy, is becoming more common as educators of children with disabilities seek more natural approaches to assessment (Segal & Webber, 1996). Play-based assessment is used in addition to the administration of standardized tests and other developmental assessments. Play-based assessment will be discussed further in chapter 5.

Assessment of children with disabilities is also affected by the No Child Left Behind Act. The issue of how to include children with disabilities in state assessments of achievement in a manner that is fair and appropriate is difficult to resolve (Education Week on the Web, 2004). Again, the limitations of standardized tests to identify and address disabilities can also affect their performance on state achievement tests.

SUMMARY

Standardized tests have a role in measuring young children. Many early childhood educators are not opposed to the use of standardized tests per se, but rather to specific tests. While teacher intuition for evaluation can be biased, systematic measurement and evaluation can have advantages. Although there are shortcomings in standardized tests used with young children, more is needed than informal measures and teacher observations, especially for young children with disabilities. The need for appropriate instruments to identify at-risk children and to plan programs for remediation will continue pressures for valid and reliable instruments.

On the one hand, information from norm- and criterion-referenced tests can be very useful in evaluating achievement and in considering instructional improvement. On the other hand, misuse of test results or lack of consideration of test errors and limitations can have a negative impact on instructional decisions affecting preschool and school-age children.

Despite ongoing concerns about their weaknesses, the use of standardized tests is increasing, and new instruments are being developed in response to pressures for accountability for the quality of education and minimum competency standards for students and teachers.

Increasingly, early childhood educators and specialists are urging the use of a variety of methods to evaluate or test children, particularly preschool children. Standardized tests have a role, but they are only one method that should be used to evaluate young children. Informal methods, such as teacher observation and teacher-designed tasks, can also be used to obtain a more accurate picture of what preschool and primary school children have learned and achieved.

REVIEW QUESTIONS

1. How do norm- and criterion-referenced tests report achievement differently?
2. Why are tests with dual referencing difficult to design?
3. Why is a normal curve used to chart the distribution of test scores?
4. What is the function of the mean on the normal curve?
5. How do standard deviations serve as reference points when interpreting test scores?
6. How are percentile ranks and stanines used with standardized test scores?
7. Why are Z scores and T scores useful?

SUGGESTED ACTIVITIES

1. Visit with an elementary school counselor to find out how standardized test results are used and reported, especially in the area of parental reporting.
2. Discuss with a teacher of children with special needs how standardized tests are used to identify and plan individual plans for children.
3. With a classmate, role play a conference between a teacher and a parent to explain a child's results on a standardized test. The responsibility of the teacher is to explain the results of the standardized test; the role of the parent is to ask questions and contribute information about a hypothetical child.

KEY TERMS

criterion-referenced test
developmental screening
diagnostic evaluation
grade equivalent
individualized instruction
mastery testing
mean
minimum-competency testing
normal distribution

norm-referenced test
percentile
percentile rank
play-based assessment
standard deviation
standard score
stanine
T score
Z score

REFERENCES

Alpern, G. D., Boll, T. J., & Shearer, M. A. (1984). *Developmental Profile II manual*. Los Angeles: Western Psychological Services.

Angaran, J. (1999). Reflection in an age of assessment. *Educational Leadership, 56*, 71–73.

Boehm, A. E. (1985). Review of *Brigance K and 1 Screen for Kindergarten and First Grade*. In J. V. Mitchell (Ed.), *Ninth mental measurements yearbook* (Vol. 1, pp. 223–225). Lincoln, NE: Buros Institute of Mental Measurement.

Boehm, A. E. (2000). *Boehm Test of Basic Concepts*. 3rd Edition. San Antonio, TX: Psychological Corp.

Bredekamp, S., & Copple, C. (1997). *Developmentally appropriate practices in early childhood programs* (Rev. ed.). Washington, DC: National Association for the Education of Young Children.

Brigance, A. H. (1982). *Brigance K and 1 Screen for Kindergarten and First Grade*. North Billerica, MA: Curriculum Associates.

Brigance, A. H. (1998). *Brigance Screens*. North Billerica, MA: Curriculum Associates.

Brown, E. G. (1983). *Principles of educational and psychological testing* (3rd ed.). New York: CBS College Publishing.

California Achievement Test, Fifth Edition. (1992). Monterey, CA: CTB/McGraw-Hill.

Check, E. (1999, September 27). In New York, a critical test gets an "F." (*Newsweek, 60*).

Comprehensive Tests of Basic Skills Fourth Edition (Level K). (1989). Monterey, CA: CTB/MacMillan/McGraw-Hill.

Cronbach, L. J. (1990). *Essentials of psychological testing* (5th ed.). New York: Harper & Row.

Dunn, L., & Dunn, L. (1997). *Peabody Picture Vocabulary Test* (3rd ed.). Circle Pines, MN: American Guidance Service.

Durkin, D. (1987). Testing in the kindergarten. *Reading Teacher, 40*, 766–780.

Education Week on the Web. (2004, January 8). Special needs, common goals. http://edweek.org/sreports/qc04/article.efm?slug=17exch.h23

Frankenburg, W. F., et al., (1990). *Denver II*. Denver, CO: Denver Developmental Materials.

Glascoe, F. P. (1995). *A validation study and the psychometric properties of the Brigance Screens*. North Billerica, MA: Curriculum Associates.

Gnezda, M, T. & Bolig, R. (1988). *A national survey of public school testing of prekindergarten and kindergarten children*. Washington, DC: National Academy of Sciences.

Goodwin, W. L., & Goodwin, L. D. (1982). Measuring young children. In B. Spodek (Ed.), *Handbook of research in early childhood education* (pp. 523–563). New York: Free Press.

Goodwin, W. L., & Goodwin, L. D. (1993). Young children and measurement: Standardized and nonstandardized instruments in early childhood education. In B. Spodek (Ed.), *Handbook of research on the education of young children* (pp. 441–463). New York: Macmillan.

Harcourt, Brace & Company. (1996). *Stanford Achievement Test Series, Ninth Edition*. San Antonio, TX: Author.

Heath, J. (1999, September, 29). Texas No. 4 on U.S. test. Austin: *Austin American–Statesman*, A1, A6.

Hopkins, K. D. (1997). *Educational and psychological measurement and evaluation* (8th ed.). Upper Saddle River, NJ: Prentice Hall.

Kaufman, A., & Kaufman, N. (1983). *Kaufman Assessment Battery for Children (K–ABC): Sampler manual.* Circle Pines, MN: American Guidance Service.

Kubiszyn, T., & Borich, G. (1996). *Educational testing and measurement: Classroom application and practice.* New York: HarperCollins.

Kurtz, M. (1999, September 30). School district offered plea deal. *Austin American–Statesman,* B1, B3.

Linn, R. L., & Gronlund, N.E. (2000). *Measurement and assessment in teaching* (8th ed.). Upper Saddle River, NJ: Merrill/Prentice Hall.

McCarthy, D. (1978). *McCarthy Screening Test.* New York: Psychological Corp.

McCarthy, D. (1983). *McCarthy Scales of Children's Abilities.* New York: Psychological Corp.

McGinn, D. (1999, September 6). The big score. *Newsweek,* 46–49.

McMaken, J. (2003, March). Early childhood assessment. Education Commission of the United States policy brief. Early learning. www.ocs.org

Meisels, S. J. (1987). Uses and abuses of developmental screening and school readiness testing. *Young Children, 42,* 68–73.

Meisels, S. J. (1994). *Developmental screening in early childhood: A guide* (5th ed.). Washington, DC: National Association for the Education of Young Children.

Meisels, S. J., & Atkins-Burnett, S. (2004, January). The Head Start National Reporting System: A critique. *Young Children, 59,* 64–66.

Meisels, S. J., Marsden, D. B., Wiske, M. S., & Henderson, L. W. (1997). *Early Screening Inventory—Revised.* Ann Arbor, MI: Pearson Early Learning.

Meisels, S. J., Steele, D.M., & Quinn-Leering, K. (1993). analysis. (2002). *Still! Unacceptable trends in kindergarten entry and placement.* Washington, DC: Author.

National Association for the Education of Young Children (NAEYC). (1988). Position statement on standardized testing of young children age 3 through age 8. *Young Children, 43,* 42–47.

Popham, W. J. (1999). Why standardized tests don't measure educational quality. *Educational Leadership, 56,* 8–16.

Popham, W. J. (2001). *The truth about testing: An educator's call to action.* Alexandria, VA: Association for Supervision and Curriculum Development.

Psychological Corporation. (1980). *On telling parents about test results.* Test Service Notebook 154. New York: Author.

Psychological Corporation. (1996). *Stanford Early Achievement Test 2 (SESAT 2), Fourth Edition.* San Antonio, TX: Author.

Raver, C.C., & Zigler, E.F. (2004, January). Another step back? Assessing readiness in Head Start. *Young Children, 59,* 58-63.

Sanford, A. R., & Zelman, J. G. (1995). *Learning Accomplishment Profile—Revised.* Chapel Hill, NC: Chapel Hill Training Outreach.

Schumacher, R., Greenburg, M., & Mezey, J. (2003). *Head Start reauthorization: A preliminary analysis of HR 2210, the "School Readiness Act of 2003."* Washington, D.C.: Center for Law and Social Policy.

Seashore, H. C. (1980). *Methods of expressing test scores.* Test Service Notebook 148. New York: Psychological Corp.

Segal, M., & Webber, N. T. (1996). Nonstructured play observations: Guidelines, benefits, and caveats. In S. J. Meisels & E. Fenichel (Eds.), *New visions for the developmental assessment of infants and young children* (pp. 207–230). Washington, DC: ZERO TO THREE: National Center for Infants, Toddlers, and Families.

Shepard, L. A. (2000). The role of assessment in a learning culture. *Educational Researcher, 29,* 4–14.

Shepard, L. A., & Graue, M. E. (1993). The morass of school readiness screening: Research on test use and test validity. In B. Spodek (Ed.), *Handbook of research on early childhood education* (pp. 293–305). New York: Macmillan.

Stanford Diagnostic Reading Test, 4th Edition. (1995). San Antonio, TX: Harcourt Brace.

Terman, L. M., & Merrill, M.A. (1973). *Stanford—Binet Intelligence Scale: Manual for third revision forms L–M.* Boston: Houghton Mifflin.

Wechsler, D. (1991). *Wechsler Intelligence Scale for Children (WISC-III).* San Antonio, TX: Psychological Corporation.

Wechsler, D. (2002). *Wechsler Preschool and Primary Scale of Intelligence (WPPSI—III).* San Antonio, TX: Psychological Corp.

Wesson, K. A. (2001). The "Volvo effect"—Questioning standardized tests. *Young Children, 56,* 16–18.

Wilson, R. (1980). *Criterion-referenced testing.* Test Service Notebook 37. New York: Psychological Corp.

5 CHAPTER

Informal Assessments

Observation

Chapter Objectives

As a result of reading this chapter, you will be able to

1. Understand the purposes for teacher assessments
2. Understand the purposes of observation
3. Use different types of observation
4. Conduct observations of physical, social, cognitive, and language development by using appropriate observation strategies

In the three previous chapters, we discussed standardized tests—tests that have been tried and tested with a population of test takers to establish standards for analyzing and reporting the results. We covered how standardized tests are developed and used, their advantages and limitations, and some of the concerns of early childhood specialists concerning their use with young children.

In chapter 2, we discussed informal ways of assessing and evaluating young children. These included instruments and other strategies designed by teachers, other school staff members, early childhood specialists, curriculum textbook writers, and others to assess what children already know, what they have learned, and what they are prepared to learn. Types of informal assessments introduced in chapter 2 included observation, checklists and rating scales, rubrics, teacher-designed tests, and performance assessments. In contrast with standardized tests, informal assessments designed by teachers are not standardized (Linn & Gronlund, 2000). It should be noted, however, that some of the assessment instruments used by teachers have been standardized. They are not standardized tests, but have established reliability and validity. Checklists and rating scales fall into this category. Although many checklists and rating scales are designed for classroom use by teachers and other educators and are considered to be informal measures, others such as the *Child Observation Record* (COR) (High/Scope Educational Research Foundation, 1992) and the *Early Childhood Environment Rating Scale—Revised Edition* (ECERS) (Harms, Clifford, & Cryer, 1998) have been developed through a formal process and have established validity and reliability.

In this chapter, we will discuss how informal assessments are used and their advantages and disadvantages. In the remainder of the chapter, we will focus on observation strategies.

USES OF TEACHER ASSESSMENT STRATEGIES

As discussed in chapters 3 and 4, standardized tests are used for two purposes: (1) to evaluate achievement in comparison to that of a sample group of children and (2) to measure a child's achievement on specific test objectives. The norm-referenced test measures achievement; the criterion-referenced test evaluates mastery of test objectives. Teachers can use criterion-referenced test results to determine an individual child's strengths and weaknesses in the content areas measured by the test. Test results provide a rough idea of the child's learning needs. However, because many objectives are measured on the standardized test, there are few test questions for each objective. Consequently, criterion-referenced test results cannot be considered a completely reliable picture of the individual child's progress and instructional needs. Teacher-conducted assessments allow the teacher to obtain more specific information about each student's knowledge and skills relative to the instructional objectives of the class. These informal assessments can be used for placement, diagnostic evaluation and instructional planning, and formative and summative evaluation.

PLACEMENT EVALUATION

At the beginning of the school year and periodically during the year, preschool and primary grade teachers must make decisions about how to place or group children. With preschool children, the teacher needs to know the skills and knowledge of each child. Because the backgrounds of the children can vary widely, the teacher will evaluate all students to determine how to plan for them in the instructional program. In preschool programs designed to prevent or deal with learning problems, the evaluation may be done to determine whether the child is eligible for the program.

For school-aged children, informal testing may result in placement in a group for reading and mathematics. The teacher or teams of teachers give tests at the beginning of the school year to determine the child's mastery of content objectives; the purpose is to group together children with similar learning needs for instruction. This type of evaluation may be repeated whenever teachers believe that regrouping is needed to improve instructional services for the children.

DIAGNOSTIC EVALUATION AND INSTRUCTIONAL PLANNING

Diagnostic evaluation is more specific than placement evaluation. When assessing for diagnostic purposes, the teacher investigates the child's ability in specific objectives. With preschool children, the teacher may assign tasks involving knowledge of colors to determine which children know the colors and which children need activities to learn them. With school-age children, the teacher may administer a paper-and-pencil test to determine which children have learned to add and which children need to be taught this skill.

FORMATIVE AND SUMMATIVE EVALUATION

Formative evaluation and summative evaluation occur after instruction on a particular objective or a series of objectives. **Formative evaluation** is done to determine how students are progressing toward mastery of objectives. After students practice a skill or learn information, the teacher evaluates them to determine which ones have achieved mastery and which need additional work through different instructional methods or learning experiences.

Summative evaluation is a final assessment of what children have learned. It is conducted after diagnostic and formative evaluation. For some grade levels, summative evaluation is done for grading purposes: The child receives a grade for performance on the objectives tested. Whether or not grades are used, it is hoped that children who have not mastered the information or skills tested will have more opportunities to learn.

ADVANTAGES OF USING INFORMAL ASSESSMENTS

Informal assessments have certain advantages over standardized tests. Although they have not been validated with large numbers of students before being used in the classroom, informal assessments include measurement opportunities that standardized tests cannot provide.

The focus of informal assessments is to encourage students to produce knowledge, rather than to reproduce knowledge. In keeping with Piaget's position that children construct knowledge, assessments can stress the child's active involvement in learning, which is exhibited through performance of tasks or samples of work, rather than through assessments that are limited to mastery of discrete skills (Goodwin & Goodwin, 1993; Wiggins, 1989, 1993). The goal of informal evaluation is to measure long-term development that occurs slowly over a period of time, rather than short-term learning that is assessed without acknowledging interrelationships in development.

One advantage of informal assessments is that they can be derived directly from the teacher's educational objectives and curriculum or from a commercial textbook curriculum. Standardized tests, by contrast, are developed to measure general objectives applicable to many children in different school districts and areas of the country. With assessments, individual teachers or groups of teachers design both the curriculum and the measures to assess children's knowledge of the curriculum. Consequently, evaluation items can focus specifically on the teacher's instruction and assessment plans. Commercial publishers also can design informal means of assessment specifically for their instructional materials.

In chapter 4, we established that standardized tests may not measure how children are being taught in the classroom. Because these tests are developed over a long period of time, the test items may reflect outdated learning objectives. As a result, teacher-designed evaluation strategies may measure learning more accurately than standardized tests.

The reality is that standardized tests are not likely to be replaced. However, teacher-designed assessments have an important role as part of an assessment program. One response is to design instruction and informal testing to maintain the integrity of a constructivist approach to learning, while also helping students to perform on standardized tests (Taylor & Walton, 1997). In the same approach, assessment specialists propose the use of sound assessments that are consistent with local educational goals in addition to the use of externally imposed standardized tests (Bernauer & Cress, 1997).

Research in reading instruction suggests that young readers use available resources such as text, prior knowledge, and environmental clues to make sense of reading material, whereas standardized tests evaluate reading as a set of discrete skills. As a result, teachers teach reading as discrete skills or teach so that students will do well on the standardized tests (Valencia & Pearson, 1987). Valencia and Pearson recommend that formal testing strategies be modified to better match reading research findings about effective instruction, but also that teachers use a combination of strategies that more accurately assess the reading process.

The developmental nature of emergent literacy is also cited as a rationale for using informal evaluation measures. Literacy includes the development of language, listening, writing, and reading, which are interrelated and concurrent. The process of literacy begins at birth and continues throughout the early childhood years. The developmental progress of literacy is followed and evaluated by using the child's performance and examples of work collected over a period of time that reflect advances toward the ability to communicate through reading and writing. More specifically, assessment of literacy occurs through emergent writing samples, emergent reading of books, and oral discussions founded on the philosophy that the child's emerging skills reflect the child's ability to construct literacy through experiences with literacy over time (Goodwin & Goodwin, 1993; Sulzby, 1990; Teale, 1988). Likewise, stages of emergent literacy that are skills related, such as knowledge of letter–sound correspondence and encoding and decoding words, are assessed through learning activities and instructional events (Schickedanz, 1989). Although federal guidelines for successful reading in the primary grades stress the importance of phonics, emergent literacy is still a very appropriate choice for developing literacy in young children (Fields & Spangler, 2000; Newman, Copple, & Bredekamp, 2000; Owocki, 2001). Moreover, emergent literacy incorporated with other strategies that use a constructivist approach can be incorporated into assessment activities. Open-ended tasks and performance activities reflect the developmental nature of emergent literacy (Shepard, 2000).

Using outdated instructional methods so that children will perform well on standardized tests can affect mathematics as well as reading. Although current theory of mathematics instruction stresses that children construct concepts by becoming actively involved with concrete materials, tests still measure knowledge of numerals (Kamii, 1985a, 1985b). School systems teach to the test, rather than follow methods that are best for children (Shepard, 2000). Moreover, the tests stress lower-order thinking, rather than higher-order thinking, and improvement in test scores reflects improvement in computation, rather than in problem solving (Dossey, Mullis, Lindquist, & Chambers, 1988; Kamii & Kamii, 1990). Although newer standardized tests, particularly achievement tests developed at the state level, have included more performance questions, particularly in writing, in general, they are still multiple-choice tests with the same limitations (Popham, 1999). Alternative assessments such as interviews, projects, games, and observations are recommended to evaluate the constructivist nature of learning in mathematics (Kamii & Kamii, 1990).

In contrast to standardized tests, informal assessments are current. Because standardized tests are developed over a period of time, there may be a lag of two years or more between test design and implementation. A test cannot be easily updated or modified. Teacher-designed evaluation measures, however, can be altered when necessary. If instructional materials are changed or learning objectives modified, the teacher can keep classroom measures current by redesigning assessment strategies to reflect the changes.

Another advantage of informal assessments is that they can be correlated with diagnostic needs. If the teacher wants certain types of information for placement, grouping, and individual instructional needs, the assessment measures can be easily adapted for these purposes. Although criterion-referenced standardized tests also serve diagnostic purposes, they are generally a starting point for effective teachers. The teacher must follow criterion-referenced results with informal strategies that provide additional diagnostic information. For preschool children who have not been given standardized tests, teacher-designed strategies are a first step in evaluation. Criterion-referenced standardized tests can be administered later, when the child has the developmental skills to take them.

The flexibility of teacher-designed assessment strategies is an important advantage. The objectives to be evaluated on a standardized test are established early in the test development process. Thereafter, objectives are not changed, and test items to measure them are evenly distributed and measure all general objectives equally. Individual teachers design both the curriculum and the measures to assess children's mastery of it; consequently, evaluation items can be tailored to the teacher's instruction and assessment plans.

DISADVANTAGES OF USING INFORMAL ASSESSMENTS

Although informal assessments have certain advantages, they also have limitations and weaknesses. Classroom teachers are more likely to use informal assessments than the results of standardized tests. Therefore, they must learn how to design and use informal measures appropriately if these measures are to be effective for evaluation and instructional planning. Improper development and implementation are the main disadvantages of informal assessments—specifically, problems centered on their validity and reliability, misapplication, and inappropriate use.

Locally designed assessment instruments are widely used in preschools and elementary schools. Since the 1970s, when informal measures such as instructional checklists first became popular, many school districts have developed their own checklists and other assessment measures. At the preschool level, teachers and administrators have devised screening tests to determine eligibility for preschool intervention programs. For example, in some states, only children who are at risk for academic failure are eligible for state-supported kindergarten programs. Local schools are expected to determine the eligibility of the 5-year-old children in their district. The screening instruments vary greatly from one community to another.

In New York, Joiner (1977) found 151 different tests and other screening procedures being used. Only 16 of the tests were considered appropriate for screening preschool children. The Michigan Department of Education (1984) found 111 different tests being used for preschool, kindergarten, and pre-first-grade programs—and only 10 of them appropriately. Meisels (1987) states that many locally designed screening tests have never been assessed for reliability, validity, or other established criteria.

There are steps that teachers and other educators in public schools can take to develop quality assessments. One method is to establish interrater reliability. Several teachers use the same instrument, such as a checklist or observation, to determine if they get similar results from using the strategy. Likewise, teachers can collaborate on developing multiple-choice or true–false test items to ensure that they locate weaknesses in test items before tests are administered. These testing strategies can be piloted with students to conduct an item analysis to retain or replace test questions as needed. More about establishing quality in assessment strategies will be discussed in the chapters that follow.

Another disadvantage of informal measures is that teachers may misuse them. Locally designed checklists are frequently used as a framework for organizing or designing the curriculum, as well as a record of evaluation of student learning. Children are tested on the checklist's objectives, and the record of their progress follows them from grade to grade. Because teachers develop their own tasks or tests to assess checklist objectives, confusion over what constitutes mastery and what kind of assessment is appropriate can cause major problems within a school or throughout a school district. In an effort to arrive at a consensus on how to assess the objectives, the strategies used by individual teachers may be severely limited. In the primary grades, teachers must frequently place a workbook page or other pencil-and-paper documentation in the child's record as proof of successful performance. This requirement eliminates the use of other informal strategies, such as teacher observation or developmental tasks, for evaluation.

The current movement to incorporate authentic or performance-based assessments in early childhood programs offers additional options for evaluating young children. Interviews, directed assignments, narrative reports, and portfolios offer new techniques that permit teachers to develop assessments congruent with their teaching style and the constructivist approach to learning (Wiggins, 1993, 1998). However, there are serious concerns about the possible disadvantages to these new approaches to informal assessment. One is that these measures may not present evidence of validity, reliability, and freedom from bias. Another disadvantage is the extensive training needed by teachers to feel comfortable with the new techniques (Winograd & Webb, 1994). Furthermore, teachers have concerns about the issue of accountability with authentic assessments. The amount of time needed to conduct the newer measures and to keep records is a concern. Finally, there are concerns about acceptance by parents, the public in general, and policymakers (Goodwin & Goodwin, 1993, 1997; Smith, 1990; Teale, 1990).

The major disadvantage of informal assessments seems to be that teachers are not prepared to develop and use them. They misuse or are unaware of the proper application of either standardized or informal measures. Some writers advocate the use of a variety of formal and informal strategies to assess young children. Observation, like other informal strategies, requires an informed, well-prepared teacher who will use it effectively. In the rest of this chapter, we discuss the purposes of observation and describe how observations are conducted and interpreted.

 ## PURPOSES OF OBSERVATION

Observation is the most direct method of becoming familiar with the learning and development of the young child. Because it requires a focus on the child's behaviors, observation allows the teacher to get to know the child as a unique individual, rather than as a member of a group.

Learning the importance of observation is important, as is developing the skills of how to observe. Many students studying to become teachers, as well as practicing teachers, do not understand how skilled observations are central to the teacher's work or what can be learned from well-conducted observations. Once the importance of observation is understood, teachers and future teachers need to develop observational skills appropriate to the objectives for the observation and the information they desire from the observation (Billman & Sherman, 1997; Harrington, Meisels, McMahon, Dichtelmiller, & Jablon, 1997). Observation can be used for three major purposes: (1) to understand children's behavior, (2) to evaluate children's development, and (3) to evaluate learning progress.

UNDERSTANDING CHILDREN'S BEHAVIOR

Because young children have not yet mastered language and the ability to read and write, they are unable to express themselves as clearly as older children and adults. They cannot demonstrate how much they know or understand through formal or informal assessments involving tasks and standardized tests. According to child development specialists, one of the most accurate ways to learn about children is to observe them in daily activities. Because children cannot explain themselves sufficiently through language, evidence of why they behave as they do is obtained through on-the-spot recording of their actions (Irwin & Bushnell, 1980).

Children communicate through their bodies. Their physical actions reveal as much about them as the things they say. Cohen, Stern, and Balaban (1997) describe how the observation of children's behavior provides information or clues to their thoughts and feelings:

> Children communicate with us through their eyes, the quality of their voices, their body postures, their gestures, their mannerisms, their smiles, their jumping up and down, their listlessness. They show us, by the way they do things as well as by what they do, what is going on inside them. When we come to see children's behavior through the eyes of its meaning to them, from the inside out, we shall be well on our way to understanding them. Recording their ways of communicating helps us to see them as they are. (p. 5)

OBSERVATION OF SOCIAL BEHAVIOR. A major accomplishment during the early childhood years is the development of social skills. Beginning as toddlers and preschoolers, young children evolve into social beings who learn to interact with each other. First efforts to become part of a social group are often ineffective, but with continued opportunity to engage in group activities, most young children develop the ability to work and play with each other. Observation of children at play or interacting in classroom centers reveals how social development and behavior are progressing. Social behavior is part of the social development included in the next section.

EVALUATING CHILDREN'S DEVELOPMENT

A second major purpose of observing children is to evaluate their development. When studying development, observation is specific. Rather than consider behavior in general, the observer's purpose is to determine the child's progress in physical, cognitive, social, or emotional development. Observation of development not only makes it easy to understand sequences of development, but also helps teachers of young children to be aware of individual growth and aids children who have delays in specific areas of development. Skilled observation of developmental domains requires a sound foundation in child development. The ability to conduct developmental observations develops with practice when the student and practicing teacher are able to match developmental characteristics and norms with the activities of the children they observe.

Beaty (1997) describes observation of development as systematic. There are specific purposes for observing and particular methods for collecting and recording observation data. Beaty proposes eight reasons for systematically observing and recording the development of young children:

1. To make an initial assessment of the child's abilities
2. To determine a child's areas of strength and areas needing strengthening
3. To make individual plans based on observed needs
4. To conduct an ongoing check on the child's progress
5. To learn more about child development in particular areas
6. To resolve a particular problem involving the child
7. To use in reporting to parents or to specialists in health, speech, and mental health
8. To gather information for the child's folder, for use in guidance and placement (p. 5)

ASSESSMENT OF YOUNG CHILDREN WITH DISABILITIES. In recent years, educators who work with children who have developmental delays or disabilities have begun to use observation as a tool for assessment. Traditionally, tests for infants and preschool children were used almost exclusively to identify and diagnose the development of children with disabilities or at risk to develop disabilities. Observation of play has been found to be more effective than testing for some types of assessment. Sometimes referred to as play-based assessment, both structured and nonstructured observations can be used to assess the young child's developmental strengths and weaknesses (Segal & Webber, 1996).

PLAY-BASED ASSESSMENT Assessment during child play, or **play-based assessment,** is particularly useful for learning about development in children with disabilities. The procedures described in this chapter can be used with children without disabilities; however, play observation provides unique ways to assess children who may be delayed in development. For example, children with disabilities and children who are developing normally can be presented with the same toys. The observer can then compare how the two groups play with the toys to determine possible deficits in children with disabilities. Toys can also be given to a child with disabilities to observe and rate the developmental sequences of play (Fewell & Glick, 1998).

Children with disabilities are usually served by a team of adults. Assessment and intervention teams have different specializations and purposes for assessment. **Arena assessment** by these teams has become a popular method of evaluating children with disabilities. In arena assessment, the professionals simultaneously observe the child's play (Foley, 1992; Linder, 1993, 1998). Transdisciplinary play-based assessment (TPBA) is used to observe characteristics of children's development in structured and unstructured play situations. A TPBA arena assessment can be used to study child–child and parent–child interactions and snack time, as well as motor play and other unstructured forms of play (Bergen, 1994; Fewell & Glick, 1998; Linder, 1993).

ASSESSING PROGRESS IN LEARNING

Once children have entered kindergarten and first grade, teachers need to acquire information on what children have learned from classroom instruction and learning activities. Although other strategies such as teacher-designed tasks and tests are commonly used, observation is also a useful tool, especially to understand the individual learning styles used by children. The teacher might use a planned observation such as the strategies described later in the chapter or an incidental observation that is employed when the teacher notices a child's activity or behavior that can provide insight into the child's learning. Both planned and incidental observation are effectively conducted during children's play. Almost every area of development can be observed through the observation of play. Teachers can observe social skills, language skills, cognitive skills, and motor skills using incidental or structured observations (Fewell & Glick, 1998). One type of activity that is effective is a performance activity whereby the child is able to demonstrate learning through some type of performance, such as motor skills on the playground or the ability to put a complex puzzle together. This type of performance assessment will be discussed in more detail in chapter 8.

A teacher can use Vygotsky's zone of proximal development (ZPD) in observations to determine the child's progress toward mastery of skills (Bodrova & Leong, 1996). Vygotsky (1978) proposed that there is a range or zone between what the child cannot do, can do with assistance, and can do independently. The teacher observes the child's activities and work to determine where the child's progress lies in the ZPD. An example in kindergarten or first grade might be the student's ability to use fine-motor skills to construct a model or make a collage. The teacher can observe the child at work to determine level of competency in drawing, cutting, and putting materials together to determine his or her ZPD in fine-motor skills needed for the task.

Because what is observed must be interpreted, the observer must know how to use observation to gather specific data. Background information on how children develop and learn is important if the observer is to convert the child's behaviors into information that can be used to understand the child's level of development and the need for experiences that will further this development.

Obviously, the quality of the information gained from an observation depends on the skills of the observer. The sophisticated observer uses knowledge of developmental theories and stages of development to identify the significant events of an observation and to interpret these events in a way that is useful in understanding the child. For example, a teacher may notice that a child is exploring or playing with a collection of buttons in making a pile of all the buttons with four holes. A knowledge of Piaget's cognitive developmental theory will enable the teacher to interpret this activity as the ability to classify objects.

Bentzen (1997) states that observation is not simply looking at something; it is a disciplined, scientific process of searching for a behavior in a particular way. The observer must know what to look for, how to record the desired information, and how to explain the behavior.

Young children develop rapidly, and their level of development changes continually. By observing frequently, teachers can track the child's development and respond to changes and advances in development with new opportunities and challenges.

ASSESSING MULTIPLE INTELLIGENCES

Howard Gardner (1993, 2000) has done extensive research in the theory of multiple intelligences. He believes that individuals can have various kinds of intelligences that can be seen in how people develop skills that are important to their lives. The intelligences work together to solve problems and result in different vocations and avocations. The purpose of schooling is to understand and develop each student's combination of intelligences and to match individuals to curriculum areas and to particular ways of teaching these subjects.

Gardner believes that children's exceptional talents can be identified in the early childhood years and profiles can be developed for individual preschoolers. Although structured games and tasks are used to assess blends of intelligence in students, observation of students in the preschool environment is the major approach. Project Spectrum, developed by researchers at Harvard's Project Zero, was established to examine children's potential to develop strength in one or more areas. Classrooms in Project Spectrum are arranged to facilitate children's opportunities to work with intelligences and combinations of intelligences. More about Project Spectrum will be discussed in chapter 10.

Teachers can evaluate how the multiple intelligences are reflected in the curriculum. Carlisle (2001) accomplished this by listing the foremost skills in each category of intelligence and then identified typical preschool activities that complemented or encouraged each ability. She then could monitor the curriculum and classroom experiences to determine if all of the eight intelligences were being addressed.

TYPES OF OBSERVATION

What happens during an observation? What does the observer actually do? When conducting an observation, the student, teacher, or researcher visits a classroom or other place where a group of children may be observed as they engage in routine activities. The observer, having already determined the objectives or purpose of the observation, the time to be spent studying the child or children, and the form in which the observation will be conducted and recorded, sits at the side or in an observation booth and watches the children. The types of observations used include anecdotal records, running records, specimen records, time sampling, event sampling, and checklists and rating scales.

ANECDOTAL RECORD

An **anecdotal record** is a written description of a child's behavior. It is an objective account of an incident that tells what happened, when, and where. The record may be used to understand some aspect of behavior. A physician, parents, or teachers may use anecdotal records to track the development of an infant or a young child in order to explain unusual behavior. Although the narrative itself is objective, comments may be added as an explanation of or a reaction to the recorded incident.

The anecdotal record has five characteristics (Goodwin & Driscoll, 1980):

1. The anecdotal record is the result of direct observation.
2. The anecdotal record is a prompt, accurate, and specific account of an event.
3. The anecdotal record includes the context of the behavior.
4. Interpretations of the incident are recorded separately from the incident.
5. The anecdotal record focuses on behavior that is either typical or unusual for the child being observed.

Figure 5–1 is an example of the form and content of an anecdotal record. Teachers can use anecdotal records in the classroom to record observed behaviors. The caregiver in an infant

FIGURE 5–1 Example of an anecdotal record

Child Name(s): <u>Robbie, Mary, Janie</u>
Age: <u>4</u>
Location: <u>Sunnyside Preschool</u>
Observer: <u>Sue</u>
Type of Development Observed: <u>Social/Emotional</u>

Incident	Social/Emotional Notes or Comments
Mary and Janie were in the House-keeping Area pretending to fix a meal. Robbie came to the center and said he wanted to eat. The girls looked at him. Janie said, "You can't play here, we're busy." Robbie stood watching the girls as they moved plastic fruit on the table. Robbie said, "I could be the Daddy and do the dishes." Mary thought for a minute, looked at Janie, and replied, "Oh, all right, you can play."	The girls play together frequently and tend to discourage others from entering their play. Robbie has learned how to enter a play group. He was careful not to upset the girls. They relented when he offered to be helpful. Robbie is usually successful in being accepted into play activities.

or toddler classroom might keep a daily logbook or index cards on a child's eating or health patterns or acquisition of a new skill to share with parents. A preschool teacher might use address labels to record a significant or changing behavior to note and place in a child's folder. Likewise, a primary-grade teacher might note a child's daily work habits in the classroom on sticky notes to record and document the ability or inability to focus on tasks, dependency on others, or improvements in a child's social behavior (Fields & Spangler, 2000; Martin, 1994).

RUNNING RECORD

The **running record** is another method of recording behavior. It is a more detailed narrative of a child's behavior that includes the sequence of events. The running record includes everything that occurred over a period of time—that is, all behavior observed—rather than the particular incidents that are used for the anecdotal record. The description is objective. An effort is made to record everything that happened or was said during the observation period. Running records may be recorded over a period ranging from a few minutes to a few weeks or even months.

The observer comments on or analyzes the behaviors separately after studying the record. His or her task is to record the situation so that future readers can visualize what occurred (Cohen et al., 1997). Figure 5–2 is an example of a running record.

Running records are also used in connection with assessment of emergent literacy. When the teacher desires to acquire information about the child's current abilities and weaknesses in reading, the teacher may wish to listen to the child read and may record errors and cor-

FIGURE 5–2 Example of a running record

Child Name(s): <u>Christopher</u>
Age: <u>4</u>
Location: <u>KinderKare</u>
Date and Time: <u>June 21, 19XX</u>   <u>8:40–9:10</u>
Observer: <u>Perlita</u>
Type of Development Observed: <u>Social and Cognitive</u>

Observation	Notes or Comments
Chris is playing with a toy. He says, "Kelly, can I keep it?" several times until he gets an answer. He moves on to a toy guitar and plays it while he supervises the other children by walking around the room. He tells everyone to sit down at the tables after the teacher says to.	Chris is polite to others. Chris is helping his classmates to follow the rules.
Chris sits by a friend and talks about eating granola bars. He watches and listens to the conversation on either side of him. He's still unaffected by the loud temper tantrum of another child. Then he notices her and watches. He tries to explain this behavior to the others by saying a plant was split.	Chris is interested in what others have to say. Chris tries to make sense of a child's behavior.
He follows teacher's directions. Then he decides he wants to be in on a secret. A boy shoves him away. Chris informs him that he *can* hear if he wants to. This has caused him to disobey the teacher. He has to sit out of the circle. He walks over to the chair, sits down, gets up immediately, comes back to the circle undetected by the teacher. He joins the circle.	Chris chooses appropriate ways to assert himself.

(continued)

rections that are made as the child reads the passage. The teacher might mark on a copy of the material that the child is reading, using a systematic method of identifying errors such as reversals, substitutions, self-corrections, or omissions. As an alternative, the teacher might use a running record form separate from the passage being read. The intent is to conduct an informal assessment when the child is actually reading (Sulzby, 1993).

FIGURE 5–2 continued

Observation	Notes or Comments
Chris tattles on a child hiding money. He is told to switch places and wants to know why. He gets up to push the chairs under the table without being asked directly. He wants to explain the temper tantrum to another child (it is still going on) who is curious.	Chris needs to know why he does some things.
Chris attends to the teacher's questions and the story that she is now reading. He begins to look around the circle and then back to the book. He plays with his socks and participates in the group answers to questions about the story (*Now One Foot, Now the Other Foot* by Tomie dePaola [he is in continuous motion with some part of his body during the story]). Now he becomes very still and attends to the story. He puts both hands over his ears when students remark about events in the story. He immediately makes his own remarks. He becomes very still again. The whole circle is quiet for the ending of the book.	Chris shows he has self-control. Chris responds to and sympathizes with the characters in the story.
As soon as the story is finished, Chris says, "I got a cut from a thorn bush." He sits very quietly but moves around. "How do we kill our plants over there?" he asks the teacher. (A plant was knocked off earlier.) "Not mine, not me!" he says.	

Running records may be used for reading instruction. A teacher might observe a child's oral reading and write down unknown words, fluency changes, or difficulty in pronouncing some words. At the end of the reading activity, the teacher has needed information to help the child immediately and in succeeding instructional periods.

FIGURE 5–3 Adaptation of a running record for reading

Child's name _Felicia_   Date _Dec 15_

Book _Catch that Frog_

PAGE:	E	Sc	M	S	V
1					
2 ✓ ✓ ✓ ✓ ✓ ✓ ✓ ✓ ✓ ✓ ✓ ✓ ✓					
3					
4 ✓✓ ✓✓ ✓✓ ✓ ✓ ✓ ✓✓ ✓					
5					
6 ✓ ✓ ✓ ✓ ✓ her/Carol's /sc ✓ ✓ ✓ ✓ ✓R ✓		1			sc
7 ✓✓✓ around/across ✓ ✓✓✓✓✓	1		⊥		
8 ✓ ✓ ✓ ✓ ✓ ✓ ✓ ✓ ✓✓					
9					
10 ✓ got/caught /sc ✓✓ ✓✓✓ along/again	1	1			✓
11					
12 ✓✓✓ ✓ ✓ ✓✓ ✓ ✓✓✓ ✓✓✓					
13					
14 ✓ ✓ ✓ ✓ ✓ ✓ ✓ ✓✓✓					
15					
16 ✓ ✓ ✓ ✓ ✓ ✓					
17					
18 ✓ ✓ after/around /sc ✓✓R ✓ that/the ✓		1	sc		
19					
20 ✓✓✓ after/around /sc ✓✓ get/after ✓✓	1	1	⊥		⊥

Analysis of Errors and Self Corrections (SC): Strategies (Meaning, Structure, Visual)

Comments:

    ✗ checks with visual and meaning clues
    this was an easy book for Felicia

Source: M. V. Fields and K. L. Spangler, *Let's Begin Reading Right: A Development Approach to Emergent Literacy,* 4th ed., p. 297. Reprinted by permission of Pearson Education, Inc., Upper Saddle River, NJ.

Marie Clay (1993) developed a standardized running record to document oral reading behaviors in the Reading Recovery Program. In this program designed to detect and correct problems at early reading stages, checks are used to mark words read correctly, while a dash is used for words missed. Figure 5–3 shows an adaptation of a running record and analysis

FIGURE 5-4 Example of time sampling

Child Name(s): <u>Joanie</u>
Age: <u>5</u>
Location: <u>Rosewood School Kindergarten</u>
Date and Time: <u>May 17, 10:45–11:00</u>
Observer: <u>Susanna</u>
Type of Development Observed: <u>Joanie Has Difficulty Completing Tasks</u>

Event	Time	Notes or Comments
Art Center—leaves coloring activity on table unfinished	10:45	Some of Joanie's behaviors seem to be resulting from failure to follow procedures for use of materials.
Library—looks at book, returns it to shelf.	10:50	
Manipulative Center—gets frustrated with puzzle, piles pieces in center—leaves on table. Pulls out Lego blocks, starts to play. When teacher signals to put toys away, Joanie leaves Lego blocks on table and joins other children.	10:55	Behavior with the puzzles may come from frustration.
	11:00	Joanie may need help in putting away with verbal rewards for finishing a task and putting materials away. Encourage Joanie to get help with materials that are too hard.

of errors and self-corrections. The left-hand side of the page shows how each word was recorded on the 20 pages of the story. Errors, self-corrections, and strategies used for identifying words are recorded in the columns at the right-hand side of the page (Fields & Spangler, 2000).

SPECIMEN RECORD

The **specimen record** is very similar to a running record. It is even more detailed and precise. Beaty (1997) defines running records as informal methods used by teachers. Specimen records, in contrast, are used by researchers who are not part of classroom activities and who are removed from the children. Researchers may later code observation information to analyze the findings. For example, specimen records were used in a study of child-care settings in Chicago. As part of the study, observation was used to determine caregiver behaviors. Researchers coded each utterance by a caregiver to a child, as well as every incident of playing, helping, teaching, touching, kissing, and hitting (Clark-Stewart, 1987).

TIME SAMPLING

The purpose of **time sampling** is to record the frequency of a behavior for a designated period of time. The observer decides ahead of time what behaviors will be observed, what the time interval will be, and how the behaviors will be recorded. The observer observes these behaviors and records how many times they occur during preset, uniform time periods. Other behaviors that occur during the observation are ignored. After a number of samplings have been completed, the data are studied to determine when and perhaps why a behavior is occurring. The observer can use the information to help the child if a change in behavior is desired.

Time sampling may be used with young children because many of their behaviors are brief. By using time sampling, the observer can gain comprehensive information about the behavior. The length of the observation can be affected by the target behavior, the children's familiarity with the observer, the nature of the situation, and the number of children to be observed (Webb, Campbell, Schwartz, & Sechrest, 1966).

Time sampling is frequently used by teachers or other school staff members when a child is behaving inappropriately at school, for example, one who behaves aggressively with other children and does not cooperate in classroom routines at certain times. It is used over a period of time during the hours of the daily schedule when the unwanted behavior occurs. After the time samples are studied, the teacher can determine what can be done to modify the behavior. Figure 5–4 is an example of time sampling as an observation method.

OBSERVING BULLYING BEHAVIOR

Oscar enjoys teasing and challenging his fellow first-graders to a fight. Although he usually picks on other boys in his own classroom, his teacher, Mary Oltorf, has been getting complaints from other teachers. Mary decides to observe how often Oscar exhibits this kind of behavior. While supervising her class during recess, she records how often Oscar bullies other children. Each time that Oscar uses an aggressive or teasing behavior she marks down the time that it occurred and the behavior used. At the end of the recess period, she evaluates the frequency of Oscar's behavior, and finds that he disturbed children five times during the play period. After making these observed time recordings every day for a week, she and the other teachers determine that Oscar bullies other children regularly and plans how to intervene and guide Oscar to more acceptable play behaviors. Mary found that she was vaguely aware that Oscar upset other children, but until she made a timed observation, she was not aware of how serious the problem was for Oscar and the other children on the playground.

In the example described, the teacher did not observe Oscar at regular time intervals as shown in Figure 5.4. Instead, she marked the times that the targeted behavior occurred during the recess period each day. Nevertheless, she was able to record the frequency of Oscar's bullying behavior for a designated period of time.

FIGURE 5–5 Example of event sampling

Child Name(s): <u>Tamika</u>
Age: <u>4</u>
Location: <u>May's Child Enrichment Center</u>
Date and Time: <u>2/4</u> <u>2:30–3:30</u>
Observer: <u>Marcy</u>
Type of Development Observed: <u>Social/Emotional</u>
   Tamika uses frequent hitting behavior

Time	Antecedent Event	Behavior	Consequent Event
2:41	Tamika and Rosie are eating a snack. Rosie takes part of Tamika's cracker.	Tamika hits Rosie.	Rosie calls to the teacher.
3:20	John is looking at a book in the Library Center. Tamika asks for the book. John refuses.	Tamika grabs the book and hits John.	John hits back and takes back the book. Tamika gets another book and sits down.

EVENT SAMPLING

Event sampling is used instead of time sampling when a behavior tends to occur in a particular setting, rather than during a predictable time period. The behavior may occur at odd times or infrequently; event sampling is commonly used to discover its causes or results. The observer determines when the behavior is likely to occur and waits for it to take place. The drawback of this method is that if the event does not occur readily the observer's time will be wasted.

Because event sampling is a cause-and-effect type of observation, the observer is looking for clues that will assist in solving the child's problem. Bell and Low (1977) use *ABC analysis* with the observed incident to understand the cause of the behavior. *A* is the antecedent event, *B* is the target behavior, and *C* is the consequent event. Using ABC analysis with event sampling permits the observer to learn how to address the problem with the child. Figure 5–5 is an example of event sampling with ABC analysis to interpret the incident. Because event sampling is used typically for inappropriate behaviors, its primary usefulness is to determine the cause of the behavior and to address the problem. For example, Sheila, age 4, frequently approached the teacher on the playground because she had "nothing to do." The teacher assumed Sheila just wanted attention until she observed Sheila's play using the ABC process and realized that she approached the teacher after being rejected by her playmates. Moreover, the other girls had noticed that Sheila "tattled" to the teacher and enjoyed the success of their actions. By probing the cause of Sheila's difficulty in group play, the teacher realized that both Sheila and the other playmates needed to change their behaviors. She helped Sheila to learn acceptable ways to be a part of the play group. At the same time, the other girls were redirected to more positive interactions with Sheila.

Figure 5–6 is an observation form that is adaptable to various types of observations. The summary of important behaviors at the bottom of the page can be expanded into a narrative report if desired. Narrative reports will be discussed in chapter 10.

CHECKLISTS AND RATING SCALES

Although chapter 6 is devoted to checklists and rating scales, it is useful to include them in this discussion of observation techniques. A **checklist** is a list of sequential behaviors arranged in a system of categories. The observer can use the checklist to determine whether the child exhibits the behaviors or skills listed. The checklist is useful when many behaviors are to be observed. It can also be used fairly quickly and easily.

The **rating scale** provides a means to determine the degree to which the child exhibits a behavior or the quality of that behavior. Each trait is rated on a continuum, allowing the observer to decide where the child fits on the scale. Rating scales are helpful when the teacher needs to evaluate a wide range of behaviors at one time. For example, a rating scale of social skills might be used to record social behaviors not yet exhibited by a child in conjunction with an observation of social play. A checklist of independent work behaviors might be used during an observation of children in the classroom to identify problematic behaviors, such as attention seeking or actions used to delay completing assigned work.

AUDIOTAPES AND VIDEOTAPES

Taping observations can be a useful tool to record activities observed during an observation. Audiotapes are helpful when children's language is important to the observation. Instead of trying to record what children say, the observer can use the tape recorder to document the language used. Later, the tape can be reviewed to analyze children's conversations.

Videotapes can also be helpful to augment an observation. Although the observer can record significant events during the observation, the videotape can provide opportunities for further study and analysis after the observation has been completed. It can also serve to assist in interpretation and analysis when several observers are working together.

 OBSERVING DEVELOPMENT

Young children develop rapidly. At this time, we need to consider the meaning of development in more detail. Development is continuous and sequential and involves change over time.

Development can be defined, in part, as the process of change in an individual over time. As the individual ages, certain changes take place. Development is thus affected by the child's chronological age, rate of maturation, and individual experiences. Children of the same chronological age are not necessarily at the same stage or level of development, possibly because they mature at different rates and have different experiences and opportunities. The child who has many opportunities to climb, run, and jump in outdoor play may demonstrate advanced motor development skills, compared to the child who spends most play periods indoors.

FIGURE 5-6 Sample observation form

Name _____

Date _____

Time _____

Location _____

Child(ren) Observed _____

_____

Age _____

Type of Development Observed: _____

Type of Observation Used: _____

Purposes of Observation:

1.

2.

3.

Questions Answered:

1.

2.

3.

Description of Observation (Anecdotal, Time Sampling, Running Record, Event Sampling):

Summary of Important Behaviors Recorded and Comments:

Developmental change can be both quantitative and qualitative. Physical growth is quantitative and cumulative. New physical skills are added to those already present. Developmental change can also be qualitative. When changes in psychological characteristics such as speech, emotions, or intelligence occur, development is reorganized at a higher level.

Development is characterized as continuous. The individual is constantly changing. In quantitative change, the individual is continually adding new skills or abilities. In qualitative change, the individual is incorporating new development with existing characteristics to create more sophisticated psychological traits.

Finally, development is sequential. Each individual develops at a different rate; however, the sequence or pattern of development is the same. All children move through stages of development in the same sequence, the characteristics of which are described by Bentzen (1997) as follows:

1. Stages or steps in development do not vary. Children do not skip a stage of development.
2. Children progress through the stages in the same order.
3. All children, regardless of cultural or social differences, progress through the stages in the same order. The stages are universal. (p. 21)

PHYSICAL DEVELOPMENT

Preschool children are in the most important period of physical and motor development. Beginning with babies, who are in the initial stages of learning to control their bodies, physical development is rapid and continues into the primary school years.

Observations of physical development focus on both types of motor development: gross- and fine-motor skills. *Gross-motor skills* refer to the movements and abilities of the large muscles of the body in physical activities. Gross-motor development includes locomotor dexterity movements that permit the child to move about in some manner, such as jumping, hopping, running, and climbing. This basic list was extended (Jambor, 1990) to include rolling, creeping, crawling, stepping up and down, bouncing, hurdling, pumping a swing, galloping, and skipping. In the preschool years, gross-motor skills advance from riding a tricycle to a bicycle. Some older preschoolers are able to roller skate and kick a soccer ball (Johnson, 1998).

Fine-motor skills involve the body's small muscles, specifically, the hands and fingers. Preschool children gain more control of finger movement, which allows them to become more proficient in using materials that require grasping and manipulating. These skills are used for eating, dressing, writing, using small construction toys, and performing other tasks. Preschool children learn to work with puzzles; cut with scissors; use brushes, pens, pencils, and markers; and manipulate small blocks, counters, and modeling clay. Fine-motor skills emerge after gross-motor skills have been mastered.

PURPOSES FOR OBSERVING PHYSICAL DEVELOPMENT. Physical development is observed for the following reasons:

1. To learn how children develop gross- and fine-motor skills
2. To become familiar with the kinds of physical activities young children engage in as they practice the use of gross- and fine-motor skills
3. To become familiar with individual differences in physical development

QUESTIONS ANSWERED BY OBSERVATION OF PHYSICAL DEVELOPMENT.
Physical development is observed to answer the following questions:

1. Observe a child on the playground. What gross-motor movements can you record?
2. What types of large-motor activities does the child enjoy using play equipment?
3. Observe a child working or playing in activity centers in the classroom. What kinds of fine-motor movements can you record?
4. Observe two children engaged in art activities. Can you see differences in fine-motor development and dexterity? Describe them.

SOCIAL AND EMOTIONAL DEVELOPMENT

Social development and emotional development are significant areas of development during the preschool years. In this period, the child moves from egocentricity to social interaction with others. When a child is able to use social behaviors, he or she influences others and is influenced by them. As children interact in various contexts, they develop and expand their repertoire of social skills.

Emotional development parallels and affects social development. The preschool child refines behaviors as he or she experiences such emotions as happiness, anger, joy, jealousy, and fear. The most common emotions in preschool children are aggression, dependency, and fear (Bentzen, 1997). *Aggression* is a behavior intended to hurt another person or property. *Dependency* causes such behaviors as clinging, seeking approval, assistance, reassurance, and demands for attention. *Fear* includes behaviors such as crying and avoiding the feared situation.

Important characteristics of social and emotional development are self-concept, self-esteem, and self-regulation of emotions. In self-concept, young children develop an awareness that they are different from other children and have individual characteristics that are defined by mastery of skills and competencies (Berger, 2000; Berk, 2001).

Self-regulation of emotions results when children develop an awareness of their feelings and are able to initiate behaviors that permit them to cope. Self-esteem emerges when children begin to make judgments about their own worth and competencies. They feel they are liked or disliked depending on how well they can do things and are influenced by parental and peer approval or disapproval. They translate accomplishments and new skills into positive or negative feelings about themselves.

PURPOSES FOR OBSERVING SOCIAL AND EMOTIONAL DEVELOPMENT. Social and emotional development is observed for the following reasons:

1. To learn how children develop social skills
2. To become familiar with how children learn about social interactions
3. To understand how children differ in social skill development
4. To become familiar with the ways preschool children handle their emotions
5. To be aware of differences in children's emotional behaviors and responses

QUESTIONS ANSWERED BY OBSERVATIONS OF SOCIAL AND EMOTIONAL DEVELOPMENT. Social development and emotional development are observed to answer the following questions:

1. How has a child demonstrated social awareness and prosocial skills?
2. How do children develop leadership skills? Observe a child who is able to lead peers in play and describe how that role was initiated.
3. How does the child resolve conflict? Observe children dealing with a problem and describe how the conflict was handled.
4. How do children use and handle aggressive behavior? Observe a child who is behaving aggressively. How does this child use aggression and what is the response of the victim?
5. What kinds of events trigger dependence or fear? Observe a child who has encountered either situation and describe how the child reacts.

COGNITIVE DEVELOPMENT

Cognitive development, which stems from mental functioning, is concerned with how the child learns about and understands the world. Cognitive abilities develop as the child interacts with the environment. Our descriptions of cognitive development are derived largely from Piaget's theory of development.

Piaget described cognitive development in terms of stages. The quality of the child's thinking progresses as the child moves through the stages. The infant is in the sensorimotor stage, which lasts until about 18 months of age. During this stage, intellectual growth occurs through the senses and innate reflexive actions. In the latter part of the sensorimotor stage, symbolic thought develops, which is characterized by improved memory.

Between the ages of 2 and 6 years, the child moves through the preoperations stage. In this stage, the ability to use language is developed. The child is egocentric, unable to view another person's perspective. Thinking is bounded by perception. Later, when the child reaches the stage of concrete operations, he or she is able to move beyond perceptual thinking. Cognitive abilities become qualitatively different. The child is now able to grasp concepts such as classification, seriation, one-to-one correspondence, and causality because he or she has attained conservation (Morrison, 1988).

The child's use of mental processes to understand knowledge develops gradually, and cognitive abilities evolve over a long period of time. Piaget attributed cognitive development to maturity, experiences, and social transmission. Therefore, the child's family, environment, and opportunities for experiences affect the development of cognitive abilities. Knowledge is reconstructed as the child organizes and restructures experiences to refine and expand his or her own understanding.

PURPOSES FOR OBSERVING COGNITIVE DEVELOPMENT. Cognitive development is observed for the following reasons:

1. To understand how children use their cognitive abilities to learn
2. To understand the differences in children's cognitive styles
3. To become familiar with how children develop the ability to use classification, seriation, and one-to-one correspondence
4. To understand how the child uses play and interaction with materials to extend his or her cognitive abilities
5. To become familiar with how children think and what they are capable of learning
6. To evaluate what children have learned

QUESTIONS ANSWERED BY OBSERVATION OF COGNITIVE DEVELOPMENT. Cognitive development is observed to answer the following questions:

1. How is the child's learning affected by cognitive abilities? Observe two children and compare how they address an activity that requires solving a problem.
2. How does the child use emerging cognitive abilities? Find examples of children using conservation, one-to one correspondence, or seriation and describe their activities.
3. How do children differ in cognitive development and cognitive characteristics? Observe two children who seem to have different levels of cognition and compare how they work with drawings, work a puzzle, or make a construction.
4. How do classroom experiences affect the opportunities for cognitive development? Study learning centers in a preschool classroom and describe opportunities for learning.
5. How is a child's cognitive knowledge demonstrated nonverbally? Observe a child and describe how the child's actions reveal that learning is occurring or being applied to an activity.

LANGUAGE DEVELOPMENT

The acquisition of language is a major accomplishment of children during the preschool and primary grade years. During the first 8 years of life, the child rapidly acquires vocabulary, grammar, and syntax. As in other types of development, the child's use of language changes, increases, and is refined over a period of time.

Whereas babies begin using speech as single utterances, toddlers and preschoolers expand their repertoire into two words, three words, and increasingly complex statements. As the child's ability to use language expands to include questions and other grammatical elements, the child uses trial and error to approximate more closely the syntax and grammar of adult speech.

Language development is also related to cognitive development. When the child's thinking is egocentric, his or her language reflects this pattern. The egocentric child talks to herself and does not use language to communicate with other children. The child who is shedding egocentric thinking uses socialized speech to communicate with others. He or she not only shares conversations with peers and adults, but also listens and responds to what others are saying.

During the preschool years, young children learn about 10,000 words. Concurrent with acquisition of a remarkable number of words, they learn the rules of their language. These rules are morphology rules, syntax rules, and semantic rules. Morphology and syntax rules relate to understanding the sounds and grammar of language; semantic rules explain vocabulary and meaning development.

Preschool children also learn the rules of conversation, or the pragmatics of language. The ability to participate in a conversation develops at an early age and is extended and refined with expanded language abilities and experiences with conversations. By age 4, preschool children understand how to carry on a conversation in their language community and culture.

PURPOSES FOR OBSERVING LANGUAGE DEVELOPMENT.   Language development is observed for the following reasons:

1. To become aware of the child's ability to use language to communicate
2. To understand the difference between egocentric and socialized speech
3. To learn how the child uses syntax, grammar, and vocabulary in the process of expanding and refining his or her language
4. To become aware of differences in language development among individual children

QUESTIONS ANSWERED BY OBSERVATION OF LANGUAGE DEVELOPMENT. Language development is observed to answer the following questions:

1. How does the child use language to communicate? Describe how two different children use language to engage in communication with a friend.
2. When do children tend to use egocentric speech? Socialized speech? Describe events when children use each type.
3. What can be observed about the child's use of sentence structure? Record several of a child's utterances and describe the sentence structure used.
4. How can errors in the use of language reveal the child's progress in refining language? Record some child conversations. Describe utterances that reveal an error that will later be expressed correctly.

ADVANTAGES AND DISADVANTAGES OF USING OBSERVATION FOR ASSESSMENT

Observation is a valuable evaluation tool. Teachers may use it to gather the kind of information that may not be available from structured methods of measurement.

When observed, children are engaged in daily activities that are a natural part of the classroom routine. The observer is able to see the typical ways children respond to learning tasks, play activities, and individual and group lessons. The observer can notice the child's behaviors and the background factors that influence the behaviors.

Learning can also be evaluated by observation. The teacher can observe the child's responses in a group during a lesson or while the child engages in exploration with construction materials. Areas of development such as gross-motor skills can be observed on the playground; language skills can be noted by listening to the language of two children in the art center.

An advantage of observation is that the observer can focus on the behavior or information that is needed. If a child is exhibiting aggression, the observer can focus on aggressive incidents to help the child to use more appropriate behaviors in interactions with other children. If a child is beginning to use prosocial skills more effectively, the teacher can observe group interactions and encourage the child to continue to improve.

Although observation allows one to concentrate on specific behaviors, it can also cause difficulties. The observer can miss details that make a significant difference in the quality of the data gathered. Because many incidents and behaviors may occur during the observation, the danger is that the observer may focus on the wrong behaviors. Or the observer may become less attentive during the observation period, resulting in variations in the information obtained (Webb et al., 1966).

Observer bias is another disadvantage. If the observer has preconceived notions about how the child behaves or performs, these ideas can affect the observer's interpretation of the information obtained from watching the child.

Observations can be misleading when the incident observed is taken out of context. Although an observed behavior is often brief, it must be understood in context. A frequent mistake of inexperienced observers is to interpret a single incident as a common occurrence. For example, the observer who witnesses a teacher losing patience with a child may interpret the incident as that teacher's normal behavior. In reality, however, this behavior may be rare. The presence of the observer can also affect children's behavior. Because children are aware that they are being watched, their behaviors may not be typical. As a result, the validity of the observation may be doubtful (Webb et al., 1966).

OBSERVATION GUIDELINES

For college students and teachers who have limited experience in conducting observations or wish to improve their observation skills, certain guidelines are now presented. The student seeking a site for observation needs to know how to go about finding a school or early childhood center and how to observe effectively once it has been selected. Classroom teachers have a ready site in their own classroom or in the classroom of a colleague. However, teachers may want to observe a different type of program and will need to visit a different setting.

DETERMINING THE OBSERVATION SITE

The observation site depends on the type of observation to be done. First, the observer must determine the purpose of the observation. He or she will want to know that children at the school or early childhood center engage in the activities of interest to the observer. For example, if the observer wishes to see activities typical of a Montessori classroom, it would be wise to find out whether these activities will be taking place during the observation period. Once the purpose of the observation has been determined, the observer must decide on an optimum location. If the objective is to learn about creativity in the young child, it is frustrating to spend time in a program in which art experiences are limited or infrequent. Likewise, if the purpose is to observe behaviors in a child-centered environment, it would be inappropriate to visit a structured program directed by the teacher.

Once the center or school has been selected, the observer should contact it ahead of time. Although many settings welcome observers on a walk-in basis, most early childhood programs request or require advance notification. Some settings do not allow observers or schedule them in ways designed to protect children from interruptions. Some schools allow observations on certain days. Others wish to be contacted well in advance because many people wish to observe their program. Many child-care centers schedule field trips frequently and wish to avoid inconveniencing their observers. Whatever the reason, it is best to contact the observation site before scheduling the observation.

OBSERVER BEHAVIORS DURING THE OBSERVATION VISIT

The observer is a guest of the center or school. Although the opportunity to study the children is important, it is also important to avoid disrupting activities in progress. The observer may want to share the purpose of the observation with staff members or the teacher in the classroom being visited. In addition, the observer should conduct the observation in a manner that is compatible with the teacher's style of leadership in the type of program being observed. For example, Montessori schools frequently restrict visitors to certain areas of the classroom and may discourage any interaction with the children. Another school or program may encourage the observer to talk to the children or to take part in their activities.

In most cases, the observer should be unobtrusive. Because children are sensitive to the presence of visitors and may alter their behaviors when a stranger is in the room, observers can minimize such changes by drawing as little attention to their presence as possible. Observers may seat themselves in a position that does not draw the children's attention. Sometimes it is helpful to avoid looking at the children for a few minutes, until they become acclimated. Postponing the writing of observation notes for a few minutes may also help prevent disruption.

Dress can make a difference. Observers dressed in simple clothing of one color rather than bright garments with bold patterns are less likely to draw undue attention to their presence. Dress should also be appropriate. Clothing that is too casual may be offensive to the adults in the early childhood center. Observers should err on the side of being dressed too formally, rather than in an unprofessional manner (Irwin & Bushnell, 1980).

ETHICS DURING THE OBSERVATION VISIT

Observers must be alert to the proper way to use the information gathered during an observation. The privacy of the children, the children's families, and school staff members must be considered. When individual children are observed, only the child's first name should be used. Information from any observation should be considered confidential and safeguarded from casual perusal by others. The child should not be discussed in an unprofessional manner with other observers, school staff members, or outsiders. It may be necessary to obtain

Observations can reveal information about different domains of development.

permission from the child's family prior to making an observation. If this is necessary, the observer should acquire the necessary forms and have them sent to the parents for their approval prior to conducting any observations.

AVOIDING PERSONAL BIAS

Personal bias can affect the observer's reaction to and report of an observation. If observers are aware of how their background and previous experiences can influence their report, they can avoid using personal opinion when analyzing the data collected during an observation.

One cause of observer bias is differences in value systems. It is easy to apply one's own value system when observing in a school. For example, a middle-class observer may misunderstand the nature of aggression exhibited by young children in an inner-city school. It is also possible to impose personal values on the language of a child from a home where cursing is a common form of communication. The observer needs to be aware of such possible biases and avoid them when interpreting observational information.

The observer's reaction to the site can also distort his or her use of observational data. Each observer has a perception of the characteristics of a "good" school or center. When observing an early childhood program that does not fit this definition, the observer may impose a negative interpretation on the information gathered. The reaction to the setting affects how the observer perceives the behaviors observed.

An observation can also be biased by the time of the observation or by the briefness of the visit. Observers frequently react to a teacher's behavior and conclude that the teacher always engages in practices that the observer considers inappropriate. Observers need to understand that what they see during a short visit may give them an incomplete, distorted perception of the teacher or setting. The observer would have to make many visits during different times of the day over a long period of time before being able to draw conclusions about the quality of teaching or the environment. One or two brief observations provide only a small glimpse of the nature of the teacher and the classroom visited.

SUMMARY

Although standardized tests are used to evaluate children's learning, informal strategies are also essential, particularly for use by classroom teachers. They provide a variety of evaluation methods by which teachers can acquire comprehensive information about their students' development and learning.

Observation is used to assess learning and to gather information regarding children's development. Because young children cannot demonstrate knowledge in a written test, teachers of preschool children use observation to learn about children's development, as well as about the knowledge the children have acquired.

Observations are of several types, each with a specific purpose. Observers can use anecdotal records, running records, time sampling, event sampling, and checklists and rating scales to gather information about young children.

REVIEW QUESTIONS

1. Why is it important to use informal assessment methods, particularly with preschool and primary-school children?
2. How do the purposes of informal assessment differ from the purposes of standardized testing?
3. Do the advantages of informal assessment strategies outweigh the disadvantages? Why or why not?
4. Describe some ways that teachers can use informal assessment strategies for instructional planning.
5. What is diagnostic evaluation?
6. What are the differences between formative and summative assessment?
7. Why do informal assessments produce immediate results, compared with standardized test results?
8. How may informal assessments be misused in elementary schools?

9. How may teachers be unaware of the proper use of formal and informal assessments?
10. Describe some purposes of using observation techniques with preschool and school-age children.
11. Why is observation of development systematic and specific?
12. Explain the purposes of the different types of observations: (a) anecdotal records, (b) running records, (c) specimen records, (d) time sampling, (e) event sampling, and (f) checklists and rating scales. What is unique about specimen records?
13. How are other types of development related to the child's cognitive development?
14. How does egocentrism affect cognitive, social, and language development?
15. How can an observer's experience and skills affect the quality of the information gained from observing young children?

SUGGESTED ACTIVITY

Conduct three observations of development. Use a different category of development for each observation. Use a different type of observation for each, selected from anecdotal records, running records, time sampling, and event sampling. Use an adaptation of the sample observation form in Figure 5.6 for each of the three observations.

KEY TERMS

anecdotal record

arena assessment

checklist

event sampling

formative evaluation

play-based assessment

rating scale

running record

specimen record

summative evaluation

time sampling

REFERENCES

Beaty, J. J. (1997). *Observing development of the young child.* (4th ed.). New York: Merrill/Prentice Hall.

Bell, D., & Low, R. M. (1977). *Observing and recording children's behavior.* Richland, WA: Performance Associates.

Bentzen, W. R. (1997). *Seeing young children: A guide to observing and recording behavior.* Albany: Delmar.

Bergen, D. (1994). *Assessment methods for infants and toddlers.* New York: Teachers College Press.

Berger, K. S. (2000). *The developing person through childhood* (2nd ed.). New York: Worth.

Berk, L. E. (2001). *Infants, children, and adolescents* (3rd ed.). Boston: Allyn and Bacon.

Bernauer, J. A., & Cress, K. (1997). How school communities can help redefine accountability assessment. *Phi Delta Kappan, 79,* 71–75.

Billman, J., & Sherman, J. A. (1997). *Observation and participation in early childhood settings.* Boston: Allyn and Bacon.

Bodrova, E., & Leong, D. J. (1996). *Tools of the mind: The Vygotskian approach to early childhood education.* Upper Saddle River, NJ: Merrill/Prentice Hall.

Carlisle, A. (2001). Using the multiple intelligences theory to assess early childhood curricula. *Young Children, 56,* 77–83.

Clark-Stewart, A. (1987). Predicting child development from child care forms and features: The Chicago study.

In D. A. Phillips (Ed.), *Quality in child care: What does research tell us?* (pp. 21–41). Washington, DC: National Association for the Education of Young Children.

Clay, M. (1993). *An observation survey of early literacy achievement.* Portsmouth, NH: Heinemann.

Cohen, D. H., Stern, V., & Balaban, N. (1997). *Observing and recording the behavior of young children* (4th ed.). New York: Teachers College Press.

Dossey, J. A., Mullis, I. V. S., Lindquist, M. M., & Chambers, D. L. (1988). *The mathematics report card: Are we measuring up?* Princeton, NJ: Educational Testing Service.

Fewell, R., & Glick, M. (1998). The role of play in assessment. In D. Fromberg & D. Bergen (Eds.), *Play from birth to twelve and beyond* (pp. 202–207). New York: Garland.

Fields, M. V., & Spangler, K. L. (2000). *Let's begin reading right.* Upper Saddle River, NJ: Merrill/Prentice Hall.

Foley, G. M. (1992). Portrait of the arena evaluation: Assessment in the transdiciplinary approach. In E. D. Gibbs & D. M. Teti (Eds.), *Interdisciplinary assessment of infants: A guide for early intervention professionals* (pp. 271–286). Baltimore: Paul H. Brookes.

Gardner, H. (1993). *Multiple intelligences: The theory in practice.* New York: Basic Books.

Gardner, H. (2000). *Intelligence reframed: Multiple intelligences for the 21st century.* New York: Basic Books.

Goodwin, W. L., & Driscoll, L. A. (1980). *Handbook for measurement and evaluation in early childhood education*. San Francisco: Jossey-Bass.

Goodwin, W. L., & Goodwin, L. D. (1993). Young children and measurement: Standardized and nonstandardized instruments in early education. In B. Spodek (Ed.), *Handbook of research on the education of young children* (pp. 441–463). New York: Macmillan.

Goodwin, W. L., & Goodwin, L. D. (1997). Using standardized measures for evaluating young children's learning. In B. Spodek & O. N. Saracho (Eds.), *Issues in early childhood educational assessment and evaluation* (pp. 92–107). New York: Teachers College Press.

Harms, T., Clifford, R., & Cryer, D. (1998). *Early Childhood Environment Rating Scale—Revised Edition*. New York: Teachers College Press.

Harrington, H. L., Meisels, S. J., McMahon, P., Dichtelmiller, M. L., & Jablon, J. R. (1997). *Observing, documenting, and assessing learning: The work sampling system handbook for teacher educators*. Ann Arbor, MI: Rebus.

High/Scope Educational Research Foundation. (1992). *Assessment Booklet Child Observation Record (COR)*. Ypsilanti, MI: Author.

Irwin, D. M., & Bushnell, M. M. (1980). *Observational strategies for child study*. New York: Holt, Rinehart & Winston.

Jambor, T. (1990). Promoting perceptual–motor development in young children's play. In S. C. Wortham & J. L. Frost (Eds.), *Playgrounds for young children: National survey and perspectives* (pp. 147–166). Reston, VA: American Alliance for Health, Physical Education, Recreation, and Dance.

Johnson, J. E. (1998). Play development from ages four to eight. In D. Fromberg & D. Bergen (Eds.), *Play from birth to twelve and beyond* (pp. 146–153). New York: Garland.

Joiner, L. M. (1977). A technical analysis of the variation in screening instruments and programs in New York State. ERIC ED 154596.

Kamii, C. (1985a). Leading primary education toward excellence: Beyond worksheets and drill. *Young Children, 40*, 3–9.

Kamii, C. (1985b). *Young children reinvent arithmetic*. New York: Teachers College Press.

Kamii, C., & Kamii, M. (1990). Negative effects of achievement testing in mathematics. In C. Kamii (Ed.), *Achievement testing in the early grades: The games grown-ups play* (pp. 135–145). Washington, DC: National Association for the Education of Young Children.

Linder, T. W. (1993). *Transdisciplinary play-based assessment: A functional approach to working with young children* (Rev. ed.). Baltimore: Paul H. Brookes.

Linder, T. W. (1998). *Transdisciplinary Play Based Assessment*. http://www.nauticom.net/www/eita/TPBA Spring, 98.html.

Linn, R. L., & Gronlund, N. E. (2000). *Measurement and assessment in teaching* (8th ed.). Upper Saddle River, NJ: Merrill/Prentice Hall.

Martin, S. (1994). *Take a look. Observation and portfolio assessment in early childhood*. Don Mills, Ontario: Addison-Wesley.

Meisels, S. J. (1987). Uses and abuses of developmental screening and school readiness testing. *Young Children, 42*, 4–6, 68–73.

Michigan Department of Education. (1984). *Superintendent's study group on early childhood education*. Lansing, MI: Author.

Newman, S. B., Copple, C., & Bredekamp, S. (2000). *Learning to read and write*. Washington, DC: National Association for the Education of Young Children.

Owocki, G. (2001). *Make way for literacy!* Portsmouth, NH: Heinemann.

Popham, W. J. (1999). Why standardized tests don't measure educational quality. *Educational Leadership, 56*, 8–16.

Schickedanz, J. A. (1989). The place of specific skills in preschool and kindergarten. In D. S. Strickland & L. M. Morrow (Eds.), *Emerging literacy: Young children learn to read and write* (pp. 96–106). Newark, DE: International Reading Association.

Segal, M., & Webber, N. T. (1996). Nonstructured play observations: Guidelines, benefits, and caveats. In S. J. Meisels & E. Fenichel (Eds.), *New visions for the developmental assessment of infants and young children* (pp. 207–230). Washington, DC: Zero to Three: National Center for Infants, Children, and Families.

Shepard, L. A. (2000). The role of assessment in a learning culture. *Educational Researcher, 29*, 4–14.

Smith, J. K. (1990). Measurement issues in early literacy assessment. In L. M. Morrow & J. K. Smith (Eds.), *Assessment for instruction in early literacy* (pp. 62–74). Upper Saddle River, NJ: Prentice Hall.

Sulzby, E. (1990). Assessment of writing and children's language when writing. In L. M. Morrow & J. K. Smith (Eds.), *Assessment for instruction in early literacy* (pp. 83–109). Upper Saddle River, NJ: Prentice Hall.

Sulzby, E. (1993). *Teacher's guide to evaluation: Assessment handbook*. Glenview, IL: Scott, Foresman.

Taylor, K., & Walton, S. (1997). Co-opting standardized tests in the service of learning. *Phi Delta Kappan, 79*, 66–70.

Teale, W. H. (1988). Developmentally appropriate assessment of reading and writing in the early childhood classroom. *Elementary School Journal, 89*, 173–183.

Teale, W. H. (1990). The promise and challenge of informal assessment in early literacy. In L. M. Morrow & J. K. Smith (Eds.), *Assessment for instruction in early literacy* (pp. 45–61). Upper Saddle River, NJ: Prentice Hall.

Valencia, S., & Pearson, P. D. (1987). Reading assessment: Time for a change. *Reading Teacher, 40,* 726–732.

Vygotsky, L. S. (1978). *Mind and society: The development of higher mental processes.* Cambridge, MA: Harvard University Press.

Webb, E. J., Campbell, D. T., Schwartz, R. D., & Sechrest, L. (1966). *Unobtrusive measures.* Chicago: Rand McNally.

Wiggins, G. (1989). Teaching to the (authentic) test. *Educational Leadership, 46,* 41–47.

Wiggins, G. P. (1993). *Assessing student performance.* San Francisco: Jossey-Bass.

Wiggins, G. P. (1998). *Educative assessment.* San Francisco: Jossey-Bass.

Winograd, P., & Webb, K. S. (1994). Impact on curriculum and instruction reform. In T. Guskey (Ed.), *High stakes performance* (pp. 19–36). Thousand Oaks, CA: Corwin Press.

Informal Assessments

Checklists, Rating Scales, and Rubrics

CHAPTER 6

Chapter Objectives

As a result of reading this chapter, you will be able to

1. Describe the purposes for using checklists for informal assessment
2. Explain how developmental checklists are used with preschool children
3. Explain the differences between the uses of checklists with preschool and primary-grade children
4. Identify the four basic steps in checklist design
5. Discuss the advantages and disadvantages of using checklists for informal assessment
6. Describe the purposes for using rating scales for informal evaluation
7. Discuss the advantages and disadvantages of using rating scales
8. Describe the purposes for using rubrics for informal evaluation
9. Discuss how rubrics are used with preschool and primary children
10. Discuss how rubrics are designed
11. Discuss the advantages and disadvantages of using rubrics

I n chapter 5, we considered the topic of informal assessment strategies. The purposes of informal assessments were discussed, as well as their strengths and weaknesses. One informal assessment strategy—observation—was described in detail. In this chapter, we discuss another type of evaluation strategy that involves the use of teacher-designed instruments: checklists, rating scales, and rubrics. Because checklists are used more extensively than rating scales by early childhood and primary school teachers, we discuss them first. A description of rating scales follows so that the reader can understand how they are designed and used and how they differ from checklists. Rubrics are used most commonly with performance assessments. They will be discussed in that context.

CHECKLISTS

PURPOSES OF CHECKLISTS

Checklists are made from a collection of learning objectives or indicators of development. The lists of items are arranged to give the user an overview of their sequence and of how they relate to each other. The lists of items are then organized into a checklist format so that the teacher can use them for various purposes in the instructional program. Because the checklists are representative of the curriculum for the grade level, they become a framework for assessment and evaluation, instructional planning, record keeping, and communicating with parents about what is being taught and how their child is progressing.

USING CHECKLISTS WITH PRESCHOOL CHILDREN

Children in the years from birth to age 8 move rapidly through different stages of development. Doctors, psychologists, parents, and developmental specialists want to understand and monitor the development of individual children and groups of children. The developmental indicators for children at different stages and ages have been established; lists and checklists of these indicators can be used to monitor development. When evaluating a child's development, many types of professionals use a **developmental checklist** format to evaluate development and record the results.

Developmental checklists usually are organized into categories of development: physical, cognitive, and social. Physical development is frequently organized into fine- and gross-motor skills. Cognitive, or intellectual, development might include language development. Some checklists have language development as a separate category. Social development checklists can also be organized to include emotional development and development of social skills.

Preschool teachers use checklists to evaluate and record preschoolers' developmental progress. The individual child's developmental progress provides important clues to the kinds of experiences he or she needs and can enjoy. For instance, the teacher keeps track of the child's use of fine-motor skills. After the child is able to use the fingers to grasp small objects, cutting activities may be introduced. In language development, the teacher can evaluate the child's speaking vocabulary and use of syntax and thus choose the best stories to read to the child.

Teachers often use checklists to screen children who enter preschool programs or to select them for programs. Developmental or cognitive tasks are used to identify children with special needs. Because these checklists include behaviors that are characteristic of a stage of development, children who do not exhibit these behaviors can be referred for additional screening and testing (Spodek & Saracho, 1994).

Checklists are also used to design learning experiences at the preschool level. The teacher surveys the list of learning objectives appropriate for that age group of children and uses the list to plan learning activities in the classroom. These checklists can be used to assess the child's progress in learning the objectives and to keep records of progress and further instructional needs. When talking to parents about the instructional program, the teacher can discuss what is being taught and how their child is benefiting from the learning experiences.

USING CHECKLISTS WITH SCHOOL-AGE CHILDREN

The use of checklists for primary school children is very similar to their use with preschool children. In fact, curriculum checklists can be a continuation of those used in the preschool grades. However, there are two differences. First, fewer developmental characteristics are recorded, and cognitive or academic objectives become more important. Second, school-age checklists become more differentiated in areas of learning. Whereas teachers are concerned with motor development, language development, social and emotional development, and cognitive development at the preschool level, at the primary level, curriculum content areas become more important. Thus, with primary grade checklists, objectives are more likely to be organized in terms of mathematics, language arts, science, social studies, and physical education (Ratcliff, 2001/2002).

Diagnosis of learning strengths and weaknesses in curriculum objectives becomes more important in the primary grades, and assessment of progress in learning may become more precise and segmented. Checklist objectives may appear on report cards as the format for reporting achievement to parents. Likewise, the checklist items may be representative of achievement test objectives, state-mandated objectives, textbook objectives, and locally selected objectives.

USING CHECKLISTS TO ASSESS CHILDREN
WITH DELAYS IN DEVELOPMENT

Checklists can be used with children who have exhibited developmental delay and are served in intervention programs. Checklists can be part of an integrated assessment system that has multiple purposes that include continuous assessment of developmental progress. The components of such a system include tracking the child's growth and development through ongoing assessment, documenting and monitoring child growth for caregivers and other professional staff, and providing a structure for families to develop and monitor goals for their children. Checklists in this context are used with a family portfolio, developmental guidelines and checklists, and summary reports of the child's progress (Meisels, 1996).

HOW CHECKLISTS ARE DESIGNED AND USED

Checklists of developmental and instructional objectives have been used in education for several decades. When educators and early childhood specialists worked with Head Start and other programs aimed at improving education for special populations of students, they developed outlines of educational objectives to describe the framework of learning that children should experience. Since that time, checklists have been further developed and used at all levels of education. Reading series designed for elementary grades include a scope and sequence of skills, and many school districts have a list of objectives for every course or grade level. Figure 6–1 is a typical checklist developed by a school district for mathematics at the elementary level.

Curriculum objectives and skills can be developed at a state or national level. The U.S. Department of Education held a reading summit in September 1998 to discuss prevention of reading difficulties in young children. The National Research Council (NRC) undertook a study of research on early reading development to provide suggestions about how to prevent reading problems in young children. Part of its report included accomplishments in reading that might be expected from birth through grade 3. Following is a partial list of second-grade accomplishments suggested by the NRC (Bickart, 1998):

Reads and comprehends both fiction and nonfiction that is appropriately designed for grade level.

Accurately decodes orthographically regular multisyllable words and nonsense words (e.g., capital, Kalamazoo).

Uses knowledge of print–sound mappings to sound out unknown words.

Accurately reads many irregularly spelled words and such spelling patterns as diphthongs, special vowel spellings, and common word endings.

Shows evidence of expanding language repertory, including increasing use of more formal language registers.

Reads voluntarily for interest and own purposes.

Rereads sentences when meaning is not clear.

Interprets information from diagrams, charts and graphs.

Recalls facts and details of texts.

Reads nonfiction materials for answers to specific questions or for specific purposes.

Takes part in creative responses to texts such as dramatizations, oral presentations, fantasy play, etc. (p. 29)

Preschool developmental checklists and curriculum checklists in the elementary grades are used in the same manner for the same purposes; however, developmental checklists add the developmental dimension to curriculum objectives. Because the young child's developmental level is an important factor in determining the kinds of experiences the teacher will use, our discussion of the purposes of checklists includes the implications of child development during the early childhood years. Those purposes are as follows:

1. To understand development
2. To serve as a framework for curriculum development
3. To assess and evaluate development and learning

FIGURE 6–1 Mathematics checklist: level 1

CHECKLIST
LEVEL 1

Name _____ Date _____

Age _____ Math Teacher _____ Unit _____

Advisor _____

Dates

I	M

NUMERATION

   0. Knows vocabulary:
     __ same   __ different   __ more   __ less   __ before   __ after

   1. Rote counts:
     __ 1 __ 2 __ 3 __ 4 __ 5 __ 6 __ 7 __ 8 __ 9 __ 10

   2. Counts objects:
     __ 1 __ 2 __ 3 __ 4 __ 5 __ 6 __ 7 __ 8 __ 9 __ 10

   3. Matches equivalent sets with concrete objects.
   4. Reproduces equivalent sets with concrete objects.
   5. Matches like pairs
   6. Matches unlike pairs
   7. Compares nonequivalent sets with concrete objects
   8. Reproduces nonequivalent sets with concrete objects
   9. Sorts objects using more than one classifying characteristic
  10. Matches numerals:
     __ 1 __ 2 __ 3 __ 4 __ 5 __ 6 __ 7 __ 8 __ 9 __ 10

  11. Identifies numerals:
     __ 1 __ 2 __ 3 __ 4 __ 5 __ 6 __ 7 __ 8 __ 9 __ 10

  12. Constructs sets for numerals:
     __ 1 __ 2 __ 3 __ 4 __ 5

  13. Names numerals:
     __ 1 __ 2 __ 3 __ 4 __ 5

MEASUREMENT

A. Linear
   1. Matches objects
     __ size   __ length   __ width   __ height
   2. Compares objects
     __ size   __ length   __ width   __ height
   3. Seriates objects
     __ size   __ length   __ width   __ height

B. Weight
   1. Classifies objects according to weight
     __ heavy   __ light
   2. Compares objects according to weight
     __ heavy   __ light
   3. Demonstrates use of balance
   4. Identifies instruments for measuring weight

CHECKLISTS AS A GUIDE TO UNDERSTAND DEVELOPMENT

All developmental checklists are organized to describe different areas of growth, including social, motor, and cognitive development. The checklist items in each area for each age or developmental level indicate how the child is progressing through maturation and experiences. When teachers, caregivers, and parents look at the checklists, they can trace the sequence of development and also be realistic in their expectations for children. See, for example, *The Work Sampling System: Preschool–4 developmental guidelines* (3rd ed.) (Marsden, Meisels, Jablon, and Dichtelmiller, 1997), which provides a checklist for physical development as shown in Figure 6–2. Figure 6–2 also includes some of the expanded explanations of checklist items.

CHECKLISTS AS A GUIDE TO DEVELOP CURRICULUM

Because developmental checklists describe all facets of development, they can serve as a guide in planning learning experiences for young children. Curriculum is not necessarily described as content areas such as science, art, or social studies, as these are commonly organized in elementary school; rather, it follows the experiences and opportunities that young children should have in the early childhood years. Thus, teachers and caregivers who study the objectives on the checklists have guides for learning activities that will be appropriate for their children.

Because checklists are organized by developmental level or age, they also serve as a guide for sequencing learning. Teachers can match the experiences they wish to use with the checklist to determine whether they are using the correct level of complexity or difficulty. They can determine what came before in learning or development and what should come next. The story retelling assessment sheet for early childhood classrooms shown in Figure 6–3 includes objectives and skills for retelling stories (Polakowski, 1993). By studying the items on the checklist and the student's level of performance in previous experiences, the teacher can plan for instruction and future activities. Moreover, because the checklist includes grades kindergarten through second, a range of levels of reading and writing ability is accommodated. Teachers can attach samples of the student's work to the checklist for use in a portfolio.

Developmental checklists help teachers and caregivers plan for a balance of activities. With the current emphasis on academic subjects even in preschool programs, teachers feel compelled to develop an instructional program that is limited to readiness for reading, writing, and mathematics. Preschool teachers are caught between the emphasis on "basics" and developmentally appropriate instruction that recognizes that young children learn through active learning based on interaction with concrete materials. Developmental checklists help the preschool teacher maintain a perspective between developmentally appropriate instruction and pressures to prepare children for first grade. Inclusion of developmental experiences helps the teacher to ensure a balanced curriculum that is best for the children's level of development.

In planning the curriculum and instruction in early childhood or preschool programs, teachers must incorporate the use of learning centers in classroom experiences. Developmental checklists with a sequence of objectives provide guidelines for selecting the materials to place in centers to support curriculum and instruction. For example,

FIGURE 6–2 Preschool checklist and developmental guidelines for physical development

D Geometry and spatial relations   F W S

1 Begins to recognize and describe the attributes of shapes. (p. 12)
Not Yet ☐☐☐
In Process ☐☐☐
Proficient ☐☐☐

2 Shows understanding of and uses several positional words. (p. 12)
Not Yet ☐☐☐
In Process ☐☐☐
Proficient ☐☐☐

E Measurement   F W S

1 Orders, compares, and describes objects according to a single attribute. (p. 13)
Not Yet ☐☐☐
In Process ☐☐☐
Proficient ☐☐☐

2 Participates in measuring activities. (p. 13)
Not Yet ☐☐☐
In Process ☐☐☐
Proficient ☐☐☐

IV Scientific Thinking

A Inquiry   F W S

1 Asks questions and uses senses to observe and explore materials and natural phenomena. (p. 15)
Not Yet ☐☐☐
In Process ☐☐☐
Proficient ☐☐☐

2 Uses simple tools and equipment for investigation. (p. 15)
Not Yet ☐☐☐
In Process ☐☐☐
Proficient ☐☐☐

3 Makes comparisons among objects. (p. 16)
Not Yet ☐☐☐
In Process ☐☐☐
Proficient ☐☐☐

V Social Studies

A People, past and present   F W S

1 Identifies similarities and differences in personal and family characteristics. (p. 17)
Not Yet ☐☐☐
In Process ☐☐☐
Proficient ☐☐☐

B Human interdependence   F W S

1 Begins to understand family needs, roles, and relationships. (p. 17)
Not Yet ☐☐☐
In Process ☐☐☐
Proficient ☐☐☐

2 Describes some people's jobs and what is required to perform them. (p. 17)
Not Yet ☐☐☐
In Process ☐☐☐
Proficient ☐☐☐

3 Begins to be aware of technology and how it affects life. (p. 18)
Not Yet ☐☐☐
In Process ☐☐☐
Proficient ☐☐☐

C Citizenship and government   F W S

1 Demonstrates awareness of rules. (p. 18)
Not Yet ☐☐☐
In Process ☐☐☐
Proficient ☐☐☐

2 Shows awareness of what it means to be a leader. (p. 18)
Not Yet ☐☐☐
In Process ☐☐☐
Proficient ☐☐☐

D People and where they live   F W S

1 Describes the location of things in the environment. (p. 19)
Not Yet ☐☐☐
In Process ☐☐☐
Proficient ☐☐☐

2 Shows awareness of the environment. (p. 19)
Not Yet ☐☐☐
In Process ☐☐☐
Proficient ☐☐☐

VI The Arts

A Expression and representation   F W S

1 Participates in group music experiences. (p. 21)
Not Yet ☐☐☐
In Process ☐☐☐
Proficient ☐☐☐

2 Participates in creative movement, dance, and drama. (p. 21)
Not Yet ☐☐☐
In Process ☐☐☐
Proficient ☐☐☐

3 Uses a variety of art materials for tactile experience and exploration. (p. 21)
Not Yet ☐☐☐
In Process ☐☐☐
Proficient ☐☐☐

B Understanding and appreciation   F W S

1 Responds to artistic creations or events. (p. 22)
Not Yet ☐☐☐
In Process ☐☐☐
Proficient ☐☐☐

VII Physical Development and Health

A Gross motor development   F W S

1 Moves with balance and control. (p. 23)
Not Yet ☐☐☐
In Process ☐☐☐
Proficient ☐☐☐

2 Coordinates movements to perform simple tasks. (p. 23)
Not Yet ☐☐☐
In Process ☐☐☐
Proficient ☐☐☐

B Fine motor development   F W S

1 Uses strength and control to perform simple tasks. (p. 23)
Not Yet ☐☐☐
In Process ☐☐☐
Proficient ☐☐☐

2 Uses eye-hand coordination to perform tasks. (p. 24)
Not Yet ☐☐☐
In Process ☐☐☐
Proficient ☐☐☐

3 Shows beginning control of writing, drawing, and art tools. (p. 24)
Not Yet ☐☐☐
In Process ☐☐☐
Proficient ☐☐☐

C Personal health and safety   F W S

1 Performs some self-care tasks independently. (p. 24)
Not Yet ☐☐☐
In Process ☐☐☐
Proficient ☐☐☐

2 Follows basic health and safety rules. (p. 24)
Not Yet ☐☐☐
In Process ☐☐☐
Proficient ☐☐☐

Source: Marsden, D. B., Meisels, S. J., Jablon, J. R., & Dichtelmiller, M. L. (2001). *The Work Sampling System: Preschool–4 developmental guidelines*, p. 19 and checklist. Used by permission. Copyright © 2001 Pearson Education, Inc., publishing as Pearson Early Learning.

FIGURE 6–3 Checklist for story retelling

Portfolio Reproducible 4.11

Story Retelling Assessment Sheet

Child's Name _____ Grade _____ Date _____

Teacher _____ Book Title: _____ Author: _____

☐ **Story was read to child**
☐ **Child read alone**

Text Difficulty:
☐ High Predictability
☐ Moderate Predictability
☐ Advanced Predictability

Response:
☐ Oral Retelling
☐ Pictorial Retelling (Attached)
☐ Written Retelling (Attached)

Story Structure	Includes	After Prompt	Comments:
Setting/Characters Starts retelling at beginning of story			
Names main character(s)			
Names other character(s)			
Tells when story happened			
Tells where story happened			
Theme Identifies goal or problem			
Plot/Events			
Includes all major events			
Tells events in sensible order			
Resolution Tells how problem was solved or goal was met			
Evaluative Comments:			

Source: Polakowski, C. (1993). Literacy portfolios in the early childhood classroom. In *Student portfolios* (pp. 47–66). Washington, DC: National Education Association, p. 64.

for 5-year-olds the sequence on a checklist for fine-motor development might be similar to the following:

Cuts and pastes creative designs
Creates recognizable objects with clay
Ties shoes
Puts together a twenty-piece puzzle

Creates or copies a pegboard design
Copies letters
Can copy numerals (Wortham, 1984, p. 33)

By studying the sequence, the teacher can determine that activities for cutting and pasting should be part of center activities earlier in the year. Later, when fine-motor skills are better developed, opportunities to copy letters and numerals should be included in centers to complement instructional activities in writing. Thus, developmental checklists help teachers to decide what to select for learning centers as the year progresses. Early in the year, the teacher may introduce simple toys, puzzles, and construction materials in centers. Later, more complex, challenging activities and materials are more appropriate. As the year progresses, the materials available in the centers should be compatible with developmental growth.

Because the rate of development varies from child to child, the sequence of development reflected in the checklists allows the teacher to vary materials for individual children. Certain games, activities, and materials can be placed in the centers and designated for a particular child's needs or interests. Materials for experiences placed in centers provide a means of individualizing learning, with checklists serving as the guide for a sequence from simple to complex. The more complex concepts or objectives lead to the selection of materials for the child whose development is more advanced.

CHECKLISTS AS A GUIDE TO ASSESS LEARNING AND DEVELOPMENT

Having information on how children are growing and learning is one of the important requirements of an early childhood program. Teachers must know how children's development and learning are progressing and must be able to discuss it with parents, other teachers, and staff members of other schools that later may teach the child. Figure 6–2, the checklist for physical development (Marsden et al., 1997), is a part of a set of developmental checklists that can be used for these purposes.

Because the checklists cover all kinds of development, they allow teachers to keep track of individual children and groups of children. When teachers keep consistent records on individual children, they can give parents information about the child's progress. Parents then have a clear idea of what is happening in school and what their child is accomplishing.

Teachers who use developmental checklists to assess, evaluate, and record children's progress may eventually realize that they have a better understanding of each child in the class than they had before. If a teacher uses a checklist for gross-motor skills to keep track of large muscle development in his or her students, systematic observation of students engaged in physical activities will make the teacher more aware of how each child is progressing and reveal individual differences in development. When reporting to one child's parent, for example, the teacher may discuss the improvement in throwing and catching a ball. In another case, the teacher may focus on the child's ability to ride a bicycle or to jump rope.

EVALUATING AND ASSESSING WITH CHECKLISTS

If a checklist is used as a framework for curriculum development and instruction, it can also be used for evaluation and assessment. The curriculum objectives used to plan instructional experiences can also be used to evaluate the children's performance on the same objectives. After a series of activities is used to provide opportunities to work with new concepts or skills, the children are assessed to determine how successful they were in learning the new skill or information. Evaluation can be accomplished through observation, during ongoing learning activities, and through specific assessment tasks.

EVALUATING CHECKLIST OBJECTIVES BY OBSERVATION

Observing young children is the most valuable method of understanding them. Because children in early childhood programs are active learners, their progress is best assessed by watching their behaviors, rather than by using a test. If you look at the items on developmental checklists, you will see that some objectives or indicators of development can be evaluated only by observing the child. For example, in the area of language development, if a teacher wants to know whether a child is using complete sentences, he or she observes the child in a play activity and listens for examples of language. Likewise, if the teacher is interested in evaluating social development, he or she will observe the children playing outdoors to determine whether they engage mostly in solitary or parallel play or whether individual children play cooperatively as part of a group.

Observation can be incidental or planned. The teacher may decide to evaluate during center time and may determine ahead of time which items on a checklist can be evaluated by observing children in the art center or the manipulative center. The teacher then places materials in those centers that are needed to observe specific behaviors and records which children are able to use the materials in the desired manner. For example, the ability to cut with scissors can be assessed by having a cutting activity in the art center. As an alternative, the teacher might use a cutting activity with an entire group and observe how each child is performing during the activity.

EVALUATING CHECKLIST OBJECTIVES WITH LEARNING ACTIVITIES

Some objectives cannot be assessed through observation alone. Objectives in a cognitive area such as mathematics may require a specific learning activity for evaluation. However, instead of having a separate assessment task, the teacher can have children demonstrate their performance on a particular skill as a part of the lesson being conducted. The teacher notes which children demonstrate understanding of the concept or mastery of the skill during the lesson. If a mathematics objective to be assessed involves understanding numbers through 5, the teacher might instruct a small group of children to make groups of objects ranging from 1 to 5 and note which children are successful.

EVALUATING CHECKLIST OBJECTIVES WITH SPECIFIC TASKS

Sometimes, at the beginning or end of a school year or grading period, the teacher will want to conduct a systematic assessment. He or she will assess a series of objectives at one time. In this situation, the teacher determines a number of objectives that can be evaluated at one time and devises tasks or activities to conduct with a child or a small group of children. The activities are presented in the same fashion as in a lesson, but the teacher has the additional purpose of updating and recording progress. Assessment tasks are organized on the basis of children's previous progress and will vary among groups of children. Some children will perform one group of activities; others will have a completely different set of activities related to a different set of objectives.

There is a time and place for each type of evaluation. The more experience a teacher has in including assessment in the instructional program, the easier it becomes. It is important to use the easiest and least time-consuming strategy whenever possible.

STEPS IN CHECKLIST DESIGN

A checklist is an outline or framework of development and curriculum. When designing a checklist, the developer first determines the major categories that will be included. Thereafter, development follows four basic steps:

1. Identification of the skills to be included
2. Separate listing of target behaviors
3. Sequential organization of the checklist
4. Record keeping

CONFLICTS ABOUT INFORMAL ASSESSMENT RESULTS

Mary Howell and Francesca Carrillo are having a heated argument in the teachers' lounge. Mary teaches first grade, and Francesca teaches second grade. At issue is the checklist from the first grade that is placed in students' folders at the end of the year, before they are promoted to second grade. Francesca's complaint is that the first-grade teachers' assessments are inaccurate. They have indicated that students accomplished first-grade objectives, but these objectives have to be retaught in the second grade because the students either never know them or forget them over the summer.

Mary clearly is offended that her professionalism has been questioned. She defends the process by which first-grade teachers determine whether the children have learned the objectives. Josie, another teacher sitting nearby, says nothing. Under her breath, she mutters, "It's all a waste of time. I wait until the end of the year and then mark them all off, anyway."

After Mary and Francesca have left, the conversation about the merits of using checklists for assessment and record keeping continues. Gunther Sachs, a third-grade teacher, supports the use of checklists for evaluating the students. He observes that he uses the checklist record when having conferences with parents. He believes that the parents gain a better understanding of what their child is learning in school when he can tell them how the child is progressing on curriculum objectives listed on the checklist. Lily Wong, another third-grade teacher, strongly disagrees. Her experience with the checklists leads her to believe that record keeping takes a great deal of time that she would rather use to plan lessons and design more interesting and challenging learning activities for her students.

IDENTIFICATION OF THE SKILLS TO BE INCLUDED

The teacher studies each checklist category and determines the specific objectives or skills that will be included. Using established developmental norms or learning objectives, the teacher decides how to adapt them for his or her needs. For example, on a checklist for language development and reading under the category of Language and Vocabulary, the following objectives might be included:

Listens to and follows verbal directions
Identifies the concept of word
Identifies the concept of letter
Invents a story for a picture book

SEPARATE LISTING OF TARGET BEHAVIORS

If a series of behaviors or items is included in an objective, the target behaviors should be listed separately so that they can be recorded separately (Irwin & Bushnell, 1980). For the objective of identifying coins, the best way to write the item would be as follows:

Identifies:
Penny
Nickel
Dime
Quarter

When the teacher is assessing the child's knowledge of coins, he or she may find that the child knows some of the coins but not others. Information can be recorded on the mastery status of each coin.

SEQUENTIAL ORGANIZATION OF THE CHECKLIST

The checklist should be organized in a sequential manner. Checklist items should be arranged in order of difficulty or complexity. If the checklist is sequenced correctly, the order of difficulty should be obvious. For example, the ability to count on a mathematics checklist might be listed as "Counts by rote from 1 to 10." At the next higher level, the checklist item would be "Counts by rote from 1 to 50."

RECORDKEEPING

A system of recordkeeping must be devised. Because a checklist indicates the objectives for curriculum development or developmental characteristics, it must have a method of recording the status of the items. Although many recordkeeping strategies have been used, commonly two columns indicate that the child either has or has not mastered the skill or behavior. Two types of indicators frequently used are a simple *Yes/No* or *Mastery/Nonmastery*. Another approach is to record the date when the concept was introduced and the date when it was mastered. In this instance, the columns would be headed *Introduced/Mastery* or could indicate an intermediate step in evaluation with three columns headed *Introduced/Progress/Mastery*. Figure 6–2 is a checklist with three columns for recordkeeping in physical development. In this example, the columns indicate when the assessment was conducted in the fall, winter, and spring. The codes *Not Yet, In Process,* and *Proficient* are used to indicate the child's progress (Marsden et al., 1997).

The teacher can use a checklist to record individual or group progress. Whether the teacher uses observation, lesson activities, or tasks for assessment, the checklist is used to keep a record of the child's progress. Checklist information can be shared periodically with parents to keep them informed about what their child is learning or is able to do.

Checklists can also be used to keep a record of all the children in the class or group. The group record lists all the children's names, as well as the checklist objectives. By transferring information about individual children to a master or group record, the teacher can plan instruction for groups of children as the group record indicates their common needs. Figure 6–4 is a checklist record for a group of students in language development.

ADVANTAGES AND DISADVANTAGES OF USING CHECKLISTS

Using checklists for assessment and evaluation has definite advantages and disadvantages or problems. Teachers must weigh both sides before deciding how extensively they will use checklists for measurement and recordkeeping purposes.

ADVANTAGES OF USING CHECKLISTS

Checklists are easy to use. Because they require little instruction or training, teachers can quickly learn to use them. Unlike standardized tests, they are available whenever evaluation is needed.

Checklists are flexible and can be used with a variety of assessment strategies. The teacher can evaluate in the most convenient manner and obtain the needed information. Because of this flexibility, the teacher can combine assessment strategies when more than one assessment is indicated.

Behaviors can be recorded frequently; checklists are always at hand. Whenever the teacher has new information, he or she can update records. Unlike paper-and-pencil tests or formal tests, the teacher does not have to wait for a testing opportunity to determine whether the child has mastered an objective.

DISADVANTAGES OF USING CHECKLISTS

Checklists can be time consuming to use. Particularly when teachers are just beginning to use checklists, they report that keeping records current on checklists reduces the time spent with children. Teachers have to become proficient in using checklists without impinging on teaching time.

Teachers may find it difficult to get started. When they are accustomed to teaching without the use of checklists, teachers often find it difficult to adapt their teaching and evaluation behaviors to include checklists. In addition, teachers can have too many checklists. They become frustrated by multiple checklists that overwhelm them with assessment and recordkeeping.

Some teachers may not consider assessment strategies used with checklists as valid measures of development and learning. For some teachers, particularly those in the primary

FIGURE 6–4 Language arts: class record sheet

NAME	LANGUAGE ABILITY													FOLLOWING DIRECTIONS			
	1. Shares personal experiences	2. Voluntarily participates	3. Voluntarily answers	4. Tells observed activity	5. Answers factual questions	6. Answers probing questions	7. Answers higher order questions	8. Answers divergent questions	9. Problem solving	10. Asks factual questions	11. Interprets story picture	12. Comprehension	13. Attention span	14. Follows simple directions	15. Carries messages	16. Two or more directions	17. Makes simple object with specified materials

grades, who are accustomed to conducting a test for evaluation, the observation and activity strategies used to measure progress may seem inconclusive. They may feel the need for more concrete evidence of mastery of learning objectives for accountability.

Checklists do not indicate how well a child performs. Unlike a paper-and-pencil test that can be used to record levels of mastery, checklists indicate only whether the child can perform adequately. For teachers who are required to give grades at the elementary level, checklists can be an incomplete strategy for assessment (Irwin & Bushnell, 1980).

Checklists themselves are not an assessment instrument. They are a format for organizing learning objectives or developmental indicators. The teacher's implementation of evaluation strategies by using a checklist makes it a tool for evaluation. In addition, recording the presence or absence of a behavior is not the main purpose of the checklist. The significant factor is what the teacher does with the assessment information recorded. If the information gained from evaluating the objectives is not used for instructional planning and implementation followed by further ongoing evaluation, the checklist does not improve learning and development.

RATING SCALES

Rating scales are similar to checklists; however, there are important differences. Whereas checklists are used to indicate whether a behavior is present or absent, rating scales require the rater to make a qualitative judgment about the extent to which a behavior is present. A rating scale consists of a set of characteristics or qualities to be judged by using a systematic procedure. Rating scales are of many forms; **numerical** and **graphic rating scales** seem to be used most frequently.

TYPES OF RATING SCALES

NUMERICAL RATING SCALES. Numerical rating scales are among the easiest rating scales to use. The rater marks a number to indicate the degree to which a characteristic is present. A sequence of numbers is assigned to descriptive categories. The rater's judgment is required to rate the characteristic. One common numerical system is as follows:

1—Unsatisfactory
2—Below average
3—Average
4—Above average
5—Outstanding

The numerical rating system might be used to evaluate classroom behaviors in elementary students as follows:

1. To what extent does the student complete assigned work?
   1   2   3   4   5
2. To what extent does the student cooperate with group activities?
   1   2   3   4   5

Numerical scales become difficult to use when there is little agreement on what the numbers represent. The interpretation of the scale may vary.

Numerical rating scales are useful in recording emerging progress in reading. In Figure 6–5, four categories of reading characteristics are assessed by using the numerical categories of Limited, Below expectation, Average, Above average, and Outstanding (Farr, 1994). A summary assessment uses three descriptors to rate progress.

GRAPHIC RATING SCALES. Graphic rating scales function as continuums. A set of categories is described at certain points along the line, but the rater can mark his or her judgment at any location on the line. In addition, a graphic rating scale provides a visual continuum that assists in locating the correct position. Commonly used descriptors for graphic rating scales are as follows:

Never
Seldom
Occasionally
Frequently
Always

The classroom behaviors described earlier would be evaluated on a graphic rating scale as follows:

1. To what extent does the student complete assigned work?
   Never   Seldom   Occasionally   Frequently   Always
2. To what extent does the student cooperate with group activities?
   Never   Seldom   Occasionally   Frequently   Always

The behavioral descriptions on graphic rating scales are used more easily than numerical descriptors. Because the descriptors are more specific, raters can be more objective and accurate when judging student behaviors; nevertheless, graphic rating scales are subject to bias because of disagreement about the meaning of the descriptors.

USES OF RATING SCALES

One of the most familiar uses of rating scales is report cards. Schools often use rating scales to report characteristics of personal and social development on a report card. Such attributes as work habits, classroom conduct, neatness, and citizenship commonly appear on elementary school report cards. Students and parents often believe that such ratings are particularly subject to teacher bias and feelings about the student.

An example of a rating scale is given in Figure 6–6. Taken from the *Early Childhood Environment Rating Scale* (Harms & Clifford, 1998), the page pictured shows a numerical scale for rating how the early childhood teacher provides for sand/water play and dramatic play, as well as the quality of the daily schedule.

An observation form (Kamii & Rosenblum, 1990) used for recording progress in numerical reasoning is another example of a rating scale that is used to evaluate concept

FIGURE 6–5 Review of portfolio reading materials

Review of Portfolio Reading Materials

Primary Level

Student's Name _____

Teacher's Name _____

Date _____   Grade _____   School _____

1 = Limited   2 = Below expectation   3 = Average   4 = Above expectation   5 = Outstanding

Assessment	1	2	3	4	5	Teacher Comments
Emergent reading skills						
Recognizes speech/print relationship						
Understands concepts of letters/words						
Handles books appropriately						
Attitudes toward reading						
Chooses reading during free time						
Reads many books/stories						
Listens attentively to stories						
Reading interests						
Has favorite books/stories						
Discusses favorite books/stories						
Participates in discussions about books/stories						
Reading skills/strategies						
Constructs meaning when reading						
Relates stories to background						
Shows confidence as a reader						

Summary Assessment

Assessment	For This Review			Since Last Review		
	Outstanding	Average	Limited	Improving	About the Same	Seems Poorer
Amount of reading						
Attitudes toward reading						
Reading skills/ strategies						

FIGURE 6–6 Examples from the *Early Childhood Environment Scale—Revised Edition*

Inadequate		Minimal		Good		Excellent
1	2	3	4	5	6	7

23. Sand/water*

| 1.1 No provision† for sand *or* water play, outdoors *or* indoors.
1.2 No toys to use for sand *or* water play. | 3.1 Some provision‡ for sand *or* water play accessible either outdoors *or* indoors.
3.2 Some sand toys accessible. | 5.1 Provision for sand *and* water play (either outdoors *or* indoors).
5.2 Variety of toys accessible for play (Ex. containers, spoons, funnels, scoops, shovels, pots and pans, molds, toy people, animals, and trucks).
5.3 Sand *or* water play available to children for at least 1 hour daily. | 7.1 Provision for sand *and* water play, *both* indoors *and* outdoors (weather permitting).
7.2 Different activities done with sand and water (Ex. bubbles added to water, material in sand table changed, i.e. rice substituted for sand). |

Notes for Clarification

*Materials that can easily be poured, such as rice, lentils, bird seed, and cornmeal may be substituted for sand. Sand or sand substitute must be available in sufficient quantity so children can dig in it, fill containers, and pour.

†"Provision" for sand and water requires action on the part of staff to provide appropriate materials for such play. Allowing children to play in puddles or dig in the dirt on the playground does not meet the requirements of this item.

‡Each room does not have to have its own sand and water table, but must be able to use a sand and water table regularly if it is shared with another room.

Questions

(3.1) Do you use sand or water with the children? How is that handled? About how often? Where is this available?

(3.2) Are there any toys for children to use with sand or water play? Please describe them.

(7.2) Do you change the activities children do with sand and water?

Source: Harms, T., Clifford, R. M., & Gryer, D. (1998). *Early Childhood Environment Rating Scale – Revised Edition.* New York: Teachers College Press, pp. 31–32. Copyright © 1998 by Thelma Harms, Richard M. Clifford, and Debby Gryer. All rights reserved. Reprinted by permission of the authors and publisher.

Inadequate		Minimal		Good		Excellent
1	2	3	4	5	6	7

24. Dramatic play*

1.1 No materials or equipment accessible for dress up or dramatic play.	3.1 Some dramatic play materials and furniture accessible, so children can act out family roles themselves (Ex. dress-up clothes, housekeeping props, dolls). 3.2 Materials are accessible for at least 1 hour daily. 3.3 Separate storage for dramatic play material.	5.1 Many dramatic play materials accessible, including dress-up clothes.† 5.2 Materials accessible for a substantial portion of the day. 5.3 Props for at least two different themes accessible daily (Ex. housekeeping and work). 5.4 Dramatic play area clearly defined, with space to play and organized storage.	7.1 Materials rotated for a variety of themes (Ex. prop boxes for work, fantasy, and leisure themes). 7.2 Props provided to represent diversity (Ex. props representing various cultures; equipment used by people with disabilities). 7.3 Props provided for active dramatic play outdoors.‡ 7.4 Pictures, stories, and trips used to enrich dramatic play.

Notes for Clarification

*Dramatic play is pretending or making believe. This type of play occurs when children act out roles themselves and when they manipulate figures such as small toy people in a doll house. Dramatic play is enhanced by props that encourage a variety of themes including *housekeeping* (Ex. dolls, child-sized furniture, dress-up, kitchen utensils); *different kinds of work* (Ex. office, construction, farm, store, fire fighting, transportation); *fantasy* (Ex. animals, dinosaurs, storybook characters); and *leisure* (Ex. camping, sports).

†Dress-up clothes should include more than the high-heeled shoes, dresses, purses, and women's hats commonly found in a playhouse area. Clothing worn by both men and women at work such as hardhats, transportation worker caps, and cowboy hats, as well as running shoes, clip-on ties, and jackets should be included.

‡The intent of this indicator is that children are provided a large enough space so that their dramatic play can be very active and noisy without disrupting other activities. A large indoor space such as a gymnasium or multi-purpose room may be substituted for the outdoor space. Structures (such as small houses, cars, or boats) and props for camping, cooking, work, transportation, or dress-up clothes may be available to the children.

Questions

(7.1) Are there any other dramatic play props children can use? Please describe them.
(7.3) Are props for dramatic play ever used outside or in a larger indoor space?

(7.4) Is there anything you do to extend children's dramatic play?

FIGURE 6–7 Observation form for tens with playing cards

OBSERVATIONAL FORM FOR TENS WITH PLAYING CARDS				
Name _____ Date _____				
	Counts-all	Counts-on	Counts-on from larger	Selects without counting (looks for)
5 + 5				
9 + 1				
8 + 2				
7+ 3				
6 + 4				
Combos ≠ 10				

Source: Kamii, C., & Rosenblum, V. (1990). An approach to assessment in mathematics. In C. Kamii (Ed.), *Achievement testing in the early grades: The games grown-ups play* (pp. 146–162). Washington, DC: NAEYC. Reprinted with permission from the National Association for the Education of Young Children, p. 151.

development in young children. The form (Figure 6–7) was developed to record the child's progress in understanding the ability to make 10 with two numbers through games with cards. The graphic indicators—Counts-all, Counts-on, Counts-on from larger, and Selects without counting—indicate the steps the child takes in being able to make combinations that equal 10. Each category describes a more complex or advanced process used by the child from counting all the symbols at the lowest level to selecting two appropriate cards without counting at the most advanced level.

ADVANTAGES AND DISADVANTAGES OF RATING SCALES

Rating scales are a unique form of evaluation. They serve a function not provided by other measurement strategies. Although some of the limitations of rating scales have already been discussed, it is useful to review their strengths and weaknesses.

ADVANTAGES OF USING RATING SCALES

Rating scales can be used for behaviors not easily measured by other means. In the area of social development, for example, a scale might have indicators of cooperative behavior.

When the teacher is trying to determine the child's ability to work with children and adults in the classroom, the scale of indicators is more usable than a yes/no response category on a checklist. Unlike an observation, which might be completely open ended, the rating scale indicators have clues to behaviors that describe the child's level of cooperation.

Rating scales are quick and easy to complete. Because the rater is provided with the descriptors of the child's behavior, it is possible to complete the scale with a minimum of effort. The descriptors also make it possible to complete the scale some time after an observation. The user can apply knowledge about the child after an observation or as a result of working with the child on a daily basis and will not always need a separate time period to acquire the needed information.

A minimum of training is required to use rating scales. The successful rating scale is easy to understand and use. Paraprofessionals and students can often complete some rating scales. The scale's indicators offer the information needed to complete the scale.

Rating scales are easy to develop and use. Because descriptors remain consistent on some rating scales, teachers find them easy to design. When using rating indicators such as always, sometimes, rarely, or never, the teacher can add the statements for rating without having to think of rating categories for each one. Figures 6–8 and 6–9 are scales with three indicators that students can use for self-assessment in mathematics. In Figure 6–8, a beginning reader can select a smiling face to evaluate his or her own work. In Figure 6–9, the same type of evaluation can be conducted by a student with more advanced reading and

FIGURE 6–8　Rating scale for data tables

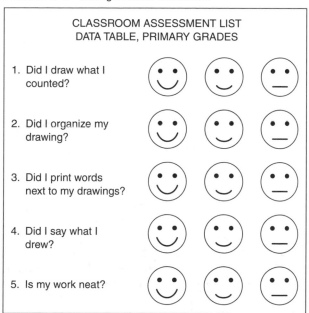

Source: Hibbard, M. K. (1996). Self-assessment using performance task assessment lists. In R. E. Blum & J. A. Arter (Eds.), *Student performance assessment in an era of restructuring* (pp. VI-6:1 to VI-6:19). Alexandria, VA: Association for Supervision and Curriculum Development, p. VI-6:17. Used by permission.

FIGURE 6–9 Rating scale for data tables

CLASSROOM ASSESSMENT LIST
DATA TABLE, ELEMENTARY SCHOOL

1. Heading
   T: I put my name and the date on my work.
   O: I left my name or the date off.
   W: I did not include my name or date.

2. Title
   T: My title says exactly what the data are about.
   O: My title gives some idea of what the data are about.
   W: I have no title or my title does not
      tell much about what the data are about.

3. Organizing The Data
   T: My data are organized into very neat rows and columns.
   O: Some of my data are organized.
   W: I need to organize my data much better.

4. Naming The Data
   T: The rows and columns have titles and all the data have
      units.
   O: Some rows and columns have titles and some data
      have units.
   W: I need to give the rows and columns titles and/or I
      need to give the data units.

Did I do my best work?

| Terrific | OK | Needs Work |

Source: Hibbard, M. K. (1996). Self-assessment using performance task assessment lists. In R. E. Blum & J. A. Arter (Eds.), *Student performance assessment in an era of restructuring* (pp. VI-6:1 to VI-6:19). Alexandria, VA: Association for Supervision and Curriculum Development, p. VI–6:13. Used by permission.

self-assessment skills. These examples are very similar to checklists, but permit the student to make a qualitative assessment on some items.

Finally, rating scales are a useful strategy for assessing progress in the child's journey into understanding the world or in reconstructing knowledge. A rating scale permits the teacher to describe the child's steps toward understanding or mastery, instead of whether the child has achieved a predetermined level or not, as is the case in the use of checklists.

DISADVANTAGES OF USING RATING SCALES

Rating scales are highly subjective; therefore, rater error and bias are common problems. Teachers and other raters may rate a child on the basis of their previous interactions or on an emotional rather than an objective basis. The subsequent rating will reflect the teacher's attitude toward the child (Linn & Gronlund, 2000).

Ambiguous terms cause rating scales to be unreliable sources of information. Raters disagree on the descriptors of characteristics. Therefore, raters are likely to mark characteristics by using different interpretations. For example, it is easy to have different interpretations of the indicator "Sometimes or rarely."

Rating scales tell little about the causes of behavior. Like checklists that indicate whether the behavior is present or absent, rating scales provide no additional information to clarify the circumstances in which the behavior occurred. Unlike observations that result in more comprehensive information about the context surrounding behaviors, rating scales provide a different type of information from checklists, but include no causal clues for the observer unless notes are taken beyond the rating scale itself.

RUBRICS

Like rating scales, rubrics are qualitative instruments that can be used for assessing student progress or scoring student work. Perhaps this purpose for scoring student work distinguishes rubrics from other types of assessment instruments such as checklists and rating scales. Wiggins (1996b) defines a rubric as follows:

> A rubric is a printed set of guidelines that distinguishes performances or products of different quality. . . . A rubric has descriptors that define what to look for at each level of performance. . . . Rubrics also often have indicators providing specific examples or tell-tale signs of things to look for in work. (p. VI–5:1)

It is clear from the definition just cited that rubrics are related to performance assessments. They provide guidelines to distinguish performance from one level to another. Although rubrics are used most frequently with students in later elementary grades and secondary schools, they can also be useful for students in kindergarten and the primary grades.

Indicators of performance can also be called the criteria for scoring. That is, they set the criteria for the score at each level. Indicators can also describe dimensions of performance—different categories of indicators leading to the desired score. In Figure 6–10, a reading rubric for first grade, two dimensions are given for scoring the student's progress in reading: (1) Comprehension of Text and (2) Appreciation/Enjoyment of Literature.

TYPES OF RUBRICS

There are generally three types of rubrics: **holistic, analytic,** and **developmental.** Each type has characteristics that distinguish it from the others.

HOLISTIC RUBRIC. This type of rubric assigns a single score to a student's overall performance. These rubrics usually have competency labels that define the level of performance. There are a number of indicators to describe the quality of work or performance at each level (Payne, 1997; Wiener & Cohen, 1997; Wiggins, 1996). Figure 6–11 is an example

FIGURE 6–10 Reading rubric

Reading Rubric Grade 1

Name _____

Date _____

Shows Comprehension of Text

1	2	3	4	5

Relies on story being read by teacher or with others

Retells with very little detail; sequences pictures to tell simple story

Does not include inferred information when summarizing

Does not differentiate real/make-believe

Does not connect story events to experiences in life

Reads independently and/or relies on story being read with others

Retells story in own words including characteristics, setting, and sequences of events

Begins to include inferred information from summarizing

Differentiates real/make-believe

Connects story events to own life experiences

Reads independently

Retells story accurately and sequentially in own words and elaborates

Includes inferred information when summarizing story

Differentiates real/make-believe and fiction/nonfiction

Connects story events to experiences in own life and elaborates

Comments:

Shows Appreciation/Enjoyment of Literature

1	2	3	4	5

Shows limited interest in being read to

Shows little interest in books

Participates minimally in oral reading of familiar stories

Limited use of classroom library

Enjoys being read to and wants to hear favorite stories repeatedly

Reads when directed to books

Participates in oral reading of familiar stories

Uses classroom library when directed

Selects books he/she wishes to have read aloud and requests favorite stories repeatedly

Voluntarily reads

Leads oral reading of favorite stories

Voluntarily uses classroom library

Comments:

Source: Wiener, R. B., & Cohen, J. H. (1997). *Literacy portfolios: Using assessment to guide instruction.* Upper Saddle River, NJ: Merrill/Prentice Hall, p. 176. Copyright © 1997 by Prentice Hall, Inc., Upper Saddle River, NJ. Reprinted by permission of Pearson Education, Inc.

FIGURE 6–11 Writing rubrics

WRITING RUBRIC
Assessment Scale
(Kindergarten)
A collection of work will demonstrate proficiency

6 Exceptional Writer
Enthusiastic, fluent, chooses to write independently; may write multiple sentences; word boundaries secure; some conventions of print and sentence sense; occasionally uses correct spelling.

5 Experienced Writer
Confident, developing fluency, sometimes writes independently; uses print from the environment in a meaningful way; begins to use the conventions of print; understands the use of spacing to define word boundaries; writes complete thoughts; primarily uses inventive spelling and begins to correctly spell high-frequency words.

4 Beginning Writer
Writes word-by-word; writes with guidance; beginning to use spacing to define word boundaries; may use beginning, middle and ending letters to represent words to demonstrate a more sophisticated understanding of sound/symbol relationships; may demonstrate a beginning awareness of conventions of print.

3 Developing Writer
Understands that oral language can be written; words are usually represented by beginning sounds; other letters may appear which demonstrate an understanding of sound/symbol relationships; writes word-by-word, but spacing to define word boundaries is not observed; can read own writing.

2 Pre-Writer
Drawing conveys message; may copy letters, words or sentences from the environment; beginning to use familiar letters and words as labels; writes familiar words from memory.

1 Inexperienced Writer
Communicates using pictures; uses scribble writing or letter-like marks; text conveys no meaning to reader; may dictate sentence to teacher.

WRITING RUBRIC
Assessment Scale
(Grade 1)
A collection of work will demonstrate proficiency

6 Exceptional Writer
Enthusiastic, fluent, writes independently; has command of many conventions of print; demonstrates sentence sense; may use a variety of techniques to engage reader; writing shows originality and an organizational plan.

5 Experienced Writer
Competent and confident; fluent writer; writes independently; begins to use conventions of print in spelling, punctuation and grammar; word boundaries secure; text conveys the message; begins to use some techniques to engage reader; writing reflects logical sequence.

4 Beginning Writer
Developing fluency; writes competently with guidance; text beginning to reflect logical sequence; uses inventive spelling to convey the message; generally observes word boundaries; writing contains more apparent meaning; sentence structure may be simple and repetitive.

3 Developing Writer
Evidence of text; uses inventive spelling almost exclusively; beginning to observe word boundaries; writing begins to convey a comprehensible message but may be difficult to read; completes sentence patterns meaningfully; may copy words, phrases and sentences from class-generated ideas.

2 Pre-Writer
Communicates using pictures; some evidence of text but may not be readable; evidence of directionality; evidence of sound/symbol relationships; may copy from the environment without understanding that text has meaning.

1 Emergent Writer
(Teacher supplies directions)

Source: Winbury, J., & Evans, C. S. (1996). Poway portfolio project. In R. E. Blum & J. A. Arter (Eds.), *Student performance assessment in an era of restructuring* (pp. VII-2:1 to VII-2: 6). Alexandria, VA: Association for Supervision and Curriculum Development, p. VII–2:5.

FIGURE 6–12 Analytic rubric

Analytic Scale for Problem Solving

Understanding the problem

1—No attempt
1—Completely misinterprets the problem
2—Misinterprets major part of the problem
3—Misinterprets minor part of the problem
4—Complete understanding of the problem

Solving the problem

1—No attempt
1—Totally inappropriate plan
2—Partially correct procedure but with major fault
3—Substantially correct procedure with major omission or procedural error
4—A plan that could lead to a correct solution with no arithmetic errors

Answering the problem

0—No answer or wrong answer based upon an inappropriate plan
1—Copying error, computational error, partial answer for problem with multiple answers; no
    answer statement; answer labeled incorrectly
2—Correct solution

Source: T., Kubiszyn, and Gary Borich, G. (1996). *Educational testing and measurement* (5th ed.), by John Wiley & Sons. Copyright © 1996 by John Wiley & Sons. Reprinted by permission of John Wiley & Sons, Inc.

of a holistic rubric in emergent writing. It has six levels of competence. The student's work is assessed using the descriptors under each level of competence.

ANALYTIC RUBRIC.   "An analytic rubric describes and scores each of the task attributes separately, uses limited descriptors for each attribute, uses a scale that can be both narrow and broad, and allows for specific diagnostic feedback" (Wiener & Cohen, 1997, p. 249). Analytic rubrics are more specific than holistic rubrics, can be used for diagnostic purposes, and can be more efficient for grading purposes. Figure 6–12 is an example of an analytic rubric for problem solving. It has three dimensions: understanding the problem, solving the problem, and answering the problem. The descriptors for each are listed with a numerical scale. This particular rubric is useful for students in the latter stages of early childhood when reading and writing skills are well developed.

DEVELOPMENTAL RUBRIC.   A developmental rubric is designed to serve a multiage group of students or to span several grade levels. The intention is to abandon mastery of skills at a particular grade level; rather, the student is assessed on a continuum that shows

FIGURE 6–13   Speaking rubric

SPEAKING RUBRIC
Assessment Scale
(Grades 1–5)

Secure Speaker
- Confident speaker
- Speaks loudly, clearly, and with expression
- Expresses ideas with elaboration and support
- Consistently makes relevant contributions to class discussions

Developing Speaker
- Competent speaker
- Speaks loudly and clearly
- Expresses ideas in complete sentences
- Takes part in class discussions and stays on topic

Beginning Speaker
- May be a reluctant speaker
- Needs to work on speaking skills (volume, clarity, eye contact)
- Rarely contributes to class discussions in a meaningful way

Source: Winbury, J., & Evans, C. S. (1996). Poway portfolio project. In R. E. Blum & J. A. Arter (Eds.), *Student performance assessment in an era of restructuring* (pp. VII-2:1 to VII-2:6). Alexandria, VA: Association for Supervision and Curriculum Development, p. VII-2:3. Used by permission.

developmental progress. Figure 6–13 shows the progression in speaking skills across elementary grade levels.

HOW RUBRICS ARE DESIGNED AND USED

Rubrics are frequently discussed as part of performance assessment and the use of portfolios. This is because they are used to assess a performance task. When an overall, general judgment is made about the performance, a holistic rubric is used. An analytic rubric applies a detailed set of criteria, usually after a holistic evaluation has been made. A developmental rubric is designed to measure evolving competencies over a span of grade levels. Each type of rubric is designed for a different type of application, but the design process is similar (McMillan, 1997).

SELECTING RUBRIC TYPE.   There are two major steps in designing a rubric. The first step is to decide what type of rubric is to be used and then design the type of rubric selected. If an overall rating is needed, then a holistic rubric scale is indicated. An analytic rubric is designed if each part of a task needs to be assessed separately, as in Figure 6–12. The three tasks to be assessed in that rubric are (1) understanding the problem, (2) solving the problem, and (3) answering the problem. Each category of the problem has different dimensions.

Figure 6–11, in contrast, is holistic. The descriptors support levels of competence, but the focus is on overall proficiency at each level.

A developmental rubric is designed when the scale covers more than one grade level or developmental level. Figure 6–13 describes levels of competency that are relevant throughout the elementary school experience. The student's progress is assessed by broad levels of achievement in speaking rather than by grade level.

DEVELOPING SCORING CRITERIA.   Teachers who are beginners at rubric design might find a generalized rubric to be a useful guide to start their rubric. The rubric can first be divided into levels of performance common to many rubrics:

No attempt
Inadequate response
Satisfactory response
Demonstrated competence

Each level has descriptions of the scoring criteria for that level of competence. This particular rubric also has a numerical rating for each level. Herman, Aschbacher, and Winters (1992) describe four common elements that characterize rubric scoring criteria as follows:

- One or more traits or dimensions that serve as the basis for the student response.

- Definitions and examples to clarify the meaning of each trait or dimension.

- A scale of values (or a counting system) on which to rate each dimension.

- Standards of excellence for specified performance levels accompanied by models or examples of each level. (p. 55)

Unlike the objectives on checklists and descriptors on rating scales, levels of performance or dimensions cannot always be predetermined when the rubric is designed. The dimensions of performance must be based on reasonable expectations of the students to be assessed using existing samples of student work and revised as necessary (McMillan, 1997; Wiggins, 1996b).

Rubrics have many uses and purposes. They can be created to assess processes such as cooperative learning and other group strategies. They are most commonly used with student work or products. Examples are individual and group projects, exhibits, and artistic products. They are also used to evaluate performances of all types. In the classroom, they can be used for oral presentations and discussions. As can be seen from the examples presented in this section of the chapter, in early childhood classrooms, they are commonly used to evaluate progress in development and learning.

ADVANTAGES AND DISADVANTAGES OF USING RUBRICS

ADVANTAGES OF USING RUBRICS

One of the many advantages of using rubrics is that they provide guidelines for quality student work or performance. Given this characteristic, other advantages can be added.

Rubrics are flexible. They can be designed for many uses and ability levels. Although teachers will conduct most of the assessments using rubrics with very young children, student self-assessment increases as students mature.

Rubrics are adaptable. They are dynamic and subject to revision and refinement. Because they are easily modified and changed, they can meet changing classroom and student needs.

Rubrics can be used by both teacher and student to guide the student's efforts prior to completion of a task or product. The teacher and student can review the expectations for quality during the process of an assignment or project so that the student is clear about what needs to be done to improve work.

Rubrics can be translated into grades if needed. If grades are not used, the rubrics can be used to discuss student work with parents and students. Periodic review of student efforts and comparison with a rubric such as a developmental rubric will add to understanding of the student's progress.

DISADVANTAGES OF USING RUBRICS

Despite its strengths, rubric design and use are not without difficulty. One difficulty is that teachers just beginning to develop rubrics may have difficulty in determining assessment or scoring criteria.

It is possible that teachers will focus on excessively general or inappropriate criteria for the rubric. In a similar fashion, the teacher might use predetermined criteria for rubric design, rather than basing them on examples of student work or modifying them as needed.

A common mistake in designing and using rubrics is to inappropriately focus on the quantity of characteristics found, rather than the indicators of quality work. The teacher focuses on the wrong characteristics of student work.

Holistic rubrics might lack validity and reliability. The teacher is forced to analyze the criteria for quality when designing an analytic rubric. The descriptors for the holistic rubric can be too general and lack specificity.

Rubrics can be used by both teacher and student to guide the student's efforts.

DEVELOPING QUALITY CHECKLISTS, RATING SCALES, AND RUBRICS

In each section of the chapter, information has been provided on how to design informal instruments for assessment. To ensure that checklists, rating scales, and rubrics are quality measures, guidelines for avoiding inappropriate design are now reviewed.

CHECKLISTS

A checklist is used when a student behavior or skill can be indicated with a "yes" or "no" or some other indicator of the presence or absence of the characteristic. Linn and Gronlund (2000) summarize the steps in appropriate development of checklists:

1. Identify each of the specific actions desired in the performance.
2. Add to the list those actions that represent common errors (if they are useful in the assessment, are limited in number, and can be clearly stated).
3. Arrange the desired actions (and likely errors, if used) in the appropriate order in which they are expected to occur.
4. Provide a simple procedure for checking each action as it occurs (or for numbering the actions in sequence, if appropriate). (p. 284)

RATING SCALES

The quality of rating scales also depends on specificity in the description of the rating. When designing a rating scale, the following steps are recommended:

1. Identify the learning outcomes that the task is intended to assess.
2. Determine what characteristics of the learning outcomes are most significant for assessment on the scale. Characteristics should be directly observable and points on the scale clearly defined.
3. Select the type of scale that is most appropriate for the purposes of the assessment.
4. Provide between three and seven rating positions on the scale. The number of points on the scale will depend on how many clear differentiations in level of accomplishment are needed for assessment.

RUBRICS

When rubric design has been completed, it should be evaluated for the appropriateness of the scoring criteria. McMillan (1997) has developed a checklist for evaluating scoring criteria for rubrics as follows:

1. Do descriptions focus on important aspects of the performance?
2. Is the type of rating matched with the purpose?
3. Are the traits directly observable?
4. Are the criteria understandable?
5. Are the traits clearly defined?

6. Is scoring error minimized?
7. Is the scoring system feasible? (p. 223)

CONSISTENCY IN CONDUCTING AND SCORING ASSESSMENTS

Steps can be taken to improve reliability in using checklists, rating scales, and rubrics. If several teachers are going to use the same instrument, the following guidelines can assist in developing consistency:

1. Before using an instrument, the teachers should review the items and indicators and reach agreement on what each is intended to measure.
2. The instrument should be piloted by the individual teacher or group of teachers to determine if there are items that are unclear or difficult to assess.
3. Scoring instructions should be reviewed prior to conducting the assessment.
4. Scoring instructions should be made according to the purposes of the assessment. If a score or grade is desired, the score will be numerical. If the assessment is to be used for student and/or parent feedback, more written information on the student's performance might be needed.

Herman et al. (1992) provided a checklist for ensuring reliability in using a rating instrument with a group of teachers:

- documented, field-tested scoring guide
- clear, concrete criteria
- annotated examples of all score points
- ample practice and feedback for raters
- multiple raters with demonstrated agreement prior to scoring
- periodic reliability checks throughout
- retraining when necessary
- arrangements for collection of suitable reliability data (pp. 93–94)

SUMMARY

Informal evaluation measures are useful for teachers who need specific information about their students to use when planning instruction. Checklists and rating scales are informal instruments that can be designed and used by teachers to obtain specific diagnostic and assessment data that will assist them in developing learning experiences for their children.

Checklists are used for more than assessment or evaluation. They are a form of curriculum outline or a framework of curriculum objectives. With checklists, teachers can plan instruction, develop learning center activities, and evaluate children's progress and achievement on specific objectives.

Rating scales allow teachers to evaluate behaviors qualitatively. Raters can indicate the extent to which the child exhibits certain behaviors.

Checklists and rating scales are practical and easy to use. Teachers can develop them to fit the curriculum and administer them at their convenience. Unlike standardized tests, checklists and rating scales are current and provide the teacher with immediate feedback on student progress.

Using checklists and rating scales also has disadvantages. Because they are not standardized, they are subject to error and teacher bias. Checklists do not include the level or quality of performance on the objectives measured. Rating scales in particular are subject to rater bias. Rating scale descriptors are ambiguous in definition. Differing interpretations of descriptors by raters lead to different responses and interpretations of children's behaviors.

Rating scales provide a multidimensional format for assessing student products and performances. They include the most complex format for assessing quality in student work. They are particularly useful in helping students to understand the expectations for quality in an assignment and to review quality indicators as a project or learning assignment is in progress. Rating scales are also useful in helping parents to understand the nature of student assignments and the criteria for quality that were developed for that assignment.

Rating scales can have drawbacks. One possible weakness is when teachers predetermine characteristics of quality, rather than using examples of typical student work to determine the indicators. Likewise, teachers can focus on less appropriate indicators of quality work or look at quantity rather than quality of work.

All three of these assessment instruments can be weakened by teacher bias and subjective judgment on the part of the teacher. Reliability in conducting an assessment with these instruments can be improved if teachers work to achieve consistency in conducting and scoring the assessments.

REVIEW QUESTIONS

1. Describe the different functions of checklists. How can checklists be used by teachers for purposes other than evaluation or assessment?
2. Why is it important to use developmental checklists in early childhood programs?
3. How do developmental checklists serve as a guide for the sequence of development and curriculum?
4. Explain the different strategies that teachers can use to measure progress with checklist objectives.
5. How does the design of a checklist affect its use as an evaluation instrument?
6. What is sequenced organization in checklist design?

7. What methods can be used to record assessment results on checklists? Which form is best?
8. Why do some teachers have difficulty in using checklists? Do you see any solution to their problems?
9. How do rating scales differ from checklists?
10. Why are rating scales vulnerable to rater error and bias?
11. Is it better to use numerical rating scales or graphic rating scales? Why?
12. Which type of rubric is more specific, a holistic rubric or an analytic rubric? Explain how they are different.
13. How do scoring criteria provide indicators of quality of student work on a rubric?

SUGGESTED ACTIVITIES

1. Collect samples of checklists used in preschool and primary classrooms. Compare the checklists in terms of objectives, evaluation strategies, and recordkeeping.
2. Develop a checklist for the first 6 weeks of school for behavior you wish to see demonstrated in a classroom or a learning center.
3. Design a rating scale to measure appropriate study behaviors in the classroom. Include five characteristics and at least three points on the scale with descriptors.
4. Design a developmental rubric for emerging reading skills in kindergarten and first-grade students. Find characteristics of beginning readers to develop the characteristics for different stages of development.

KEY TERMS

analytic rubric
developmental checklist
developmental rubric

graphic rating scale
holistic rubric
numerical rating scale

REFERENCES

Bickart, T. (1998). *Summary report of preventing reading difficulties in young children.* Prepared for U.S. Department of Education Reading Summit. Washington, DC: Teaching Strategies.

Farr, R. C. (1994). *Portfolio assessment teacher's guide grades K–8.* Orlando, FL: Harcourt Brace Jovanovich.

Harms, T., Clifford, R. M. & Gryer, D. (1998). *Early Childhood Environment Rating Scale—Revised.* New York: Teachers College Press.

Herman, J. L., Aschbacher, P. R., & Winters, L. (1992). *A practical guide to alternative assessment.* Alexandria, VA: Association for Supervision and Curriculum Development.

Irwin, D. M., & Bushnell, M. M. (1980). *Observational strategies for child study.* New York: Holt, Rinehart & Winston.

Kamii, C., & Rosenblum, V. (1990). An approach to assessment in mathematics. In C. Kamii (Ed.), *Achievement testing in the early grades: The games grown-ups play* (pp. 146–162). Washington, DC: National Association for the Education of Young Children.

Linn, R. L., & Gronlund, N. E. (2000). *Measurement and assessment in teaching* (8th ed.). Upper Saddle River, NJ: Merrill/Prentice Hall.

Marsden, D. B., Meisels, S. J., Jablon, J. R., & Dichtelmiller, M. L. (1997). *The work sampling system: Preschool–4 developmental guidelines.* Ann Arbor, MI: Rebus.

McMillan, J. H. (1997). *Classroom assessment: Principles and practice for effective instruction.* Boston: Allyn & Bacon.

Meisels, S. J. (1996). Charting the continuum of assessment and intervention. In S. J. Meisels & E. Fenichel (Eds.), *New visions for the developmental assessment of infants and young children* (pp. 27–52). Washington, DC: ZERO TO THREE: National Center for Infants, Toddlers, and Families.

Payne, D. A. (1997). *Applied educational assessment.* Belmont, CA: Wadsworth Publishing.

Polakowski, C. (1993). Literacy portfolios in the early childhood classroom. In *Student portfolios* (pp. 47–66). Washington, DC: National Education Association.

Ratcliff, N. J. (2001–2002). Using authentic assessment to document the emerging literacy skills of children. *Childhood Education 98,* 66–69.

Spodek, B., & Saracho, O. N. (1994). *Dealing with individual differences in the early childhood classroom.* New York: Longman.

Wiener, R. B., & Cohen, J. H. (1997). *Literacy portfolios: Using assessment to guide instruction*. Upper Saddle River, NJ: Merrill/Prentice Hall.

Wiggins, G. (1996a). Creating tests worth taking. In R. E. Blum & J. A. Arter (Eds.), *Student performance assessment in an era of restructuring* (pp. V:6-2 to V:6-9). Alexandria, VA: Association for Supervision and Curriculum Development.

Wiggins, G. (1996b). What is a rubric? A dialogue on design and use. In R. E. Blum & J. A. Arter (Eds.), *Student performance assessment in an era of restructuring* (pp. VI-5:1 to VI-5:13). Alexandria, VA: Association for Supervision and Curriculum Development.

Wortham, S. C. (1984). *Organizing instruction in early childhood*. Boston: Allyn & Bacon.

7 CHAPTER

Informal Assessments
Teacher-Designed Strategies

Chapter Objectives

As a result of reading this chapter, you will be able to

1. **Describe why teacher-designed assessments and tests are used**
2. **Understand the relationship between teacher-designed assessments and curriculum and instruction**
3. **Design assessments for preschool and primary-grade students**
4. **Understand the process of mastery learning**
5. **Write an instructional or behavioral objective**
6. **Develop formative and summative tests and learning, enrichment, and corrective activities for learning objectives**

Another type of informal evaluation to be discussed is teacher-designed assessments. In assessing and evaluating children from birth through the primary grades, measures other than paper-and-pencil tests are generally more appropriate. As children progress through the primary grades, however, they develop skills in reading and writing that will make it possible for them to demonstrate learning on a written test. In this chapter, we discuss how teachers design their own assessments of classroom instruction and use commercially designed classroom tests.

PURPOSES OF TEACHER-DESIGNED ASSESSMENTS AND TESTS

Although all types of evaluation, both formal and informal, are used to measure and evaluate children's behavior and learning, there are circumstances under which teacher-designed assessments or written classroom tests are especially useful for the teacher. Paper-and-pencil tests, when given to students who are able to use them, can supplement other types of evaluation and provide teachers with information that the other types lack. These purposes include providing objective data on student learning and accountability and providing additional information for making instructional decisions.

Teacher-designed assessments support other evaluation measures, enabling the teacher to make more accurate decisions for the instruction of individual students. The teacher uses observation, tasks during group instruction, and manipulative activities to determine a child's progress in learning. A written test used with older children can reinforce or support the teacher's evaluation with an objective assessment. Objective testing complements the teacher's more subjective, personal evaluation, which can be subject to individual impressions or biases.

Classroom assessments can also support teachers' decisions that may be questioned by parents or school staff members. The teacher may understand, from ongoing work with a child, that the child needs to be instructed at a different level or requires extended experiences with a concept that other children have mastered. Although the teacher is confident in making the decision, a task or paper-and-pencil assessment can support it and, at the same time, help the parents to understand the nature of the problem. The teacher-designed assessment thus can increase the teacher's accountability for decisions that affect students' learning.

Teachers must make instructional decisions, both immediate and long term. As they teach, they must decide how long to spend on a particular science unit or math concept. In addition to using informal evaluation strategies, such as individual tasks and ongoing observations of class progress, they can use written tests to provide more information that will help them to decide whether to include more experiences, use review activities, skip planned activities, or conclude the current topic and move on to a new one.

Unfortunately, at present, the increased emphasis is on grading young children. Although kindergarten children may be exempt, primary-grade students are being given letter or numerical grades in many schools, and the practice has expanded with the recent emphasis on higher instructional and grading standards. Teachers find it difficult to assign letter grades to primary-school children. Whether the practice should continue is debatable; nevertheless, testing can help the teacher make decisions about student achievement. To use only written evaluations for grading would be inappropriate for all the reasons discussed throughout this book; however, when combined with other developmentally appropriate evaluation strategies, paper-and-pencil tests add supporting information on which grades can be based.

In the same fashion, tests can be used to support diagnostic decisions about student needs. The classroom teacher can supplement information from standardized tests and informal evaluations to determine student strengths and weaknesses in content areas. Assessments can be designed that correspond to local instructional objectives and that provide specific information on student accomplishment and instructional needs. Once diagnostic information has been analyzed, the teacher can place students more accurately into instructional groups and regroup periodically as students move through the program at different rates.

Finally, teacher-designed assessments allow evaluation of the local instructional program. Unlike standardized tests, which reflect general objectives suitable for a broad range of school programs at a state, regional, or national level, the teacher-designed test assesses specific or local learning objectives. These objective-based tests evaluate more closely the effectiveness of the local educational program. Without evaluation measures designed for the classroom, there is no ready method to assess local curriculum objectives.

TYPES OF TESTS USED WITH PRESCHOOL AND PRIMARY-GRADE CHILDREN

Teacher-designed assessments for preschool children must match the way these children learn—through active interaction with concrete materials. Children who do not yet read cannot demonstrate their learning effectively with a paper-and-pencil test. The teacher constructs assessment activities that allow the child to manipulate materials, explain understanding orally, or point to the correct response if expressive language is limited.

Teacher assessments using tasks or oral responses can be conducted during a teaching activity, as part of a learning center experience, or as a separate assessment or series of assessments (Wortham, 1984). For example, for the objective of recognizing uppercase and lowercase letters, the teacher may present a set of cards with five letters and ask the child to match the uppercase and lowercase letters. Figure 7–1 pictures an array of cards that can be used for this purpose.

To demonstrate an understanding of counting, the preschool child is given objects to count. The teacher can conduct the assessment in two ways. He or she may either select five objects and ask the child to count them or ask the child to group five of the objects.

Pictures also may be used for assessment tasks with nonreaders. To assess knowledge of shapes, a pictured array of basic shapes could be used. If the objective is to identify shapes, the teacher can ask the child to find a given shape by saying, "Show me a triangle." The

FIGURE 7-1 Uppercase and lowercase letters

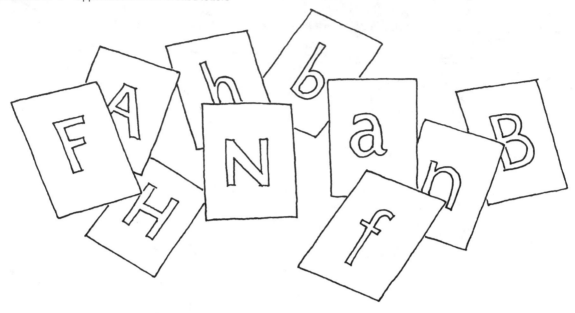

FIGURE 7-2 Array of basic shapes

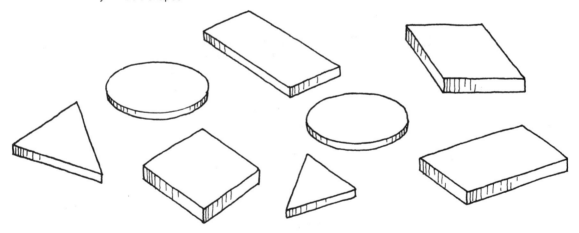

teacher can also point to the shape and ask the child to name it if the objective is to be able to name shapes. Figure 7–2 shows an array of shapes that can be used to identify circles, squares, triangles, and rectangles (Wortham, 1984).

For some preschool assessments, an oral response may be most appropriate. For example, a common preschool objective is for the child to know his or her first and last name. The teacher would ask the child to give this information.

FIGURE 7–3 Sequencing pictures

For the objective of sequencing events in a story, the teacher shows the child a set of three to five pictures that have a logical sequence and asks the child to put them in order. The child then is asked to tell the story. Figure 7–3 shows a series of pictures that can be used for sequencing the cards and providing a verbal description.

As children learn to read, the teacher's assessments begin to include printed test activities with pictures and some written words. Instead of a physical response using concrete materials or an oral response, the child uses a pencil with a printed test. These written assessments may be commercially produced materials designed for classroom use with basal textbooks or as supplementary resources. The teacher must also be able to design his or her own tests to evaluate his or her own or individual learning objectives most effectively.

Paper-and-pencil tests must be adapted to the child's limited reading and writing skills. Therefore, tests designed for children in the primary grades use a format that provides pictorial or visual clues to assist the student in selecting or writing the correct response. To prepare beginning readers and writers for written tests, the teacher introduces key words such as *circle* or *draw* that are commonly used in paper-and-pencil assessments. More words are taught until the child is able to read written instructions. Throughout the primary grades,

FIGURE 7–4 Examples of assessments for students with limited literacy skills

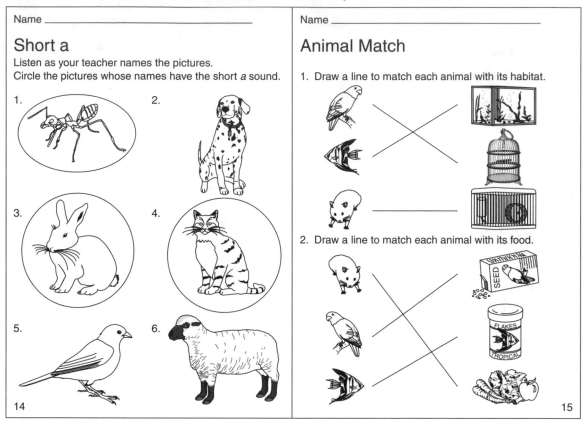

Source: Chamot, A. U., Cummins, J., Kessler, C., O'Malley, J. M., & Fillmore, L W. (1997). *Accelerating English language learning*. White Plains, NY: Pearson Education. Copyright © 1997 by Pearson Education. Reprinted by permission of Pearson Education, Inc. White Plains, New York.

the teacher will introduce the assessment page with the children before asking them to complete the page independently.

Once the students can successfully complete a written assessment, the teacher may use a commercially prepared activity or design one. Regardless of which type is chosen, certain tasks are used to accommodate the child's limited reading and writing abilities. The most common tasks include marking or circling a response, drawing a line to a response, and writing simple numeral or word answers. Although both commercial and teacher-designed tests use these responses, most of the following examples are from commercial sources. Later in the chapter the process of preparing teacher-designed assessments and tests is described.

Children can circle pictures in response to questions before they have learned to read and write. This type of response is continued in the grades where beginning reading skills are acquired. Figure 7–4 presents a page from a commercially designed test in which the child is asked to circle the correct responses and to draw a line to match pictures. On the

FIGURE 7–5 Putting an X on the correct answer

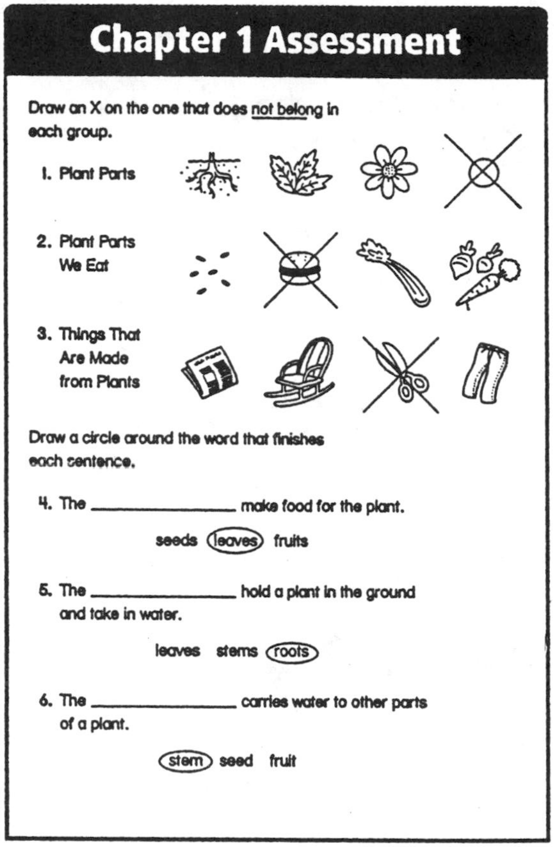

Chapter 1 Assessment

Draw an X on the one that does <u>not belong</u> in each group.

1. Plant Parts

2. Plant Parts We Eat

3. Things That Are Made from Plants

Draw a circle around the word that finishes each sentence.

4. The _____ make food for the plant.

        seeds (leaves) fruits

5. The _____ hold a plant in the ground and take in water.

        leaves stems (roots)

6. The _____ carries water to other parts of a plant.

        (stem) seed fruit

Source: Scott Foresman Science Teacher's Edition, Grade 1; Teacher's Assessment Package, p. 5. Copyright © 2000 Addison Wesley Educational Publishers, Glenview, Illinois. Reprinted by permission of Pearson Education Inc.

left-hand side of this figure, the child is asked to circle the correct pictures as the teacher says the name of each. On the right-hand side of the figure, lines are drawn to match animals with their food and habitat. The example is for first-grade students. Although the instructions are printed on the page, the teacher rather than the student would provide the information needed to complete the tasks.

A similar type of response can be made by marking a test question with an X or making the correct choice to complete a sentence. Figure 7–5 uses a multiple-choice format. At the top of the page the student must put an X on the picture that does not fit a group. At the bottom of the page a circle is drawn around the correct word to fill a blank in a sentence. In Figure 7–6, a teacher-designed assessment for reading vocabulary, the student must determine whether to write each word under the people or places category. In Figure 7–7, part of a science test, the student must select the correct word at the top of the page to write in the blank to complete each sentence.

FIGURE 7–6   Teacher-designed assessment for reading vocabulary

---

PEOPLE AND PLACES

Write each vocabulary word under People or Places below.

People   Places   Words

                                                        bank
                                                        fireman
                                                        friend
                                                        grocery store
                                                        neighbor
                                                        park
                                                        policeman
                                                        post office
                                                        school
                                                        sister

---

FIGURE 7–7   Writing a word for a response

Chapter 1 Assessment

Each sentence tells about a part of the earth.
Write a word from the box.

| water | air | land | ocean |

6. This is the part of the earth that has soil.

   People can walk on it. _____

7. Most of the water on the earth is found here.

   It is salty. _____

8. This is a liquid that covers most of the earth.

   People drink it. _____

9. This is a gas that is all around the earth.

   People breathe it. _____

10. Circle the helpful thing to do.

Source: Scott Foresman Science Teacher's Edition, Grade 1: Teacher's Assessment Package, p. 42. Copyright © 2000 Addison Wesley Educational Publishers, Glenview, Illinois. Reprinted by permission of Pearson Education Inc.

All the examples of written assessments for the primary grades follow the same guidelines. Not only must the child have visual clues to be able to respond, but an example is usually given to help the child to understand the task. Also, although there are written instructions for the child to read, in reality the teacher may need to read and discuss the instructions with the students to ensure that they understand what is required. In the following section, we discuss the design of teacher-constructed assessments and tests.

HOW TESTS ARE DESIGNED AND USED

Classroom tests are closely matched to curriculum objectives and content. Whether designed by the teacher or obtained from a textbook or other commercial source, they are used to measure the student's ability to benefit from classroom instruction.

Unlike standardized tests that provide general information about student achievement, classroom tests measure student accomplishment and learning needs in relation to specific classroom objectives. Classroom tests can be used for placement and diagnosis, formative testing, and summative testing (Linn & Gronlund, 2000).

Placement and diagnostic testing have a similar function. In placement testing, the student is assessed to determine the instructional group into which he or she should be placed. Tests are given to determine what the student already knows and is ready to learn. Diagnostic testing is used to determine student weaknesses that need to be corrected. The same tests can be used for both purposes unless learning difficulties are persistent and need more extensive diagnosis by the school diagnostician or psychologist. Placement and diagnostic testing in the classroom are similar to criterion-referenced testing using standardized tests; however, the tests may assess selected learning objectives, rather than objectives for an entire grade level.

Formative and summative tests are related to mastery learning (Bloom, Madaus, & Hastings, 1981). **Formative tests** are given periodically while teaching specific objectives to monitor student progress. These tests measure a limited number of objectives at a time so that the teacher can identify which objectives have been mastered and which call for additional work or activities. They provide feedback and are not used for grading purposes.

The **summative test**, in contrast, is the final test given on completion of a unit of work. The unit of work may be organized for a single objective or for a small group of objectives. The summative test is given after instruction and formative testing reveal that the material has been mastered. It is administered as the final step to verify the student's achievement on the material covered in the unit or by a group of objectives.

The information gained from diagnostic, placement, formative, and summative testing provides the teacher with current, relevant information for instructional planning. It allows the teacher not only to group students for instruction effectively, but also to determine how long the class needs to continue working on objectives and whether alternative types of experiences are needed to correct learning weaknesses in particular students. Unlike standardized tests that are administered once a year, classroom tests provide ongoing, criterion-related information about student progress on objectives being covered in a particular classroom. To use classroom testing effectively, the teacher must know how to design appropriate tasks that match the students' ability to use paper-and-pencil tests. The teacher must also know what kinds of tests will accurately measure the students' progress or mastery of each learning objective.

STEPS IN TEST DESIGN

Teacher-designed classroom assessments, although less rigorously constructed than standardized tests, must accurately measure objectives for classroom instruction. Whether the teacher is organizing assessment strategies for preschool or primary-school students, tests are carefully designed to fit the learning objectives. Although in this section of the chapter we discuss teacher assessment in terms of test design, we refer to evaluation strategies for preschool students who are nonreaders, as well as for students in the primary grades who are beginning to read and write.

Several steps in test design must be followed if a test is to measure student learning accurately. Based on Bloom's model of mastery learning (Block, 1971), the process includes the following:

1. Determination of instructional objectives
2. Construction of a table of specifications
3. Design of formative and summative evaluations
4. Design of learning experiences
5. Design of correctives and enrichment activities

DETERMINING INSTRUCTIONAL OBJECTIVES.   In chapter 5, we discussed objectives relative to skills continuums and checklists. The same types of sources are used to develop instructional objectives that will be used to design classroom tests. Although the term *learning outcomes* has replaced instructional objectives in many states and school districts, they have the same purpose. School districts have various sources to draw from when determining curriculum objectives for each grade level.

One common source of curriculum objectives is basal textbook series used in the classroom. Most textbooks in reading, mathematics, social studies, and science are based on learning objectives appropriate for that grade level in school districts in many states. A commonly accepted pool of learning objectives can be found in the content areas for each grade level; however, objectives can vary markedly among different basal series. Textbooks are organized around these objectives, and teachers' editions of the textbooks contain activities to implement instruction for the objectives and tests to evaluate student learning on the objectives.

School districts, particularly large, urban ones, establish their own learning objectives in various content areas for each grade level. These objectives may draw on commercial resources, which are supplemented with other objectives that are deemed important in the school district.

The state's department of education may produce learning objectives for each grade level in each content area. The state-mandated curriculum objectives are followed by each school district. These objectives may be the minimum required by the state. If this is so, local districts may have the freedom to supplement state learning objectives with commercial and local sources for additional objectives.

The *Addison-Wesley Mathematics, Teacher's Edition* for first grade (Eicholz et al., 1985) includes sets of skills divided into 14 chapters or units. Chapter 2 of the text covers "Sums to 5." The objectives for the unit are as follows:

2.1 Recall addition facts through sums to 5.
2.2 Solve problems using cumulative computational skills.

The teacher using this textbook can use these objectives, plus others, to determine the learning objectives for mathematics in the first-grade classroom. The objectives will be followed in designing instructional experiences and testing procedures to evaluate achievement.

WRITING BEHAVIORAL OBJECTIVES. **Behavioral** or **instructional objectives** provide the framework for curriculum and instruction and the measurement of the effectiveness of instruction and learning. According to Kubiszyn and Borich (1996), instructional objectives should have the following characteristics:

> An instructional objective should be a clear and concise statement of the skill or skills that your students will be expected to perform after a unit of instruction. It should include the level of proficiency to be demonstrated and the special conditions under which the skill must be demonstrated. Furthermore, an instructional objective should be stated in observable, behavioral terms, in order for two or more individuals to agree that a student has or has not displayed the learning outcome in question. In short, a complete instructional objective includes:
>
> an observable behavior (action verb specifying the learning outcome)
> any special conditions under which the behavior must be displayed, and
> a performance level considered sufficient to demonstrate mastery. (p. 51)

For example, a common objective for preschool children is to be able to sort objects into two groups by using some type of criterion. An instructional or behavioral objective could be written as follows:

> Given an array of nuts, the student will be able to sort the nuts correctly into two groups of nuts with smooth shells and nuts with rough shells.

An analysis of the objective would identify the components of an instructional objective as follows:

> Given an array of nuts (condition), the student will be able to sort the nuts correctly (100% performance standard implied) into two groups of nuts with smooth shells and nuts with rough shells (behavior).

An objective for physical development might include the ability to catch a ball with both hands. Stated behaviorally, the objective might be worded as follows:

> Following a series of activities throwing and catching large rubber balls, the child will be able to catch the ball with both hands in four out of six tries.

To analyze the parts of this objective, it would be described as follows:

> Following a series of activities throwing and catching large rubber balls (condition), the child will be able to catch the ball with both hands (behavior) in four out of six tries (standard of performance or performance level).

Before a learning objective or outcome can be measured, then, it must be stated clearly in terms of its content and the desired behavior. The *content* refers to the knowledge or skill to be learned. The *behavior* is what the student does to demonstrate that the knowledge or skill has been attained. In the objectives described for the *Addison-Wesley Mathematics, Teacher's Edition* for first grade, the content is clearly stated but the required behavior is missing. Objective 2.1, "Recall addition facts through sums to 5," describes the required skill, but does not specify how the student will demonstrate it or the performance standard. If the statement is changed to read, "The student will recall addition facts through sums to 5 by correctly adding sums in 10 problems," the desired behavior and performance standard have been described.

ANALYZING OBJECTIVES TO DETERMINE PREREQUISITE SKILLS. The teacher must not only develop the learning objective, but also determine what must be taught for the student to master it. Part of the planning for instruction involves studying the learning objective to decide what prior knowledge or skill the student must have to be able to learn the new information. In Objective 2.1, "Recall addition facts through sums to 5," the teacher will plan instruction to help students to learn to combine all possible groups of numbers that equal five. In addition, the teacher determines what the student must already know to understand and use addition skills. Prior skills to be considered include the following:

1. Knowledge of numbers through 5
2. Identification of numerals through 5
3. Understanding that small groups can be combined to make a larger group

The teacher must decide whether the students have the prerequisite skills to be able to master the targeted learning objective. If not, the prior skills will have to be taught, or re-taught if necessary, before the new objective is introduced. A pretest or a diagnostic test may be used to determine student readiness for the learning objective.

SETTING A STANDARD FOR MASTERY. The final step in determining the instructional objectives is to set the level of mastery that will be expected for the student to learn the objective. In the section on writing behavioral objectives, information was included on how to include the performance level for the objective. In this context, the process for determining the level of performance desired or required is discussed. The level of accomplishment may be set by the teacher, the school district, or the state department of education. This is the minimum standard required to pass the objective. The learning objective can reflect the established standard for mastery. If 80% is established as the minimum standard for mastery, the learning objective can be stated to reflect the standard. Objective 2.1, the mathematics objective for first grade, can be rewritten to include the standard of mastery as follows: "The student will be able to recall addition facts through sums to 5 by correctly completing eight of ten addition problems." If each objective does not include the written standard of mastery, the standard can be set separately for all of the learning objectives.

CONSTRUCTING A TABLE OF SPECIFICATIONS. After the learning objectives for a unit of study or the content of an entire course has been described behaviorally, the teacher or curriculum developer is ready to outline the course content. Before a test can be organized to measure the curriculum objectives, it is necessary to understand more accurately what concepts or skills are to be measured and to what extent the student will be expected to perform to demonstrate mastery of the objective. Will the student be expected to remember information, use the information to solve problems, or evaluate the information? The test items will reflect the level of understanding that is required to master the objective.

Analysis of objectives to determine the level of understanding is commonly done by constructing a **table of specifications** (Linn & Gronlund, 2000). Here learning objec-

FIGURE 7–8 Explanation of Bloom's taxonomy

Level of Understanding	Descriptive Terms	
Knowledge Recognition and recall The ability to remember or recognize information	Tell List Name	Define Identify Locate
Comprehension The ability to translate information in your own words Show that you understand	Restate Discuss Explain Review	Describe Summarize Interpret
Application The ability to use information or apply learning to new situations and real-life circumstances	Demonstrate Construct Imply	Dramatize Practice Illustrate
Analysis The ability to break down information into parts To identify parts of information and its relationship to the whole	Organize Differentiate Compare Distinguish	Solve Experiment Relate

Synthesize
The ability to assemble separate parts into a new
  whole
The ability to take information from various sources
  and present it in a created form
	Design
	Plan
	Develop
		Compile
		Create
		Compose

Evaluation The ability to make judgments about information To be able to evaluate based on criteria or standards	Decide Conclude Appraise Choose	Judge Assess Select

Source: Bloom, B. S. (Ed.). (1956). *Taxonomy of educational objectives: The classification of educational goals. Handbook I: Cognitive domain.* New York: McKay.

tives are charted by using Bloom's *Taxonomy of Educational Objectives* (Bloom, 1956). This work describes levels of understanding in the cognitive domain, ranging from the ability to recall information (the knowledge level) to the highest level of understanding (evaluation). Figure 7–8 is an explanation of the levels of Bloom's taxonomy, with examples of terms that characterize each level. In Figure 7–9, an adaptation of the taxonomy is used to make a table of specifications for the mathematics unit covering addition

FIGURE 7–9 Table of specifications for a unit on sums to 5

Sums to 5	Know	Comprehend	Apply	Analyze	Synthesize	Evaluate
2.1 Recall addition facts through sums to five	X	X	X			
2.2 Solve problems using cumulative computational skills	X	X	X	X		

sums to 5. The two objectives for the unit are listed to the left of the figure. The columns to the right describe how the objectives are charted on the taxonomy. The first objective requires that the student be able to recall addition facts and problems, understand the facts and problems, and apply that understanding. The second objective also requires that the student be able to analyze or solve problems. When designing test or assessment items, the teacher must know the type and level of understanding that test items will reflect and must organize the test so that the described levels of understanding are adequately sampled. Figure 7–10 is a table of specifications for a unit on classification at the kindergarten level.

DESIGNING FORMATIVE AND SUMMATIVE EVALUATIONS. After the teacher has determined what is to be measured by designing a table of specifications for the learning objectives to be taught, it is time to design the formative and summative evaluations. Both types of evaluations are derived from the table of specifications. Assessment items will be designed to measure the student's achievement at the levels of Bloom's taxonomy, as described in the table of specifications. The assessment items on the two forms are equivalent, but the evaluation purposes differ. The formative evaluation is not a test; it is a checkup or progress report on the student. The teacher uses the formative evaluation to decide whether the student needs further work with the objective.

If the student needs additional experiences, more activities, known as **correctives**, are implemented. Correctives are learning resources designed to approach the objective differently from the original instruction. The intent is to provide various kinds of activities to meet individual students' needs.

If the student's responses indicate mastery on the formative evaluation, the teacher provides **enrichment activities**. The student engages in activities that are at a higher level on Bloom's taxonomy than are required for mastery. Thus, if the mastery level in the table of specifications is at the application level, students who master the information after an initial period of instruction may benefit from activities at the analysis, synthesis, or evaluation levels (Bloom et al., 1981).

The summative evaluation is the final assessment or test of what the student has learned or accomplished. It is given after all instruction has been concluded. Although formative and summative evaluations are interchangeable in content, only the summative form is used as a test. The decisions to be made about both assessments include the format, selection of assessment items, determination of length, and assembly of the assessment.

FIGURE 7–10   Unit objective: classifying objects by common attributes in a table of specifications

Behavioral Objectives	Knowledge	Comprehension	Application	Analysis	Synthesis	Evaluation
A. Classifying 1. The student will describe the object by naming one of its attributes.	X	X				
2. The student will construct a set from various objects by classifying together those with common attributes.	X	X	X			
B. Noting Differences 1. From a set of four objects, the student will remove the one object that is different from the others.	X	X	X	X		
C. Classifying by Name 1. The student will classify a group of pictures into two categories, using class names.	X	X	X			
D. Classifying by Design 1. The student will classify objects into sets according to design, such as stripes, dots, etc.	X	X	X			

TEST FORMAT.   Earlier in the chapter, we talked about test formats for use with children in the primary grades. When the teacher is ready to design classroom tests, the appropriate format will have to be determined. Most preschool children respond best to concrete tasks and oral questions. With first graders, the teacher must limit student responses to tasks that require little or no reading and writing, such as circling pictures, marking the correct response, and drawing lines to correct responses. Later in the year, and for children in second and third grades, more writing and reading can be incorporated into the test format. If several different tasks are to be used, more than one format may be used for a test. Figure 7–11,

FIGURE 7–11   Teacher-designed test on coins

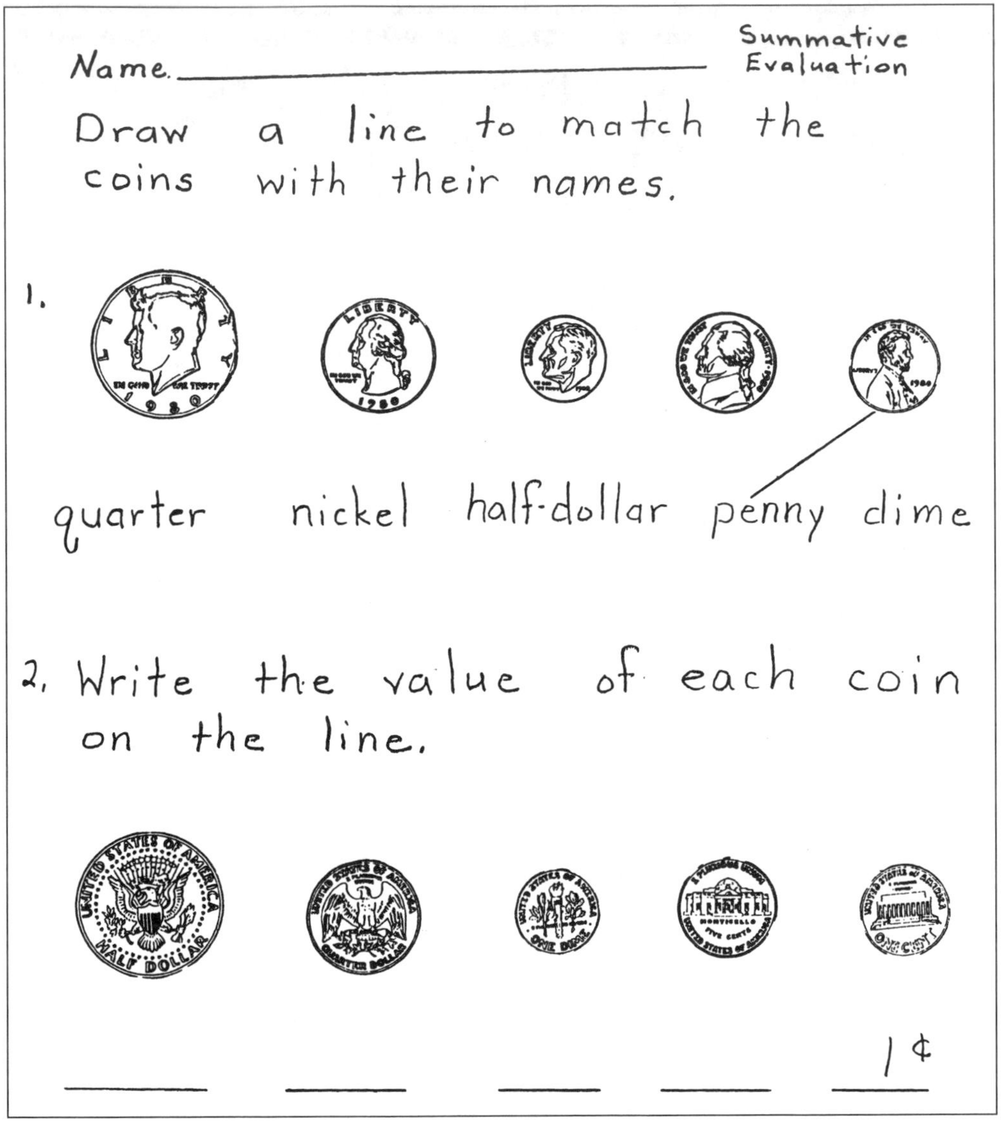

Name._____   Summative Evaluation

Draw a line to match the coins with their names.

1.

quarter   nickel   half-dollar   penny   dime

2. Write the value of each coin on the line.

1 ¢

_____   _____   _____   _____   _____

designed for an assessment of a second-grade unit on money, shows the format used. The student must draw a line from the coin to its name and write the numerical value below the coin.

ASSESSMENT ITEMS.   In addition to determining the format or formats to be used in the assessment, the teacher must develop the items that reflect the table of specifications describing the objectives to be tested. Figure 7–12 and 7–13 are examples of an assessment that fulfills a cell of the table of specifications developed for the unit on coins. In Figure 7–12, Objective 5 requires the student to count collections of coins up to 99 cents. In Figure 7–13,

FIGURE 7–12 Unit on coins: table of specifications

OBJECTIVES	KNOWLEDGE	COMPREHENSION	APPLICATION	ANALYSIS	SYNTHESIS	EVALUATION
1. The student will be able to identify the five coins (half-dollar, quarter, dime, nickel, penny) by sight with 100% accuracy.	X					
2. The student will be able to match the five coins with their letter names with 100% accuracy.	X					
3. The student will be able to match the five coins to their number value using a cent sign (¢) with 100% accuracy.	X	X				
4. The student will be able to classify like coins by counting: pennies by ones, nickels by fives, dimes by tens, and quarters by twenty-fives, with 80% accuracy.	X	X	X	X		
5. The student will be able to differentiate like/unlike coins by switch counting from twenty-fives to tens to fives to ones in necessary order to count collections of coins up to 99¢ with 80% accuracy.	X	X	X	X		
6. The student will be able to analyze and solve story problems by counting coins with 80% accuracy.	X	X	X	X		

the directions require the student to count the value of the coins and to record the total on the line provided with each of the six collections of coins.

At the preschool level, Figure 7–10 shows a table of specifications for a unit on classification. Objective B specifies that the student will be able to remove the object that is different from a set of four objects. Figure 7–14 pictures a group of objects that may be used to evaluate the child's performance on the objective. The child chooses or points to the object that does not belong in the group.

TEST LENGTH. After determining the format and developing a pool of items to provide the levels of understanding expected from the table of specifications, the test developer

FIGURE 7–13 Test on coins

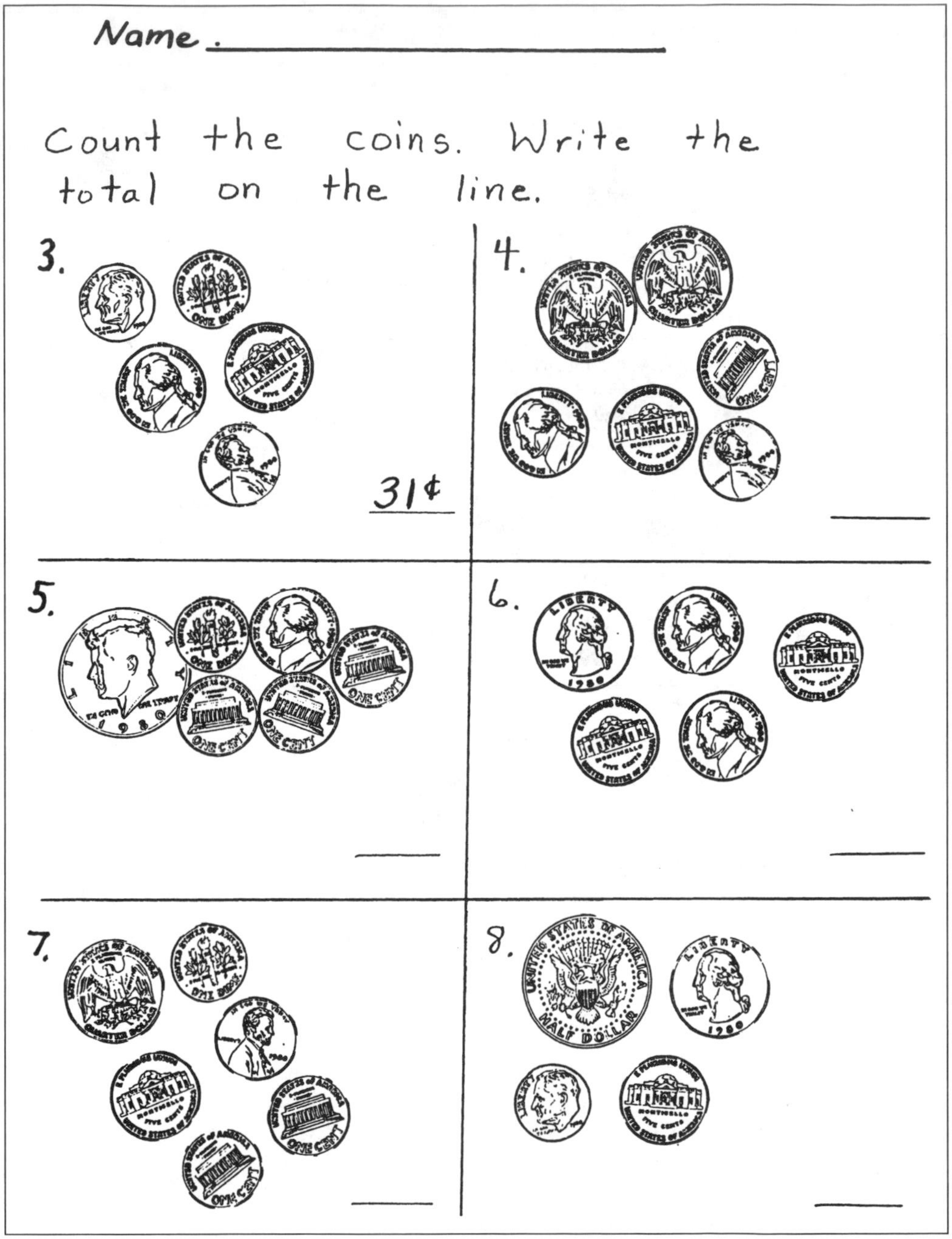

Name ._____

Count the coins. Write the total on the line.

3.

31¢

4. _____

5. _____

6. _____

7. _____

8. _____

FIGURE 7–14 Unit on classification: array of objects

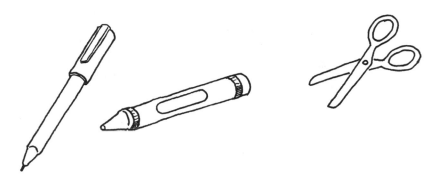

must determine how many test items or tasks will be included in the test. For young children, a balance is reached between the number of items needed to demonstrate the child's responses to determine understanding and a reasonable length that will not overtax the child's ability to attend to the task. For preschool and primary grades, the test length should not exceed the time normally needed to complete classroom activities and assignments. A maximum of 20 to 30 minutes is reasonable in testing primary-school students. Commercial tests designed to evaluate these students commonly are one page long.

ASSEMBLY. The final step in test design is to assemble test items into both a formative and a summative form. The teacher should construct enough items so that both forms of the test can be put together at the same time. The formative evaluation, conducted after the students have had some work with the objective, will enable the teacher to assess how well the students are learning the information. After the formative assessment has been examined, the teacher can reteach, provide different types of experiences or practice for some students, or move on to the summative test if the students show adequate progress. The teacher should have enough items to obtain the feedback needed to monitor student learning and mastery. The formative and summative assessments should be equivalent in terms of the level of understanding required and the types of items used.

When assembling the tests, the teacher must decide how instructions will be given to the students. If written instructions requiring reading skills will be used, they must be simply stated to match the students' reading ability. Pictures used must be clear and easily interpreted. Poorly drawn or inappropriate pictures will hamper the child's ability to respond correctly and distort the child's performance on the test. If the teacher is unable to draw simple pictures, he or she should obtain them from another source or ask a colleague for help.

DESIGNING LEARNING EXPERIENCES

After the table of specifications and the formative and summative evaluations have been constructed, the teacher collects and prepares the activities and instruction that will enable the student to learn the information designed in the objective. Instruction also matches the level given in the table of specifications. Instruction to introduce and work with the objectives includes teacher instruction and other resources normally used by the teacher to help children to practice and master new concepts and skills.

The instructional objective contains the structure for the learning experiences that will be provided for the students to interact with and master concepts. The teacher-directed lessons and child-centered activities enable the child to work with information and skills. When planning the activities, the teacher will want to establish some type of format to describe each activity and how it will be used. The activity description will include the objective, the materials needed, and any other relevant information.

For example, one objective of the unit on classifying objects discussed earlier could be used to describe appropriate activities. Figure 7–10 had the objective under "B. Noting Differences" as follows: From a set of four objects, the student will remove the one object that is different from the others. Figure 7–14 shows an assessment task that uses an array of objects to permit the child to demonstrate understanding of the objective. Figure 7–15 describes an activity that can be used for young children to experience the same concepts, first as a teacher-directed activity and later in a learning center.

FIGURE 7–15   Example of a learning activity

Objective
From a set of four objects, the student will remove the one object that is different from the others.

Materials Needed
A group of 2-inch blocks, 5 of one color, 1 of a different color
Several socks of different types and sizes, 1 shoe
An array of leaves of one type, 1 leaf of a different shape and size

Type of Activity
Teacher-directed, to be placed later in the math–science center. Small group.

Activity Description
The teacher will introduce the concept by using the group of blocks. The words *alike* and *different* will be modeled to describe the blocks.

Next, the socks and the shoe will be explored, with children encouraged to identify the one that is different. The leaves will then be used for the same activity.

As a final step, the teacher will ask each child to find examples in the classroom that are alike and different and to make a group similar to the examples that have been used: three things that are identical and one that is different. Each child is encouraged to describe his or her collection.

DESIGNING CORRECTIVES AND ENRICHMENT ACTIVITIES

Corrective activities for students who need additional work after initial instruction and formative evaluation provide learning alternatives. These include audiovisual resources, games, workbooks, peer tutoring, student–teacher discussions, and other opportunities that are different from the original instruction and activities. The purpose is to provide different or alternative ways for the student to learn the information in the learning objective.

Examples of corrective activities and enrichment activities may use the objective cited previously: From a set of four objects, the student will remove the one object that is different from the others. A child who needs additional activities to internalize the concept would benefit from opportunities to practice, but with alternative types of experiences. If the teacher-directed activities have focused on concrete objects, a corrective activity might consist of a card game of several sets of four cards that could be played by two children. Another corrective might use a flannel board and have the child remove the item that is different from an array of four items.

Enrichment activities provide opportunities for higher-level thinking. If additional complexity is desired, the number of items might be increased to five, with two items that are different, rather than one. Another way to increase complexity is to make the difference in the item more difficult to identify. Only a slight difference is evident between the three identical items and the one that is different. For example, if the four pictured items are gift-wrapped boxes, the ribbon on one of the boxes is different or part of the ribbon is missing.

Enrichment activities also allow students who easily mastered the objective initially to engage in challenging and more creative activities. The students can work on individual projects that allow them to problem solve and apply their own ideas in various types of activities that emerge from their own efforts (Block, 1977). Students might engage in developing pictures of items that are alike and different or write a story in which each page has a different category of items with one that is different.

ADVANTAGES AND DISADVANTAGES OF USING TEACHER-DESIGNED ASSESSMENTS

Teacher-designed assessments in the classroom have several advantages over commercially produced tests developed for the same purpose. The advantages are related to the flexibility of the tests constructed for the teacher's own classroom.

When a teacher plans an assessment activity or test, the objective or objectives to be tested may be selected to suit individual class needs. Unlike commercial tests, which may be programmed to fit student progress in a grade-level textbook, the teacher-designed test can vary from the structure or plan of the book. A teacher may be concerned about an objective outside the textbook sequence and feel compelled to conduct an evaluation. Because he or she is developing tests to fit classroom needs, the targeted objective can be tested within the teacher's assessment plans whenever needed.

In addition, teacher-constructed assessments can be designed for a particular class. If the children are nonreaders but have advanced concepts that normally are introduced to children who have reading skills, the teacher can write the test to accommodate their abilities. If the students are advanced readers, the test can be designed to take advantage of their reading skills. The most common difficulty with commercial classroom tests is that they are set for a certain reading level or penalize the child for being unable to perform well because pencil-and-paper skills are required. The teacher can modify test tasks to include manipulative activities, oral responses, and assessment within instructional periods if the child understands concepts but cannot yet respond on a written test.

Teacher-designed assessments can be improved whenever needed. Each time the teacher administers a test, student responses provide feedback on its effectiveness. The test can be changed and improved whenever students' responses indicate problems with the format or test items.

ASSESSMENTS FOR INSTRUCTIONAL OBJECTIVES: HOW USEFUL ARE THEY?

Norris teaches kindergarten. He and the other kindergarten teachers have been sent to a training session on designing assessments for instructional objectives using mastery learning. In the session, the teachers have reviewed how to write behavioral objectives and how to construct a table of specifications based on Bloom's taxonomy of educational objectives. Working with the table of specifications prepared them to design assessment strategies for the objectives.

On the way home after the training session, Norris and the other teachers voice skepticism. How can this kind of testing be used with kindergarten children? Norris comments, "I can see how some areas, such as math, can be organized and assessed by behavioral objectives, but how do you decide what 80% accuracy is on learning the Pledge of Allegiance, or what they learn from art or using concepts in science?" Jane, another kindergarten teacher in the group, agrees in principle, with the strategies they have learned. She remarks, "I can see why they want us to learn the process. It forces us to be more specific in our understanding of what the objectives are meant to accomplish. My problem is that I'm afraid we are going to end up teaching to objectives and fragmenting the curriculum with the children."

Norris finally decides that it is a matter of common sense. The teacher can apply the strategies with some parts of the curriculum in kindergarten, but not others. The question is whether the school's principal and the kindergarten coordinator will share his perspective. He and the other kindergarten teachers decide to talk to teachers at other grade levels to determine how they are implementing the assessment strategies. Afterward, they want to study their curriculum and decide where they can use assessments based on a table of specifications. They want to meet with the principal and the coordinator to discuss where the process will work and which parts of the curriculum do not lend themselves to that type of assessment.

When Norris and the other teachers meet with the principal and the kindergarten coordinator, they present tables of specifications and assessments for mathematics and units in science. After they explain their reluctance to use the process with their reading program and other curriculum components, the kindergarten coordinator supports their position. The principal is more reluctant, but decides to let the coordinator work with the teachers to determine how and where the assessment strategies will be implemented at the kindergarten level.

Young children benefit from assessments that use real objects.

Teacher-designed tests also have disadvantages; potential weaknesses generally focus on the teacher's skill in designing classroom assessments. Because teachers do not generally have extensive experience in developing their own tests, the evaluations they design may not be effective in evaluating student learning.

Because of the abundance of commercially designed tests that accompany curriculum texts and kits, teachers are not always required to construct their own tests. Teachers become dependent on commercial tests and do not consider the necessity of designing their own. As a result, the teacher may not clearly understand the purpose of the tests or the levels of knowledge that are tested.

Teachers may lack the training in test design that affects both the understanding of the purpose of the commercial tests and the skills needed to construct tests. For example, teachers may not have learned how to use a table of specifications for curriculum objectives. When they design tests, they are not aware of the levels of knowledge in the curriculum that need to be part of the evaluation process. This lack of awareness may be more true of early childhood teachers than of teachers in intermediate grades and secondary school. Teachers of preschool and primary-grade children need to be aware of the various levels of cognitive understanding, as well as alternative methods of evaluation that are developmentally suited to young students.

Finally, the process of developing good classroom tests, especially for younger students, is time consuming. Because test items must be developed to accommodate emerging reading and writing skills, each item must be carefully considered for both content and method or format. This consideration takes more time than developing items for students who have good reading and writing skills. The method of presentation is as important as the concepts and skills being tested.

A discussion of the weaknesses of teacher-designed assessments must include mention of the issues surrounding the use of mastery learning in early childhood education. Because mastery learning requires that the teacher analyze learning objectives and determine the level of mastery to be achieved, it would seem to be in conflict with the philosophy that early childhood educators should provide developmentally appropriate classroom experiences; that is, the teacher is encouraged to provide learning experiences that are consistent with the child's level of development, rather than to ask the child to fit into a predetermined style of learning that requires specific types of responses to achieve mastery.

The interest in providing developmentally appropriate practices also extends to the use of behavioral or instructional objectives specifically. One criticism of the objectives is the division of learning into small, skill-based objectives, rather than more global constructivist learning. The performance standard or level of mastery seems limiting when compared to the emphasis on child-centered learning that emerges from the child's interests and previous experiences.

Although these issues first applied to preschool classrooms, they are also a concern with primary-grade teachers. Constructivist learning or a "thinking curriculum" (Linn & Gronlund, 2000) focuses on the student's active involvement in constructing meaning, rather than mastery of specific skills. Thus, students should be engaged in more divergent types of learning and more complex types of outcomes. Performance assessment, discussed in chapter 8, addresses this issue.

Certain components of the preschool classroom curriculum lend themselves to the mastery learning approach. Concept development, particularly in mathematics, has sequential objectives that can be taught within the mastery learning format. Nevertheless, many early childhood educators object to attempts to limit early childhood programs to this approach. The need for exploratory and inquiry-based experiences, originating from the child's opportunity to initiate activities both indoors and outdoors and using self-directed learning, is essential in early childhood classrooms. In fact, these experiences are essential for both preschool and primary-grade levels.

Teachers must ultimately be able to understand and use their own assessments appropriately to match the curriculum and their students' development. Mastery learning must also be used appropriately in early childhood programs.

Despite their weaknesses, teacher-designed evaluations have an important place in early childhood classrooms. An answer to the difficulties in using these assessments may be to help teachers to understand the process of test design and to support their efforts to develop tests.

DEVELOPING QUALITY TEACHER-DESIGNED ASSESSMENTS

The steps in test design described in this chapter provide a guide to developing quality assessments that are directly linked to the learning process. Test items and learning activities are linked to the same learning objectives so that teachers are teaching and testing to the same levels of knowledge on Bloom's taxonomy. Similar steps can be taken for all teacher-designed assessments. Following are some suggestions for teachers to consider when designing assessment tasks and tests.

CONCRETE TASKS FOR PRESCHOOL

- Be sure that the task is at the same level of difficulty as the learning activities designed for the learning objective.

- Have a variety of objects and/or concrete materials so that the assessment task can be administered several times.
- When possible, administer tasks for a number of learning objectives. Have materials for a number of tasks organized and available.

TESTS FOR PRIMARY-GRADE CHILDREN

- Be sure that test items match the child's reading level. (Use the lowest possible reading level.)
- Use clear directions, even if they will be read by the teacher.
- Response items for multiple-choice-type assessments have one correct answer.
- Response options for multiple-choice-type assessments are the same length and are brief.
- The list of items is brief for matching exercises.
- The list of items for matching exercises is homogeneous.
- The length of blanks is the same for completion test items.
- Use only one blank for each completion item.

SUMMARY

Although written tests are the least commonly used method of evaluating the learning of young students, there is a place for these tests once children have mastered some reading and writing skills. Teachers and parents can use written tests as sources of objective information of student progress.

Like standardized tests, teacher-designed and commercially produced classroom assessments are developed through the use of procedures that ensure they are correct in content and method of evaluation. Test design begins with careful analysis and description of learning objectives for the curriculum. The objectives are examined for the prerequisite skills that must be mastered prior to their use and for how the content and skills must be taught. In addition to determining the level of mastery for the learning objectives, the test developer must use a developmentally appropriate test format that will maximize the performance of students who are learning to read and write.

Before test items are constructed, the test designer must describe the level at which the student must demonstrate the new knowledge. A table of specifications organized for the learning objectives is used for this purpose. While constructing the formative and summative evaluations, the teacher must consider length, equivalent items for both evaluations, and what types of test instructions are most appropriate.

Because paper-and-pencil tests may not be the most effective way to evaluate or assess children through the primary grades, teachers must understand when and how such tests are appropriate. The teacher must have acquired the skills to develop such tests if they are to measure learning accurately and appropriately. Teachers of young students must also understand the limitations of written tests and become skilled in combining them with alternative evaluation methods to ensure that each student is tested with procedures that are most appropriate for his or her own level of development and ability to respond.

REVIEW QUESTIONS

1. How do written tests serve a purpose different from other types of tests and evaluation methods?
2. Why should teachers be careful when using written tests with students in the primary grades?
3. How do written tests provide records of student learning that facilitate teaching accountability?
4. Why is the description of content and student behavior important in using learning objectives for assessment design?
5. How does the standard of mastery affect both the learning objective and the test developed to measure achievement of the objective?
6. What is a table of specifications? How is it used with learning objectives?
7. Why do teachers need to understand the levels of knowledge used to chart objectives on a table of specifications?
8. Describe different formats used in written tests developed for beginning readers.
9. What kinds of guidelines should the teacher consider when determining the length of a test for primary grade children?
10. Can more than one format be used in an assessment?
11. How are formative and summative tests alike? Different?
12. Why are written tests for primary-grade children difficult to design?
13. Why do classroom teachers tend not to develop their own tests?
14. How can teacher-designed tests be more effective than commercially designed tests that evaluate the same objectives?
15. When should teachers use written tests? When should they not use written tests?

SUGGESTED ACTIVITIES

1. Write behavioral objectives for the following: (a) The child will be able to match uppercase and lowercase letters; (b) The child will be able to sort objects by color; (c) The child will be able to match sets of objects with the correct numeral.
2. Develop a teacher-designed assessment for a learning center.
3. Develop a mastery learning unit based on three objectives. The unit should include a table of specifications, two learning activities for each objective, two correctives for each objective, and two enrichment activities for each objective.

KEY TERMS

behavioral objective
correctives
enrichment activity
formative test

instructional objective
summative test
table of specifications

REFERENCES

Block, J. H. (1971). Introduction to mastery learning: Theory and practice. In J. H. Block (Ed.), *Mastery learning: Theory and practice* (pp. 2–12). New York: Holt, Rinehart & Winston.

Block, J. H. (1977). Individualized instruction: A mastery learning perspective. *Educational Leadership, 34,* 337–341.

Bloom, B. S. (Ed.). (1956). *Taxonomy of educational objectives: The classification of educational goals. Handbook I: Cognitive domain.* New York: McKay.

Bloom, B. S., Madaus, G. E., & Hastings, J. T. (1981). *Evaluation to improve learning.* New York: McGraw-Hill.

Chamot, A. U., Cummins, J., Kessler, C., O'Malley, J. M., &

Fillmore, L. W. (1997). *Accelerating English language learning.* Glenview, IL: Scott, Foresman.

Eicholz, P. E., O'Daffer, P., Fluxor, C., Charles, R., Young, S., & Barnett, C. (1985). *Addison-Wesley mathematics teacher's edition. Book I.* Menlo Park, CA: Addison-Wesley.

Kubiszyn, T., & Borich, G. (1996). *Educational testing and measurement: Classroom application and practice* (5th ed.). New York: Harper-Collins.

Linn, R. L., & Gronlund, N. E. (2000). *Measurement and assessment in teaching* (8th ed.). Upper Saddle River, NJ: Merrill/Prentice Hall.

Wortham, S. C. (1984). *Organizing instruction in early childhood.* Boston: Allyn and Bacon.

Informal Assessments

Performance-Based Strategies

8 CHAPTER

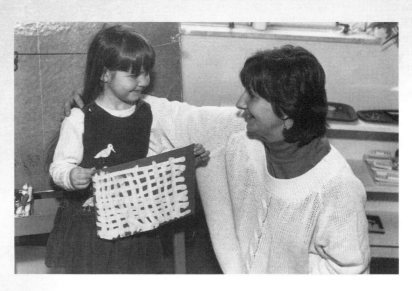

Chapter Objectives

As a result of reading this chapter, you will be able to

1. Understand the relationship between authentic learning and authentic assessment

2. Understand the definition of and purposes for performance-based assessment

3. Describe several types of performance-based assessments and how they are used

4. Understand the advantages and disadvantages of using performance-based evaluation tools

In chapters 5, 6, and 7, we discussed types of informal evaluations such as observation, checklists and rating scales, and teacher-designed assessments. In this chapter, we discuss how these informal evaluations contribute to a broader strategy—performance-based assessment. Each informal assessment discussed in previous chapters contributes to the collection of assessment information that is part of performance-based assessment. The strategies used to conduct these assessments permit the teacher to measure a child's performance.

Before proceeding further, I should explain what is meant by performance-based assessment and how it is seen as a positive alternative to the use of standardized tests to measure children's development and learning.

Traditional formal methods of measuring learning have focused on assessing what the child knows. Achievement tests are accurately labeled in that they measure what the child has achieved. Performance assessment is advocated as a contrast to high-stakes testing. Meisels (2000) deplores the current situation in which tests determine what teachers teach, what children learn, and whether children will fail or be promoted. Rather than depend on tests that are a single indicator of what a child has learned, Meisels proposes that the teacher should have a generative or transformed role with children. The teacher–learner process permits the learner to use his or her own skills to learn new skills.

Performance assessments require more in that they measure what the child can do or apply, in addition to what the child knows (Herman, Aschbacher, & Winters, 1992; Pierson & Beck, 1993; Wiggins, 1993, 1998). Moreover, performance assessment includes completion of a task in a realistic context. Another term frequently used for this type of assessment is **authentic assessment** or **authentic performance assessment.** Bergen (1994) proposes that a good authentic performance assessment must have some connection to the real world and be an application of learning. Furthermore, it possesses the following qualities (p. 99): (1) It is integrative, measuring many facets simultaneously; (2) it is applied, having the complexity of real-world roles; and (3) it may be individual, but is often group based, and the performance of every group member is essential for success as both individual and group performance effectiveness is evaluated. An important element in authentic assessment is that it is linked directly to authentic learning. Before we discuss performance-based assessment, this relationship between learning and assessment will be discussed.

AUTHENTIC LEARNING AND AUTHENTIC ASSESSMENT

Advocates of authentic assessment propose that **authentic achievement** must accompany authentic assessment. As described by Neill (1997):

> Assessment to enhance student learning must be integrated with, not separate from curriculum and instruction . . . Schools need to ensure the development of "authentic instruction," which involves modes of teaching that foster understanding of rich content and encourage students' positive engagement with the world. (p. 35)

If we are to use authentic or performance assessment to understand how children can apply or use what they have learned, the learning experiences they are provided must also be authentic or meaningful. Meaningful learning includes intellectual accomplishments that are similar to those undertaken by successful adults and involve tasks and objectives that engage the mind (Checkley, 1997; Jones & Fennimore, 1996; Newmann, 1996). When children are engaged in authentic learning, they are given opportunities to link new information to prior knowledge and engage in problem solving.

Authentic learning is based on construction of knowledge and focuses on higher-order thinking. The purpose is to move beyond the knowledge level and to construct new knowledge (Wehlage, Newmann, & Secada, 1996). This type of learning includes communication of their construction of knowledge and application of knowledge in meaningful contexts, such as some type of performance (Kulm, 1994; Wehlage et al., 1996).

Like authentic learning, authentic assessment is meaningful. It is "designed to present a broader, more genuine picture of student learning" (Zessoules & Gardner, 1991, p. 49). It requires a different role for the teacher in that there is continual interaction with student work. The teacher engages in dialogues, questioning, suggesting, observing, and guiding to encourage students (Palmer, 1996). The purpose of this approach is to enable students to demonstrate how they can use what they understand and to represent that learning in some type of product or performance. Teachers not only use performance assessments to reflect authentic learning, but the results of these assessments are used as resources to extend and deepen student learning.

Performance-based assessment is considered to be particularly useful with young children because it measures progress as well as achievement. Children in the early childhood years are proceeding through rapid changes in development that are described as complex because of the interaction between maturation, experience, and learning (Hills, 1993). Performance assessments provide a vehicle for measuring developmental progress in addition to progress in learning new concepts. Performance assessments permit teachers to understand the processes children use to learn and how they actively construct meaning through analysis, synthesis, and evaluation (Brown, 1989; Harrington, Meisels, McMahon, Dichtelmiller, & Jablon, 1997; Meisels, 1993).

PURPOSES FOR PERFORMANCE-BASED ASSESSMENT

What, then, are the purposes for using **performance-based assessment** with young children? First, the importance of measuring young children appropriately has been an ongoing theme in this text. Contrary to many of the standardized tests and more formal strategies that have been criticized as inappropriate to the young child's development, performance assessments can be good tools for evaluating progress in development. Because they are designed to measure a child's performance of a real or designed task or activity relevant to the desired learning, performance observations are directly related to the child's development and achievement (Harrington et al., 1997).

Second, performance assessments are integrally related to instruction. The performance activity is a natural outcome of ongoing curriculum and instruction and not a separate, unrelated type of experience that is unfamiliar to the child. Krechevsky (1991, p. 45) characterizes the close relationship as "blurring the line between curriculum and assessment." When using performance-based evaluation, the classroom teacher needs to know how to design appropriate, related assessment tools, interpret assessment results to understand the child's progress and plan for further instruction, and interpret performance assessment results to parents and administrators (Hills, 1993).

Finally, performance assessments are used to evaluate whether preschool programs are meeting the needs of the young students. Good performance assessment tools help to clarify the goals of preschool programs to provide developmental curriculum. Progress assessment reflects both individual developmental progress and accomplishment of developmental program goals (Harrington et al., 1997; Schweinhart, 1993). The teacher then has the responsibility to report program accomplishments in a meaningful way to administrators (Hills, 1993).

In the next sections, we discuss types of evaluation strategies that use performance assessments. Although most of the tools are selected or created by the teacher, others use examples of the child's work. Some are planned by both teacher and child, while others are spontaneous and not preplanned when the teacher takes advantage of an ongoing activity or event to conduct an assessment.

TYPES OF PERFORMANCE-BASED ASSESSMENT

Many strategies can be used to conduct performance-based assessments. Like checklists and observations, performance-based evaluation has been used for many decades; however, in this context, it may have a broadened purpose or a more comprehensive role as part of a system of evaluation. The assessment strategies appropriate for use with young children are interviews, contracts, directed assignments, games, work samples, projects, and portfolios.

INTERVIEWS

Teachers use **interviews** to find out what children understand about concepts. Interviews are especially appropriate for young children who are just beginning to develop literacy skills and cannot yet express themselves with a paper-and-pencil activity. The strategies followed in interviews complement the techniques used by Piaget to understand children's thinking. By questioning and asking more questions based on children's responses, Piaget was able to determine not only what the child understood, but the thinking processes used to organize responses to the questions (Seefeldt, 1993).

Interviews can be described as **unstructured, structured,** or **diagnostic.** An *unstructured interview* can occur when children are playing, working in centers, or otherwise engaged in classroom activities. The teacher becomes aware that it is an opportune time to engage the child in an interview and takes a few minutes to question the child.

Structured interviews are preplanned by the teacher and conducted to acquire specific understandings about the child. For example, the teacher might want to determine the beginning reader's understanding of a story. After a reading of the story, the teacher asks probing questions to elicit the child's thoughts about the meaning of the story (Engel, 1990). Likewise, concepts in mathematics can be assessed through a structured interview when the teacher asks oral questions about a concept or process and explores the child's responses with further questions. Kamii and Rosenblum (1990) described an activity to determine the kindergarten child's understanding of small addends by dropping beads into two glasses. The child was interviewed about the sum of the two groups of beads to assess the child's progress in mental arithmetic.

Diagnostic interviews serve an additional purpose: to determine the child's instructional needs. The interview may be informal or structured. The teacher's questioning is directed more at understanding what kind of help the child needs through responses to questions. If the teacher notices that the child is confused or making errors, the diagnostic interview can reveal the difficulty the child is experiencing in thinking about the concept or skill.

Teachers can use several techniques to enhance the effectiveness of interviewing for assessment. In addition to taking notes when conducting an interview, teachers can make an audiotape of the child's responses for later review. Seefeldt (1993) suggests that when interviewing children about a social studies concept, responses need not be limited to talking. The child could act out a concept, find an example of the concept in pictures, or draw the things he or she knows about the concept. These possibilities would be helpful for children who are first speakers of another language or otherwise have difficulty expressing themselves verbally.

Interviews with young children should be short. Engel (1990) suggests that 10 minutes is an appropriate length of time. Other tips are to (1) continue questions after the child's initial responses to find out more than whether the child's response is correct or not and (2) give the child plenty of time to think about and respond to the teacher's questions. The child needs to feel comfortable with the process if pertinent responses are to be elicited.

CONTRACTS

Contracts serve a dual purpose. They provide a plan between the teacher and the child and a record of the child's progress. Contracts of activities the child will engage in are designed for a period during a day, for the whole day, or for several days. Preschool children will need pictures or other visual representations of activities that are to be completed. Primary-grade children can follow simple written instructions. After the child has completed an activity, some type of check-off system can be used to record the accomplishment.

Contracts can also be used to keep a record of accomplishment of skills and concepts. The teacher and the child can use the contract as a guide for conferences and interviews or as a recording system for the teacher to indicate when the child has completed an objective or needs more opportunities to interact with a concept. Over a period of time, completed contracts can provide information on progress and accomplishments.

DIRECTED ASSIGNMENTS

Directed assignments are an extension of teacher-designed assessments, discussed in chapter 7. They are also similar to interviews, except that a specific task is involved in acquiring the child's understanding, rather than an interview. Children who are beginning to read independently might be asked to read a story and discuss it. Preschool children might be asked to use concrete objects to solve a problem in mathematical thinking. The important point is that the teacher makes a specific assignment or task for the purposes of assessment. Discussion and questioning may be a part of the process, but the child's ability to carry out the assignment is the focus of the assessment process (Hills, 1992).

GAMES

Games can be used to understand children's progress with a skill or a concept. Although more than one child will be playing the game at one time, the teacher can use observation to assess the child's abilities and thinking. Kamii and Rosenblum (1990) suggest that the teacher use games for systematic observation of an entire class. Two children or a slightly larger group play the game until all the children have been assessed. The ability to make 10 with two numbers is one example of a skill that can be assessed through the child's performance in a game. Cards from one to nine are arranged in groups of nine at one time. The child shows all the pairs that can be combined to make 10. In addition to determining whether the child has mastered the skill, the teacher can observe the process the child uses

Teachers can design games to be used to learn concepts and for assessment.

to solve the problem. If the child arranges combinations quickly, a higher level of progress of mental addition has been achieved than that of a child who must count up from the first card to get the sum with the second card. Figure 6.7 shows a form for recording levels of understanding for this concept.

Games may be used for concepts and skills in other content areas. Over many decades, games have been developed for reading skills. Card games to identify letter knowledge are one ready example. Board games can be adapted or developed for language arts, mathematics, and social studies. A game similar to Trivial Pursuit, in which children must respond to an oral or a written question related to a topic being studied, is an example of how games can be used to test the child's ability to perform a task or solve a problem as an assessment activity.

WORK SAMPLES

Teachers and students are equal participants in the use of **work samples** for performance assessment. Work samples are examples of all types of children's work that can demonstrate the child's developmental progress or accomplishments. For preschool children, work samples may be clay models of animals that reflect the child's understanding of concepts in a thematic study related to animals. Other work samples include paintings, emergent writing, and dictated interpretations of wordless books (Ratcliff, 2001/2002). Primary-grade children might have samples of book reports, creative writing that has been illustrated, and work pages of computation problems. Grace and Shores (1991) suggest using other visual media, such as photographs, videotapes, and tape recordings or audiotapes.

Work samples are often included in discussions about portfolios because portfolios become the means through which work samples and other types of information related to performance assessment are stored. A system for selecting and organizing work samples is important if the collection is to serve appropriately for performance assessment (Meisels, 1993).

ASSESSING PROGRESS WITH GAMES

Joan Harrison, a first-grade teacher, is using a board game to assess reading words. The purpose of the game is to assess children's knowledge of words that have been used in reading activities. Each student has an individual bank of words from books he or she has read. Kim Soo and Martha are playing the game. The children take turns drawing a word card. If they name the word correctly, they can advance one square on the board. The first child to reach the end wins the game. Words that are missed are put in a separate pile, and Joan notes them in her notebook so that she can work with the words in small-group activities.

PROJECTS

A **project** is an activity conducted by a student or a group of students that is more lengthy than a classroom activity conducted during a single class period. The project can be part of a unit of study, such as a science or social studies unit, or part of a theme that is studied by a class. A product of some type results from the project. For example, a second-grade class might study spring wildflowers. A group of students might elect to gather samples of the flowers, identify them, and describe their characteristics. Each flower would be dried and attached to the completed information. The completed booklet of wildflowers would become the product of the project that could be evaluated.

PORTFOLIOS

The **portfolio** was one of the most popular methods of authentic assessment in the 1990s. In looking for alternatives to standardized tests, drill worksheets, and other assessment measures that reflect skills development, rather than developmental progress evolving from the student's own demonstrations of performance, school districts across the United States have implemented portfolios as a preferred type of performance-based evaluation. Some states have initiated performance assessment to replace standardized tests (Givens, 1997).

Portfolios are a process or method whereby student performance information can be stored and interpreted. Portfolios may be a folder very similar to collections of student work that many teachers have used for decades for reporting to parents. They may contain examples of papers that students have completed, as well as checklists, anecdotal records, summary reports for a grading period, and any other materials that students and teachers think are relevant to demonstrate the student's performance.

Portfolios may also be the vehicle used for assessing and reporting the student's progress and accomplishments to parents and administrators. How portfolios are designed and used will be discussed in chapter 9.

UNDERSTANDING THE INTERRELATED NATURE OF PERFORMANCE ASSESSMENTS

Different types of informal and performance-based assessments have been discussed in both this chapter and earlier chapters. At this point, it is important to describe how these assessments are used in an interrelated manner to understand characteristics of a child's performance. For example, observation can be the basis for assessing a child's performance on a directed assignment, whereas a checklist might be used to record the child's progress on the same assignment. In the following sections, we explore the characteristics of performance assessments and how they are used by the teacher to evaluate the development and achievement of the whole child.

THE ROLE OF THE TEACHER

The teacher has the primary role in selecting the types of performance assessments to be used and how they will be used. Because teachers assess and use the assessment information, they also have the responsibility to decide which strategies will be most effective for their purposes.

Performance assessment occurs continually in the early childhood classroom. Information is collected throughout the day when children are working in centers, playing outdoors, participating in small-group instruction, and during whole-group activities. The teacher is observing and participating in these activities to acquire the information about each child's progress and the child's own thinking about what and how he or she is learning.

Collecting information is only part of the teacher's role. Interpreting and using the data are another responsibility. First, the teacher must obtain enough information to know the child's abilities and needs so that appropriate planning can further growth and development. Second, the teacher must collect comprehensive information about each child so that all areas of development and learning are addressed (Harrington et al., 1997). The teacher's goal is to design and implement a program that is appropriate for the child's physical, intellectual, and social development. Likewise, the program should be developmentally appropriate for all the children. In summary, Hills (1992) describes the teacher's role and responsibilities for assessment:

1. To integrate instruction and assessment fully in planning and carrying out the program
2. To use knowledge of young children to choose or design assessment processes
3. To analyze the results to find their meaning for the program and the children
4. To apply what has been learned to planning next steps and improving the program
5. To communicate with parents and involve them in an exchange of information about their child's learning and development (p. 46)

Meisels (2000) adds another dimension to the teaching role. The teacher's role is transformed in that the teacher's approach to teaching is different in authentic learning and assessment. The teacher provides meaningful learning experiences that children would never have experienced otherwise. At the same time, the teacher empowers the children to learn more independently and spontaneously.

Assessments that are consistent with a relationship of trust and authority between teachers and children also have a different approach. Early childhood educators should be aware of the following (Meisels, 2000):

- In an early childhood setting it is essential to address yourself to the personal and unique attributes of the children in your care.
- You need to learn to listen, diagnose, examine, hypothesize, intervene, evaluate, and then reflect and redesign.
- Your goal should be to try to create a relationship of trust with children—one upon which learning is based. (p. 18)

Thus, in performance assessment, teaching, learning, and evaluation result from a partnership relationship between teacher and child. Moreover, the teacher uses performance assessment strategies to collaborate with children on the nature of their accomplishments and the next steps in their learning.

A TEACHER'S ASSESSMENT ROLE IN A KINDERGARTEN CLASSROOM

Upon entering the classroom of 5-year-olds, a buzz of activity captures the visitor's attention. Children working in small groups are busily pursuing a number of activities. One group is drawing illustrations for the big book that the class wrote describing their trip to Pizza Hut. Another group is creating menus for the restaurant they are setting up in the dramatic play area. "Don't forget to put 'We have pepperoni' on your menu," one child says. The other children nod their heads and continue drawing and writing on their papers. One child is bent over a large sheet of construction paper, marker in hand. He is carefully copying the words "Pizza Hut" from the word wall the children have created. When finished, he tapes the paper to two chairs he has placed in front of the dramatic area. "Here's the sign," he tells the others. Three other children are looking at a recipe book, discussing the "gredients" they will need to make the pizzas. Another group is looking at books about restaurants in the literacy corner.

Source: Ratliff, N. J. (2001/2002). Using Authentic Assessment To Document the Emerging Literacy Skills of Young Children. *Childhood Education, 72*, 66–69.

The teacher in this classroom is focusing on emerging literacy skills. The strategies that are being used for performance assessment are checklists, observations, videotapes, audiotapes, and work samples.

The teacher uses checklists to document reading and writing skills. Children drawing an illustration for a big book demonstrate their understanding between pictures and text. As children write menus for the "Pizza Hut," the teacher can observe and document left-to-right skills in their writing skills or the use of uppercase and lowercase letters.

Observations with anecdotal notes can provide more detail about the process a child uses in reading or writing. A videotape or audiotape can record an entire episode. This type of documentation provides information on various children engaged in an activity that can be analyzed for assessment of what children can do.

Finally, work samples provide the teacher with specific evidence of accomplishment. In the classroom activities described in the scenario, the teacher would have work samples of big book illustrations, menus, and a Pizza Hut sign for documentation of performance.

CLASSIFICATION AND ORGANIZATION OF PERFORMANCE ASSESSMENTS

Although all performance assessments are considered to be informal measures, they can be categorized as structured or unstructured and direct or indirect. These organizational patterns are similar to structured and unstructured interviews but are more comprehensive in the types of assessments that are included.

One approach to categorizing assessments is by the type of activity used for assessment. Lee (1992) describes **unstructured** (or nonstructured) **performance assessments** as those that are part of regular classroom learning activities, such as writing samples, projects, checklists, and teacher-designed tasks and tests. **Structured performance assessments** are predetermined or designed to include questions or tasks that require problem solving, synthesis, and analysis. Questions are open ended, and all students are administered the questions through similar test administration procedures.

Another perspective of the two classifications is as spontaneous or structured. Similar to Lee's definition, spontaneous assessments evolve from the teacher's natural day-to-day interactions and observations in the classroom. Structured performance assessment not only is preplanned, but also must meet the standards for reliability and validity required of standardized measurement instruments. Such assessments are carefully designed and have specified scoring criteria, as well as well-defined behaviors that are to be measured.

Performance assessments can also be classified as direct or indirect. On the one hand, **direct performance measures** require students to use knowledge in some type of application. On the other hand, **indirect performance measures** measure what students know about a topic. An example of an indirect measure is a paper-and-pencil test. An example of a direct measure is taking measurements of a table to determine how large to make a tablecloth to fit the table. The distinction between these performance measures is assessing knowledge versus assessing application of knowledge (Pierson & Beck, 1993).

THE ROLE OF OBSERVATION

Strategies for observation were discussed in chapter 5, and the importance of using observation to evaluate the development of young children was emphasized. A discussion of the role of observation within performance assessments reinforces that importance. When considering the measurement of the young child's performance, observation is the most effective strategy (Harrington et al., 1997; Hills, 1992; Segal & Webber, 1996). Observation behaviors such as attending, examining, heeding, considering, investigating, monitoring, studying, and watching enable the teacher to understand and know the child and what the child can do in real-life circumstances and common learning situations (Hills, 1993).

Observation should occur throughout the day in all types of classroom activities. Strategies for observation, including anecdotal records, running records, observation with checklists and rating scales, and time and event sampling, can all have a role in performance assessment. To ensure that the desired performance is observed and recorded, Hills

Portfolios can be used to share a child's performance with parents.

(1993) recommends that the following components be determined prior to conducting the observation:

- **Purpose**   What do we want to know?
- **Focus**   Who or what is being observed? Exhibits what behaviors? When? Where?
- **Record/documentation**   What information is needed? How will it be recorded? How frequently?
- **Use of the observation**   What does the observed event mean for the child's progress and needs? What next steps would we take to further the child's development? (p. 27)

Gathering and documenting information through observation is not enough. Analysis and use of assessment data must also be facilitated as a result of the observation. Therefore, the child should be observed at different times and places and using different materials before determining whether new knowledge has been developed (Bergan & Feld, 1993; Segal & Webber, 1996). In addition, teachers should spend time reflecting about the information that has been gathered. The purpose of this reflection is so that teachers will use assessment in an intentional manner to plan for children's future learning opportunities. To properly collect and reflect on observation data, teachers might include the following steps (Hills, 1992, p. 50): (1) establish purpose and focus; (2) observe and record; (3) compile what was recorded, both for individual children and for the group; and (4) reflect on the records and refocus teaching and learning activities.

Observation is the foundation of performance assessment. It is used with interviews when the teacher observes the child's responses and behaviors. It is integral to directed assignments as the teacher observes the child completing the assignment or task. Observation enables the teacher to understand the child's thinking and knowledge when engaging in assessment games. Observation complements other strategies used for unstructured and structured and direct and indirect performance assessments. Finally, checklists and rating scales and teacher-designed assessments of various types incorporate observation as part of or all of the process of understanding the child's performance.

THE ROLE OF RUBRICS

In chapter 6, rubrics were described as essential to performance assessment. Different types of rubrics were defined and the process used to develop rubrics was discussed. Examples of different kinds of rubrics were provided to demonstrate their flexibility and adaptability to different developmental stages and content areas in preschool and primary grades.

In this section, it might be helpful to reemphasize why rubrics are essential for performance assessment. When we look at checklists, rating scales, and teacher-designed assessments, they tend to focus on whether a developmental milestone or skill has been achieved or how well it has been achieved.

Performance assessments, on the contrary, focus on process and progress in development and learning. Teachers must be grounded in how children develop as well as how children use emerging mental processes to acquire knowledge and new concepts. Rubrics provide the framework to assess processes of learning that focus on child-initiated accomplishments. The assessment strategies discussed earlier in the chapter—interviews, contracts, directed assignments, games, work samples, and projects—can be used with rubrics.

For example, Figure 6.10 can be used in structured interviews. The teacher might read a story to the class and then interview children individually to discuss the story. By asking questions such as "What happened (to a character) in the story?" or "Can you tell me the story in your own words?" the teacher can assess comprehension of text in an emerging reader.

Likewise, a kindergarten teacher can use Figure 6.11 for a developmental assessment using work samples or a directed assignment. The teacher can use children's writing efforts to assess progress in the emerging ability to write.

When working with children who engage in thematic projects, the teacher might use the following range of four points or levels to establish the structure of a rubric to evaluate the projects:

Begin again
Revision needed
Acceptable
Well done

For example, a kindergarten class might be studying the topic of "homes." After investigating different types of homes in the surrounding neighborhood, small groups selected a type of home to study. Construction of a model of a type of home is the task of small groups to represent what they have learned. The teacher designs the following rubric to establish performance standards:

1. *Begin again*
   Group is unable to initiate task.
   Teacher redirection is needed to initiate an appropriate approach.
   Initial efforts show little evidence of understanding the task.
2. *Revision needed*
   Project work is incomplete; needs elaboration.
   Project does not reflect the information learned.
   Additional planning is needed to achieve the desired results.

3. *Acceptable*
   Project is completed.
   Project reflects the purpose of the task, although details and elements are missing.
   Information about the project could be expressed more clearly.
4. *Well done*
   Project shows clear understanding of the concepts learned.
   Project fully accomplishes the purposes of the task.
   Project includes details and elements essential to communicate learned information.

This rubric is generic in that it can be applied to different types of thematic studies. Although it can be applied to projects reflecting the study of homes, it can also be adapted to other projects and topics. It can be simplified or made more detailed as circumstances indicate.

ADVANTAGES AND DISADVANTAGES OF USING PERFORMANCE-BASED ASSESSMENT

ADVANTAGES OF USING PERFORMANCE-BASED ASSESSMENT

There are definite advantages in using performance-based evaluation for assessment of young children. Although performance assessment is recommended for children of all ages, it is particularly suitable for children in preoperational and concrete operational stages of development. Because young children learn best by acting on the environment, it logically follows that assessment that permits the child to demonstrate ability by performing some action is most compatible with developmental capabilities. Performance assessments, then, are fitting for the development of children in the early childhood years. Some arguments for using performance assessments for evaluation are the following:

1. Performance assessments are conducted in the context of what children are experiencing, rather than in isolation from classroom curriculum. Earlier in the chapter, it was recommended that assessment be an integral part of curriculum and instruction. Whenever possible, performance assessments are conducted as part of a lesson, during center activities, or serendipitously when the teacher observes desired learning demonstrated spontaneously. Performance assessments are meaningful and timely.

2. Performance assessments take advantage of the premise that children construct their own understanding. Early childhood educators today prepare curriculum activities with the comprehension that knowledge is not transmitted by the teacher; instead, the child gradually forms or produces new knowledge through repeated encounters with concepts and information. Performance assessment provides the teacher with tools to observe and document the child's progress. This provision means that assessment goes beyond assessing whether the child has mastered the teacher's learning objectives. The child's progress toward mastery using Vygotsky's (1983) zone of proximal development can also be evaluated. The zone described by Vygotsky refers to the variability between what the child can currently do and what the child can master potentially in the future.

The teacher can determine whether the child is unable to demonstrate an ability or understanding, whether the child can show some of the desired behaviors with assistance, or whether the child can perform independently (Hills, 1992). Also, the focus of the assessment is on the child, and not on the child's responding to the teacher. The teacher still plays a major role in the assessment, but the child's performance is the key and the teacher responds to what the child is doing.

3. Performance assessments provide a variety of means whereby the child can demonstrate what he or she understands or can do. The child's ongoing work examples, art products, play, conversation, emergent writing, and dictated stories are a few examples of ways that children can perform. Some of the performances can be recorded as a result of the teacher's observation or interviews, whereas others can be documented by work samples. Because assessment is integrated with instruction and daily activities, the possibilities for observing and interpreting accomplishments are almost unlimited.

4. Performance assessment is continuous or ongoing. Unlike more formal assessments such as tests, end-of-chapter assessments, and reporting period evaluations, performance assessments reflect daily opportunities to be aware of the child's thinking and work.

5. Performance assessments provide meaningful information for parents to understand their child's progress and accomplishments. They also enable parents to contribute and participate in the assessment process. Teachers can use performance assessments of all types in parent conferences. Likewise, parents can become more aware of behaviors their child is using at home that demonstrate developmental advancement and share their observations with the teacher. Once parents understand the significance of the child's activities and their relationship to development and learning, they can be partners with the teacher and child in facilitating opportunities for the child.

DISADVANTAGES OF USING PERFORMANCE-BASED ASSESSMENTS

Performance assessments have their disadvantages or limitations. Like all informal assessments, they are subjective; teacher bias and interpretation are part of the process. Teachers must be constantly alert for the need for objectivity when evaluating young children. Also, performance assessments increase the responsibility and accountability of the teacher in administering and interpreting evaluations. This opportunity for more meaningful assessments is accompanied by the need for teachers to be skilled in the assessment process.

Although some of the strategies used to evaluate children in performance assessments are not new, the approach as the primary means to assess and give grades to students is considered to be an innovation. Like any educational innovation, problems and difficulties can cause teachers and administrators to become disenchanted with the process and to doubt the effectiveness of the practice. Therefore, it is important to be aware of and understand the implications and limitations of performance assessment, as well as the benefits. Following are some of the concerns that measurement specialists propose about the use of performance assessments:

1. Performance assessments are time consuming. Teachers need time to conduct observations, record data, and interpret information in planning future instruction. All

performance assessments require extensive involvement of the teacher. Recordkeeping adds to paperwork responsibilities; moreover, teachers must consider how to fit assessment into otherwise busy days. Teachers must develop the ability to do several things at once and to keep up with reflection on information and ideas they gain from studying the child's performance activities.

2. Authentic assessment can be more complex than more traditional types of assessment. Because assessment is integrated into instruction, teachers must clearly understand what they are looking for in assessment. Assessment with young children might be interdisciplinary or measure more than one type of development when it is a part of integrated curriculum and child-centered activities. The teacher must predetermine explicit standards of performance for development and learning objectives, no matter how incidental or integrated the assessment process. The more complex and integrated the curriculum is, the more difficult the performance assessment process will be in terms of interpreting the implications of the child's performance (Bergen, 1994). A related issue is in scoring performance assessments. A common concern is who will determine the quality of performance assessments when they are used for grading or state-level evaluations (Givens, 1997).

3. More traditional forms of assessment have had the goal of evaluating the child's achievement. Performance assessment has the goal of evaluating progress, as well as achievement. Teachers may have difficulty incorporating this new role of understanding the child's progress and implications for curriculum planning for that child. Teachers must not only develop new competencies in acquiring assessment information, but also become more competent in using progress information to further the child's development. Teachers may find this requirement to be very confusing and be uncertain about how skillfully and appropriately they are using performance assessments (Bergen, 1994).

4. There are also concerns about the validity and reliability of performance assessments. Schweinhart (1993) proposes that early childhood assessment tools must be developmentally appropriate, valid, reliable, and user friendly. As described in the previous section, the difficulty of using performance assessments would raise doubts about how user friendly they are. To be valid, the tools must correlate with concurrent measures being used to assess young children. Likewise, assessments should be internally consistent and assessed similarly by various assessors. Informal procedures used in performance assessments must provide evidence of validity, reliability, objectivity, and freedom from bias if they are to be considered feasible (Goodwin & Goodwin, 1993). The probability that public school systems will understand this necessity and undertake the extensive work needed to ensure quality seems doubtful (Givens, 1997).

5. Parental involvement and education are a requirement when implementing performance-based evaluation. Parents are familiar with traditional evaluation and reporting practices. School districts must plan to educate and prepare parents before moving into performance assessments. Parents need to be knowledgeable and comfortable with how the innovative assessment process is used before they encounter it in their child's grade report or in a parent–teacher conference. Unfamiliar terminology and assessment procedures can cause a lack of confidence in and support for the school and teachers.

Most of the disadvantages and limitations discussed previously seem related to proper preparation and training for performance assessments. Too often in the past, schools have embraced and implemented curriculum and instruction innovations without training

FIGURE 8–1 Summary of advantages and disadvantages of performance assessment

Advantages	Disadvantages
• Performance assessments are conducted in context of experience	• Performance assessments are time consuming
• Performance assessments are based on constructivist learning	• Performance assessments can be more complex
• Performance assessments demonstrate what a child understands and can do	• Performance assessments can be difficult to evaluate when scores or grades are required
• Performance assessments provide a variety of demonstrated learning	• Assessing a child's progress using performance assessment can be confusing to some teachers
• Performance assessment is continuous	• It can be difficult to establish validity and reliability in performance assessments
• Performance assessment reflects meaningful learning	• Performance assessments can be difficult for parents to understand

teachers and administrators properly. Some of the authors cited in this chapter consistently discuss the need for extensive training and preparation prior to using new performance assessments. Like any change or new approach to curriculum or assessment, adequate training and knowledge about performance assessments can do much to ensure that they will be a successful and appropriate alternative for assessment of young children. Because performance assessments inherently have the potential to measure young children's development and learning in a realistic and meaningful way, the limitations can become either difficult obstacles or perceptive cautions that can be used to facilitate appropriate and skilled use of new tools.

DEVELOPING QUALITY PERFORMANCE ASSESSMENTS

An important step in developing quality performance assessments is to use rubrics both to describe the performance and to serve as evaluation tools. Suggestions for developing quality rubrics were given in chapter 6. Additional suggestions can be listed for performance assessments as a whole. Following are a few guidelines:

- Base assessments on instructional goals
- Use fully developed task descriptions for performance assessments
- Review assessment criteria against instructional goals
- Score systematically and recheck scoring strategies periodically

- Compare rubric and other performance scoring with other informal assessments when appropriate
- Use more than one assessment in making important decisions
- Conduct assessments that are consistent for all students to eliminate bias (Herman et al., 1992)

SUMMARY

The time has come for us to adopt a new assessment paradigm: *performance assessment.* Performance assessments document activities in which children engage on a daily basis. They provide a means for evaluating the quality of children's work in an integrated manner. They are flexible enough to reflect an individualized approach to academic achievement. They are also designed to evaluate many elements of learning and development that standardized tests do not capture well. As active constructors of meaning, children analyze, synthesize, evaluate, and interpret facts and ideas (Brown, 1989). Performance assessment allows teachers the opportunity to learn about these processes by documenting children's interactions with materials and peers in the classroom environment. In short, performance assessment puts assessment back where it belongs: in the hands of teachers and children, and in the classrooms that they inhabit. (Meisels, 1993, p. 36)

In this chapter, we have discussed performance-based evaluation as an alternative or authentic method of assessing young children. Meisels, quoted previously, believes that this approach to assessment makes teachers more powerful and in control of the learning-evaluation process.

A number of methods or strategies can be used to evaluate a child's development or learning through performance of what he or she understands and can do. Interviews, contracts, directed assignments, games, work samples, projects, and portfolios are among the assessment activities that will permit young children to demonstrate their ability to understand and apply new skills and information.

Performance assessments complement each other in how they focus on the child's progress and accomplishments. In addition, informal assessment methods, such as observation, checklists and rating scales, and teacher-designed assessments, are used in the process of assessing through performance.

Performance assessment transfers responsibility to teachers for the instructional and assessment process. This empowerment of the teacher facilitates the teacher's opportunity to design assessment that includes all areas of development and that is appropriate for the level of development of each child. It also allows the teacher to make a close connection between curriculum and evaluation.

Although performance assessment is more relevant and appropriate than traditional formal methods of measuring learning, it can also be more difficult. Teachers must accept the time that is needed to organize and conduct this type of evaluation; moreover, they must overcome limitations related to validity, reliability, and accountability. Care must be exercised in planning and implementing performance assessment if it is not to become an educational fad that fades after a few years.

REVIEW QUESTIONS

1. Explain the definition of performance assessments or performance-based assessments.
2. Why is performance assessment suited for children in the early childhood years?
3. Why do measurement specialists describe performance and instruction as closely related?
4. Interviews can be used for evaluation in several ways. Discuss three types of interviews and when they are appropriate.
5. How are interviews helpful for understanding children's thinking processes?
6. Why can it be said that directed assignments are designed by the teacher, but contracts are designed by the teacher and child?
7. How is assessment through games different from assessment through an interview?
8. Explain the role of observation in performance assessments.
9. What is meant by interrelated assessments? Describe two assessments that can be interrelated.
10. Explain the difference between direct performance measures and indirect performance measures.
11. How do you believe performance assessments will be advantageous to you as a teacher of young children?
12. Explain how performance assessments can be difficult to interpret.
13. How can teachers ensure that performance assessments are accurate?
14. Why is it possible that performance assessments can lack validity and reliability?
15. What role should parents have in using performance assessments? Explain.

SUGGESTED ACTIVITIES

1. Visit a classroom where performance assessments are used. Identify the assessments used that demonstrate what the child *knows* and those that demonstrate what the child *can do* or *can apply.*
2. Select a learning objective suitable for a child in the first grade. Design assessments that use observation, an interview, and a game. Describe how you would conduct the observation and analyze the results.

KEY TERMS

authentic achievement
authentic assessment
authentic performance assessment
contract
diagnostic interview
directed assignment
direct performance measure
game
indirect performance measure

interview
performance-based assessment
portfolio
project
structured interview
structured performance assessment
unstructured interview
unstructured performance assessment
work sample

REFERENCES

Barbour, A., & Desjean-Perrotta, B. (1998). The basics of portfolio assessment. In S. C. Wortham, A. Barbour, & B. Desjean-Perrotta, *Portfolio assessment: A handbook for preschool and elementary educators* (pp. 15–30). Olney, MD: Association for Childhood Education International.

Bergan, J. R., & Feld, J. K. (1993). Developmental assessment: New directions. *Young Children, 48,* 41–47.

Bergen, D. (1994). Authentic performance assessments. *Childhood Education, 70,* 99, 102.

Brown, R. (1989). Testing and thoughtfulness. *Educational Leadership, 7,* 31–33.

Checkley, K. (1997). Assessment that serves instruction. *Education Update, 39,* 1, 4–6.

Engel, B. (1990). An approach to assessment in early literacy. In C. Kamii (Ed.), *Achievement testing in the early grades* (pp. 119–134). Washington, DC: National Association for the Education of Young Children.

Givens, K. (1997). Performance assessment tests: A problematic panacea. *Contemporary Education, 69,* 27–29.

Goodwin, W. L., & Goodwin, L. D. (1993). Young children and measurement: Standardized and nonstandardized instruments in early childhood education. In B. Spodek (Ed.), *Handbook of research on the education of young children* (pp. 441–463). New York: Macmillan.

Grace, C., & Shores, E. F. (1991). *The portfolio and its use.* Little Rock, AR: Southern Association on Children Under Six.

Harrington, H. L., Meisels, S. J., McMahon, P., Dichtelmiller, M. L., & Jablon, J. R. (1997). *Observing, documenting, and assessing learning: The work sampling system handbook for teacher educators.* Ann Arbor, MI: Rebus.

Herman, J. L., Aschbacher, P. R., & Winters, L. (1992). *A practical guide to alternative assessment.* Alexandria, VA: Association for Supervision and Curriculum Development.

Hills, T. W. (1992). Reaching potentials through appropriate assessment. In S. Bredekamp & T. Rosegrant (Eds.), *Reaching potentials: Appropriate curriculum and assessment for young children* (pp. 43–64). Washington, DC: National Association for the Education of Young Children.

Hills, T. W. (1993). Assessment in context: Teachers and children at work. *Young Children, 48,* 20–28.

Jones, B. F., & Fennimore, T. (1996). The new definition of learning: The first step for school reform. In R. E. Blum & J. A. Arter (Eds.), *Handbook for student performance assessment in an era of restructuring* (pp. III-7:1 to III-7:11).

Alexandria, VA: Association for Supervision and Curriculum Development.

Kamii, C., & Rosenblum, V. (1990). An approach to assessment in mathematics. In C. Kamii (Ed.), *Achievement testing in the early grades: The games grown-ups play* (pp. 146–162). Washington, DC: National Association for the Education of Young Children.

Krechevsky, M. (1991). Project Spectrum: An innovative assessment alternative. *Educational Leadership, 48,* 43–48.

Kulm, G. (1994). *Mathematics assessment: What works in the classroom.* San Francisco: Jossey-Bass.

Lee, F. Y. (1992). Alternative assessments. *Childhood Education, 69,* 72–73.

Meisels, S. J. (1993). Remaking classroom assessment with the Work Sampling System. *Young Children, 48,* 34–40.

Meisels, S. J. (2000). On the side of the child. *Young Children, 55,* 16–19.

Neill, M. (1997). Transforming student assessment. *Phi Delta Kappan, 79,* 34–40.

Newmann, F. M. (1996). Introduction: The school restructuring study. In F. M. Newmann & Associates, *Authentic achievement: Restructuring schools for intellectual quality* (pp. 1–16). San Francisco: Jossey-Bass.

Palmer, J. (1996). Integrating assessment and instruction: Continuous monitoring. In R. E. Blum & J. A. Arter (Eds.), *Handbook for student performance assessment in an era of restructuring* (pp. IV-6:1 to IV-6:12). Alexandria, VA: Association for Supervision and Curriculum Development.

Pierson, C. A., & Beck, S. S. (1993). Performance assessment. The realities that will influence the rewards. *Childhood Education, 70,* 29–32.

Ratcliff, N. J. (2001/2002). Using authentic assessment to document the emerging literacy skills of young children. *Childhood Education, 78,* 66–69.

Schweinhart, L. J. (1993). Observing young children in action: The key to early childhood assessment. *Young Children, 48,* 29–33.

Seefeldt, C. (1993). *Social studies for the preschool-primary child* (4th ed.). Upper Saddle River, NJ: Merrill/Prentice Hall.

Segal, M., & Webber, N. T. (1996). Nonstructured play observations: Guidelines, benefits, and caveats. In S. J. Meisels & E. Fenichel (Eds.), *New visions for the developmental assessment of infants and young children* (pp. 207–230). Washington, DC: ZERO TO THREE: National Center for Infants, Toddlers, and Families.

Vygotsky, L. (1983). School instruction and mental development. In M. Donaldson, R. Grieve, & C. Pratt (Eds.), *Early childhood development and education: Readings in psychology* (pp. 263–269). New York: Guilford.

Wehlage, G. G., Newmann, F. M., & Secada, W. G. (1996). Standards for authentic achievement and pedagogy. In F. M. Newmann & Associates, *Authentic achievement: Restructuring schools for intellectual quality* (pp. 21–48). San Francisco: Jossey-Bass.

Wiggins, G. P. (1993). *Assessing student performance.* San Francisco: Jossey-Bass.

Wiggins, G. P. (1998). *Educative assessment.* San Francisco: Jossey-Bass.

Zessoules, R., & Gardner, H. (1991). Authentic assessment: Beyond the buzzword and into the classroom. In V. Perrone (Ed.), *Expanding student assessment* (pp. 47–91). Alexandria, VA: Association for Supervision and Curriculum Development.

Assessment Systems

9 CHAPTER

Portfolio Assessment

Chapter Objectives

As a result of reading this chapter, you will be able to

1. **Understand the limitations of report cards for reporting student progress**
2. **Understand the importance of developing alternative reporting systems**
3. **Design and use portfolios for assessing and reporting student progress**

W hat is the best way to assess the young child's progress and develop an evaluative report for that child? In early chapters of this text, we discussed standardized measures, how they are developed and used, and when they are not appropriate for evaluating young children. We also discussed some strategies for conducting informal assessments. In chapter 8, we described performance assessments and how informal strategies are a part of or complement performance assessments.

In this chapter and the next, we address how to take the data we collect by using informal or performance assessments and construct a holistic picture of a child's progress that can be reported to parents and school district administrators periodically throughout the school year. These alternative types of reporting are suggested as more suitable for communicating the development and learning of children in the early childhood years. They are equally important for children in elementary schools. First, we will discuss why we need alternative types of reporting, particularly to report cards. Then the majority of the chapter will be devoted to one type of assessment and reporting system, portfolios.

UNDERSTANDING THE NEED FOR ALTERNATIVE ASSESSMENT AND REPORTING SYSTEMS

We are in a period of new trends in curriculum and instruction that have implications for assessment. As the work of Piaget (1952, 1962, 1963) and Vygotsky (1978) has resulted in a more constructivist approach to student learning, early childhood teachers have been reinforced in using child-centered learning. An emphasis on constructivism is reflected in whole language, emergent reading and writing, the use of manipulatives, and attention to individual learning styles (Lescher, 1995). Teachers are more aware of the cultural, linguistic, and ability diversity in their students and are designing activities that complement the strengths that accompany this diversity. Alternative informal and performance assessments (discussed in chapters 5 through 8) and strategies to report performance (addressed in this chapter) are partly in response to the limitations and concerns about standardized tests and partly to fulfill the need for more appropriate methods of measuring the new trends in curriculum and instruction (Glazer, 1994).

USING ALTERNATIVE ASSESSMENTS APPROPRIATELY

In this period of transition in curriculum and instruction and assessment, particularly with children in the preschool and primary years, the fundamental task for educators is to make a knowledgeable shift from more traditional forms of assessment and reporting to alternative strategies. Basic to any transition is first determining what method of reporting achievement and progress to parents is to be used. If the traditional report card is to be maintained, assessment records will have to be compatible with that type of report. That is, if grades or some type of scale to compare progress among students is the profile to be reported, teachers must be accountable for how they determined the child's grade. If an alternative process such as a portfolio, rather than a report card, is to be used to present the child's profile of progress, there must be understanding and consensus as to what the report means and how parents can share in the communication of the child's development and achievement.

Administrators and teachers must be clear about the purposes for and methods of assessment. School districts that are moving toward a constructivist approach and integrated curriculum in elementary classrooms, but are expecting teachers to be accountable for letter grades, particularly in primary-grade classrooms, must understand the incompatibility of methodology and assessment and reporting. In sum, the trend toward holistic, developmental, and integrated learning must be accompanied by sensible assessment and evaluation strategies provided in the alternative assessments defined as authentic and performance based.

LIMITATIONS OF LETTER GRADES AND REPORT CARDS

Currently, teachers in school districts all over the United States are reviewing and redesigning report cards. A primary motive for this endeavor is the difficulty teachers have in following new trends in curriculum and instruction and in trying to report the child's progress in terms of isolated skills or letter grades based on more traditional teaching methods.

Curriculum and instruction for children in the early childhood years in quality programs are shifting from an academic approach, in which children are expected to learn the same information at the same time, to a developmental approach. The developmental approach reflects the understanding of development and learning as a continuum along which each child progresses via an internal clock and an individual cognitive process that depends on maturation and previous experiences. Each child's understanding of new knowledge is based on the cognitive information stored from previous encounters in the environment. There is a basic incompatibility between developmental programs reflected in constructivist curriculum and instruction that are organized to respond to the individual child's development and child-initiated learning and letter grades that require competence in skills development based on a timetable established by the teacher or the school district. Seidel et al. (1997) describe student work as disposable under conditions that result in grades on report cards. Student work is graded and returned with no further value to the teacher or the student.

Letter grades can reward students for correct answers and discourage risk taking and experimentation. Newer trends in curriculum and instruction stress the student's willingness to use ideas and develop problem-solving strategies as part of the process of learning. Grading undermines these instructional practices because students are unwilling to take the chance of making errors and possibly receiving low grades.

Letter grades are also limited because they only measure achievement. They do not reflect the student's strengths and weaknesses or the effort made to earn the grade. Critics believe that grades tend to limit how many students can do well. Not only does the system tend to sort students into categories, but also slower students lose their motivation to learn as a result of continuing negative feedback. In addition, they get labeled as poor students, and teacher expectations are lower for them than for students who make higher grades (Willis, 1993).

Alternative systems of reporting that use authentic or performance assessments provide more than letter grades. They can include (1) a continuum of development and learning, (2) information about the whole child, not just about skills that have been mastered, (3) diagnostic information that allows the teacher to adjust instruction and activities, and, most important, (4) examples of what the child has done to demonstrate understanding.

Report cards themselves are changing as teachers and administrators find more flexible and meaningful types of reporting. Figure 9–1 shows a continuum or hierarchy of skills for language arts, math, science, and social studies. The report is used as an ongoing tool to report progress. The continuum begins at the bottom of the page, and the complexity or difficulty increases as the indicators or objectives move up the page. After the child has mastered a concept or a skill, it is checked off. Progress is the important factor, rather than a letter grade given if mastery is demonstrated during a reporting period. Likewise, the child can progress along the hierarchy of objectives above or below grade level. The reporting form shown is at the piloting stage. As teachers and administrators become more knowledgeable and skilled, more indicators of development may be included, along with refinements in the objectives presently listed.

Once school district policymakers, administrators, and teachers determine that performance assessments are to be included in the evaluation process, decisions are then made on how to use performance assessments and develop a comprehensive picture of the child's progress. Collection and interpretation of data relevant to the child's performance require organization of an evaluation system that permits the teacher to describe growth in a meaningful manner. Portfolios are one such assessment.

PORTFOLIO ASSESSMENT

Portfolios are a collection of a child's work and teacher data from informal and performance assessments to evaluate development and learning. A portfolio may be kept just by and for the child, with samples of work over a period of time. It may also be organized by the teacher and contain observation reports, checklists, work samples, records of directed assignments, interviews, or other evidence of achievement. There are child portfolios, teacher portfolios, and combinations that include entries made by both the child and teacher.

PURPOSES FOR PORTFOLIO ASSESSMENT

How the contents of a portfolio are used depends on the purpose. Portfolios can be used for assessment and evaluation, for self-assessment and reflection, and for reporting progress.

USING PORTFOLIOS FOR ASSESSMENT AND EVALUATION.   A portfolio collection is used to develop a holistic picture of activities the student has engaged in over a period of time. The portfolio should include many examples of a student's work that will

FIGURE 9–1 A first-grade reporting system

	Language Arts	Math	Science	Social Studies
FIRST GRADE				
6.0	❏ Recognizes vowels ❏ Reads primer level simple sentences ❏ Understands antonyms ❏ Writes phrases ❏ Arranges events in sequential order ❏ Alphabetizes according to initial letter ❏ Acquires basic sight vocabulary ❏ Engages in creative dramatic activities and nonverbal communication ❏ Responds to nonverbal cues	❏ Knows greater than/less than ❏ Writes numerals 1 - 20 ❏ Recognizes simple color and size patterns ❏ Recognizes and sorts plane figures ❏ Finds differences by separating and comparing objects ❏ Solves problems involving addition and subtraction with manipulatives ❏ Uses numeral sentences	❏ Acquires data through the use of senses ❏ Identifies careers related to theme: mayor, construction workers, business people, etc. ❏ Identifies internal organs and their functions (brain, heart, lungs) ❏ Identifies skeletal parts (skull, ribs, pelvis, spine) ❏ Classifies food into pyramid levels ❏ Classifies events in a consistent, organized fashion while making observations (plant growth)	❏ Is aware of others' needs ❏ Identifies kinds of work of school personnel and family members ❏ Knows birth date ❏ Knows geography of school campus ❏ Identifies name of school ❏ Knows geographical location of home in relation to school/community ❏ Identifies and accepts one's classroom responsibilities ❏ Completes assigned tasks ❏ Identifies positive traits of self and others
6.3	❏ Selects topics of interest to self and others ❏ Understands opposites ❏ Understands naming words (people, places, things, animals) ❏ Recognizes a sentence ❏ Understands action words ❏ Identifies the main idea in speaker's words ❏ Uses basic phonics: media/message/final consonants ❏ Uses pronouns properly ❏ Contributes ideas and information in group discussion	❏ Finds sums by combining groups and counting ❏ Finds differences by separating and comparing objects ❏ Estimates and predicts quantities ❏ Identifies lines of symmetry ❏ Measures/estimates mass using standard units ❏ Develops concept of conservation (measuring capacity using containers) ❏ Constructs picture graphs	❏ Creates an order of events in a logical continuum while making observations ❏ Collects information to make reasonable interpretations ❏ Makes accurate measurements and uses them appropriately as descriptors ❏ Manipulates laboratory materials and equipment ❏ Uses information and observations to make reasonable interpretations	❏ Contributes to group activities ❏ Understands food processing ❏ Discusses visuals (pictures, charts) ❏ Knows how animals are used for clothing, food, etc. ❏ Understands and distinguishes animal habitats ❏ Uses terms concerning time (today, tomorrow, yesterday) ❏ Knows months of the year ❏ Knows the days of the week ❏ Knows N, S, E, W ❏ Knows the four seasons

provide multiple assessments of concepts, skills, and projects that result in an accurate picture of what the student understands and is able to use in a meaningful context (Micklo, 1997; Valencia, 1990). In addition to the child and the teacher assessing the child's achievement, the portfolio can be used to evaluate the teacher. The child is given an opportunity to provide feedback to the teacher.

USING PORTFOLIOS FOR SELF-ASSESSMENT AND REFLECTION. Portfolios, particularly those that are used over a period of several years, make it possible for the student to observe growth and progress by comparing work samples and drawings longitudinally (Hebert & Schultz, 1996). Many teachers in kindergarten and primary grades have students make a drawing of themselves at the beginning of a school year. At the beginning of each subsequent reporting period, another drawing is made. Students can look back and see how their efforts have improved. Samples of writing provide the same type of comparison. Students at the end of second or third grade may not even recognize their earlier efforts at the beginning of the year.

USING PORTFOLIOS FOR REPORTING PROGRESS. At the beginning of the chapter, we discussed how alternative reporting methods to report cards are needed to report student progress to parents. Portfolios are a comprehensive alternative approach. When parents are engaged with their child and teacher in selecting and reviewing what has been completed during a grading period, they are able to see the work and assessment examples that have been used (Gilkersen & Hanson, 2000). If grades are required, the work in the portfolio can document the assessments used to determine the grade. More about communicating with parents about student progress will be discussed in chapter 10.

ORGANIZING PORTFOLIOS

Portfolios have become a popular trend in elementary schools in the last few years, particularly in the language arts. Although abundant literature is available on how to use the portfolio for assessment in language arts, particularly for the whole language and emergent literacy approaches, less has been offered for other developmental or content area categories. More recently, portfolios have been used for many content areas in the curriculum. It is just as appropriate to use portfolios for social studies, science, and mathematics as it is to use alternative or authentic strategies for assessment for all types of curriculum and instruction.

TYPES OF PORTFOLIOS

As teachers and students use portfolios to fulfill the three purposes for portfolio assessment described earlier, they make decisions about the type of portfolio that best serves their purposes. Among these possibilities are working portfolios, evaluative portfolios, archival portfolios, and showcase portfolios. The portfolios can be organized by the teacher, by the teacher and child, and by the child alone.

Decisions must be made as to who will determine portfolio contents and purpose. Will the portfolio be maintained and used by the teacher alone? Will the teacher and child make choices for the portfolio together? What role will parents play in the process? Will parents be encouraged to make selections for a portfolio and bring samples of work done at home to be included? These considerations can be included for each of the types of portfolios described next.

WORKING PORTFOLIOS.   A working portfolio is used to collect examples of student work for future evaluation. During an interval of a reporting period, the work is collected without making final decisions as to what will be kept and what will be discarded. Samples are collected by both teacher and child. Progress notes and planning for subsequent work are important components (Gronlund, 1998). The items in the working portfolio later can become part of another type of portfolio.

EVALUATIVE PORTFOLIOS.   This is the most commonly understood type of portfolio. An evaluative portfolio permits the teacher to make an assessment of the student's progress, both formative and summative. The teacher is able to use the materials included to evaluate the student's developmental advances and needs for future growth and learning. The evaluative portfolio is used for reporting to parents and administrators and for planning for curriculum and instruction (Barbour & Desjean-Perrotta, 1998).

SHOWCASE PORTFOLIOS.   A showcase portfolio is used to exhibit the child's best work. Showcase portfolios are most frequently used to share the child's accomplishment with parents. They can also be used for school open-house events or occasions when children from different classrooms and grade levels share what they are learning and doing. Showcase portfolio contents are frequently chosen by the child (Barbour & Desjean-Perrotta, 1998; Gronlund, 1998).

ARCHIVAL PORTFOLIOS.   In some preschools and elementary schools, student portfolios follow students from one year to another. This type of portfolio can be called an archival or pass-along portfolio because it can provide information for the child's next teacher and/or other future teachers (Puckett & Black, 2000; Seidel et al., 1997).

Examples of children's work can be used in portfolio assessment.

Portfolios can be organized by developmental category, by content area, or by topics or themes if an integrated curriculum is followed. As is true for curriculum design, the goals of the program and objectives for development and learning serve as the foundation for instruction and assessment. As teachers understand more about the emergent nature of cognition and development, their task is to become comfortable with using characteristics of emerging development and how that is reflected in the work they and the children can collect for assessment. In this respect, understanding the principles and characteristics of development become essential if the teacher is to comprehend how to assess the child's developmental progress. In the following sections, examples of organization of a developmental portfolio and content area portfolio are provided.

ORGANIZING PORTFOLIOS USING A DEVELOPMENTAL APPROACH

A sensible approach to organizing portfolios for preschool and primary-grade children is by developmental category. Thus, the teacher might provide dividers in the portfolio for motor development, social and emotional development, language development, and cognitive development. Grace and Shores (1991), citing Meisels and Steele (1991), make the following suggestions for organizing such a portfolio (pp. 21–25):

Art Activities (Fine-Motor Development)

- Drawings of events, persons, and animals. The child might dictate descriptions or explanations of the drawings to the teacher or a parent or classroom volunteer. Or the child might write such explanations. (The teacher may need to make notes if the child writes his own picture caption.)
- Photos of unusual block constructions or projects, labeled and dated
- Collages and other examples of the child's use of various media when designing a picture
- Samples of the child's manuscript printing. (The appearance and placement of the letters on the page are evaluated in the context of a developmental continuum.)

Movement (Gross-Motor Development)

- Notes recorded by the teacher or videotapes of the child's movement activities in the classroom or on the playground, which reflect the child's developing skills
- Notes, photographs, videotapes, and anecdotal records that demonstrate the child's skills and progress in music activities and fingerplays
- Notes from teacher interviews with the child about his on her favorite active games at school

Math and Science Activities (Concept Development)

- Photographs of the child measuring or counting specific ingredients as part of a cooking activity
- Charts on which the child has recorded the planting, care, watering schedule, periods of sunlight, etc., of plants in the classroom or on the school grounds
- Work samples demonstrating the child's understanding of number concepts. An example is the numeral four formed with beans glued to a sheet of paper and the appropriate number of beans glued beside the numeral.

- Work samples, teacher notes, taped pupil interviews illustrating, in a progressive fashion, the child's understanding of mathematical concepts
- Photographs and data gathered from checklists and taped pupil interviews that document the child's conceptual understanding, exploring, hypothesizing, and problem solving. (The documentation will depend on the child's developmental stages during the life of the portfolio.)

Language and Literacy

- Tape recordings of a child rereading stories that she "wrote" or dictated to a parent, teacher, or classroom volunteer
- Examples of the child's journal entries
- Copies of signs or labels the child constructed
- A log of book titles actually read by the child or read to the child by a teacher, parent, or other adult
- Copies of stories, poems, or songs the child wrote or dictated
- Taped pupil interviews that reveal the child's increase, over time, in vocabulary and skill in use of the language

Personal and Social Development

- Teacher notes and anecdotal records that document interactions between the child and her peers. Such interactions can indicate the child's ability to make choices, solve problems, and cooperate with others.
- Teacher notes, anecdotal records, and videorecordings that document events that occurred on field trips. Such incidents may illustrate the child's social awareness.
- Notes from teacher–parent conferences

ORGANIZING PORTFOLIOS USING A SUBJECT AREA APPROACH

The teacher may prefer to organize portfolios using a subject area approach. If this approach is taken, the choice must be made whether to include all subject areas or to dedicate a portfolio to a single content area. If a comprehensive collection of the child's work, teacher assessments, and other evaluation data is desired, Batzle (1992) recommends the following contents for the portfolio:

1. **Required Tests and Accountability Measures**
   - Standardized Tests
   - Minimum Competency Tests
   - Criterion-Referenced Tests
   - Chapter or Unit Tests

2. **Samples Across the Curriculum**
   - Language Arts
     Reading Responses
     Reading Logs
     Home Reading Logs
     Oral Reading Tapes
     Writing Folders
     Writing Samples

Spelling Work
- Math
- Fine Arts
- Content Areas

3. **Teacher Observations and Measures**
   - Kid Watching and Anecdotal Records
   - Running Records
   - Retellings
   - Progress Checks
   - Teacher-made Tests
   - Rubrics
   - Conference Records
   - Summary of Findings

Inventories and Other Forms
- Reading Inventory
- Informal Reading Inventory
- Writing Inventory
- Parent Surveys, Comments, and Evaluations

Additional Items
- Cassette or Photo of Drama Presentations
- Oral Presentation, Book Talk
- Oral Language Inventory
- Oral "Publishing" (p. 35)

It should be noted that this example includes possibilities for several subject areas to be included; nevertheless, some subjects, such as social studies, are omitted. Moreover, the predominant categories suggested are related to language arts. It should also be observed that inclusion of results of standardized tests is recommended.

The pamphlet "Portfolio Assessment," published by Teaching for Excellence (1992), has more complete ideas for a portfolio that include all subject areas. The ideas proposed could focus on specific subjects or integrated subject areas. Possibilities suggested are the following:

- Self-evaluation through an "All About Me" portfolio in which students choose items which express themselves, such as their likes, dislikes, hobbies, personality and family.
- Written literacy portfolios, with such works as timed writing samples, best notes, log and journal entries, essays, critiques and short stories.
- Math portfolios, with such items as statistical studies, graphic representations, diagrams of problem-solving steps, written descriptions of math investigations, and responses to open-ended questions and problems.
- Creative expressions such as art, music, dance and photography.
- Projects such as science and social studies investigations. A fun way to teach and test applications is to assign job role simulations, such as an archaeologist who must find the culture or time period of an artifact, or a policy analyst who must predict the future in a country being studied.
- Videotapes and written analysis of progress for physical skills such as soccer, gymnastics, volleyball, etc.

Organization of student portfolios can focus on a single content area, and there are options for how to organize the contents. Farr (1993) suggests some organization patterns for student portfolios for a reading and writing system as follows:

1. **Organization by topic.** Students might put reading and writing materials on sports in one section, school topics in another, and mysteries in another.
2. **Organization by genre.** Students might arrange materials according to whether they are stories, letters, articles, songs, and other genres for reading and writing.
3. **Organization by difficulty.** One section might include those things that were easy to do; in another those that were more difficult; and in a third those that were very difficult.
4. **Chronological organization.** Students use weeks or some other time period as the organizational pattern.
5. **Organization by preference.** Students use one section for reading and writing activities they liked a great deal, another for those they felt neutral about, and a third for those they disliked.
6. **Multiple-level organization.** Students arrange materials first by topics and then within topics by genre, preference, or difficulty. (p. 13)

SETTING UP PORTFOLIOS

The decision to initiate the use of portfolio assessment should be approached thoughtfully. If the process of implementing portfolio assessment is to be successful, a good climate needs to be present in the early childhood center or school that will support the change (Seidel et al., 1997). The purposes of portfolio assessment and how they are associated with a philosophy of learning and instruction need to be understood and accepted by the teachers before embarking on a new and complex assessment approach.

STEPS IN GETTING STARTED

Once the decision has been made to use portfolio assessment and the teacher understands the implications of undertaking the changes, several decisions must be made prior to beginning the process. The first steps are to select the purpose, format, and storage system for portfolios. Then the teacher will need to determine what will go into the portfolio by selecting portfolio contents and to decide how student work will be collected, organized, and reviewed. Finally, the teacher will need to decide how assessment of student progress will be reported.

SELECTING THE PURPOSE. The purpose for the portfolio is determined by the objectives the teacher has for assessment. If the purpose is to assess development for a reporting period, an evaluative portfolio with a developmental format will be chosen. If the purpose is for the student to initiate learning objectives and engage in reflection and self-evaluation, a working portfolio might be the obvious choice. If portfolios are implemented for parent conferences and are not the major source of assessment, a showcase portfolio might be indicated.

In reality, the teacher might determine multiple purposes for a portfolio. The portfolio might be used both for assessment and as a showcase. For this type of portfolio, both the teacher and the student might have sections of student work. As an alternative, there might be a section for assessment and another for showcase entries. There are all kinds of possibilities. The teacher will want to consider what purpose or purposes will best serve his or her objectives for assessment.

SELECTING THE FORMAT. After the teacher has decided why and how the portfolio is to be used for assessment, some decisions will be made as to how to organize the contents. For an evaluative portfolio in preschool, a chronological organization might be the best choice to display student progress in developmental domains. If the teacher uses a thematic curriculum, the materials placed in the portfolio might be organized by thematic topic. If a portfolio is to serve as the assessment system for a single content area, the genre approach to organization will permit division of the contents into reading, writing, skills practice, and so forth. Organization by difficulty might be the preference for a mathematics portfolio.

Once the format has been determined, it can be further organized using a table of contents. The following could be used for various formats:

* A table of contents
* A title page that identifies the student and explains what can be found in the collection and the purpose of the portfolio
* Dividers with labels that identify contents of each section
* Dates on all entries
* A review or assessment section that includes both teacher and child assessments to include teacher comments (Seidel et al., 1997; Wortham, 1998)

SELECTING THE STORAGE SYSTEM. An important decision is how to store portfolios. The purposes for the portfolio and types of materials to be stored will influence the type of storage containers to be used. A writing portfolio that is composed primarily of student writing samples can be housed in a file folder; in contrast, a portfolio that contains project work or video- and audiotapes might require a box. Some suggested storage containers include the following (Barbour & Desjean-Perrotta, 1998; Grace & Shores, 1991):

* Expandable file folders
* X-ray folders
* Pizza boxes
* Grocery bags stapled inside each other
* Large mailing envelopes
* Office supply boxes
* Paper briefcases
* Shoe boxes containing file folders
* Plastic crates
* CD ROM

IDENTIFYING PORTFOLIO COMPONENTS. Based on the purposes and format of the portfolio, decisions must now be made about portfolio contents. Will the portfolio for 4–year-olds include all developmental domains or just literacy? Will the content area portfolio be for math and science or language arts? Will the portfolio include only student work, or will teacher assessments be included? There are many possibilities for determining what will go into the portfolio that will vary according to the developmental level of the child and the purposes for the portfolio. As the use of portfolios evolves, teachers will modify the components they will include. In some cases, they may find that they are collecting too many types of materials. In other cases, they may find that they need to expand the examples that are to be included.

Teachers might find it useful to develop a checklist for reviewing the steps they have taken in getting started in using portfolio assessment. Lescher (1995) provides one model for such a checklist as pictured in Figure 9–2.

FIGURE 9–2 Checklist for portfolio design

Portfolio Design Worksheet
Your student portfolios must answer at least four questions.
Your team can use this worksheet to begin to design your student portfolios.

1. What needs to be assessed?
   _____
   _____
   _____
   _____

2. Who will be involved in the assessment process?
   _____
   _____
   _____

3. How will data be collected and analyzed?
   _____
   _____
   _____

4. What components will be included in the portfolio?
   ☐ observational/anecdotal records   ☐ informal skill assessments
   ☐ checklists   ☐ student self-assessments
   ☐ work samples   ☐ conference logs and records
   ☐ formal skill assessments   ☐ various types of journals and learning
   ☐ _____   logs
   ☐ _____   ☐ _____
   ☐ _____   ☐ _____

5. _____?
   _____
   _____
   _____

(Add other questions that you think are important)

Source: Lescher, M. L. (1995). *Portfolios: Assessing learning in the primary grades.* Washington, DC: National Education Association, p. 9. Copyright © 1995 by National Education Association. Used by permission.

COLLECTING AND ORGANIZING WORK

When the portfolio process is getting underway, the teacher and children make decisions about how they will collect and organize entries for the portfolio. Periodically, during a grading period or other designated time, pieces are selected for the portfolio. The teacher can likewise select samples for the portfolio from assessment activities or tests that have been administered, checklists, rating scales, essays, and other evidence of work. Rubrics for individual and group work will be included in the assignments. When it is time to finalize the portfolio, the teacher, child, or teacher and child will make final choices for the portfolio.

Over the duration of the school year, more decisions will be made as to which materials will remain for the entire year and which will be replaced by better or more advanced work. If a longitudinal review is desired at the end of the year, work completed at intervals throughout the year will be retained for comparison over time. If the portfolio is for archival purposes, decisions are made about what will be passed on to the next teacher and what will be eliminated. Size and amount become important factors in all portfolio collections, but archival portfolios require careful selection.

SELECTING PORTFOLIO ASSESSMENTS

A major task for the teacher is to determine which assessments will be included in the portfolio. Depending on the purpose for the portfolio, the teacher decides what types of assessments will be included. Barbour and Desjean-Perrotta (1998) suggest that there should be a balance between process and product. The portfolio contents should include traditional assessment measures, performance assessments, and observation results. The assessments that are chosen should correspond to the possibilities or purposes for their use. It is at this point that all the assessment possibilities that have been included in this text can be analyzed and considered for the portfolio. Although most of the assessment types are performance based, teacher-designed tests and tasks and other assessment instruments are included in the total range of possibilities. Figure 9–3 shows a range of assessments and the purposes that they can serve for portfolio assessment.

A kindergarten teacher desiring to select assessments for a comprehensive preschool or kindergarten portfolio might consider several types of assessments. For example, the pattern of emergence in writing and reading can be organized into a checklist, rubric, or other recordkeeping form to determine the child's progress in emergent literacy (Farr, 1993; Sulzby, 1993; Wortham, 1998). Figure 9–4 is a form for keeping a record of a child's emergent and conventional reading (Sulzby, 1993), and Figure 9–5 is a rubric that can be used to select materials for a learning center and assess emergent writing. Figure 9–6 is an example of an interview form that might be used with a child in kindergarten or first grade. Figure 9–7 provides a rating scale to determine the child's level of development in emergent reading (Polakowski, 1993).

If the teacher wishes to track the acquisition of skills development and project work in science, a checklist might be developed to assess accomplishments and participation in projects. Figure 9–8 shows two different checklists that evaluate both developmental skills and performance work in group projects (Cliatt & Shaw, 1992). Figure 9–9 provides for self-assessment by the child (Farr, 1993).

FIGURE 9–3 Portfolio assessment purposes

PURPOSES FOR PORTFOLIO ASSESSMENTS

Work Samples
To assess and evaluate
To make a diagnosis
To assess longitudinal progress
To conduct student self-evaluation
To understand student thinking processes
For self-selection of important work

Diaries
For student reflection
To trace progress
To express understanding
For problem solving
For self-evaluation
For self-expression

Interviews
For specific feedback
To evaluate conceptual understanding
To observe thinking processes
To assess skills
To assess progress

Interactive Journals
For communication and feedback
For peer editing
For building support
To stimulate creativity
For problem solving

Checklists and Rating Scales
To assess and report progress and mastery
To assess and report development
To record task list results
For instructional planning
To assess teaching processes

*Teacher-Designed Tests, Tasks, and
    Observations*
To assess skills
To assess cognitive processes
To document progress
To determine eligibility for special programs
For screening
To establish zone of proximal development (ZPD)

Contracts
For behavior management
To conduct student self-assessment
To assess student work habits
To conduct student self-initiated planning
For student management of learning activities
For feedback on student activities
For feedback on student interests
For recordkeeping

*Audio/Video/Photographs/Computer
    Assessments*
For assessment through observation
To determine progress
To assess learning processes
For self-assessment
For reporting to parents
To demonstrate skills
To maintain an electronic portfolio

Performance/Criterion-Related Tasks
To conduct a demonstration or exhibit
To conduct application of learning in context

Group Assessments
To assess group performance
To evaluate instruction
To evaluate program progress
To assess skills
To assess student progress in learning how to learn
To assess student progress in cooperative group
    learning

Narrative Summary
For teacher reflection on student progress
For summative assessment
For reporting to parents
To screen for special programs

FIGURE 9–4 Teacher's record of child's reading

Student	
BOOKS THE CHILD HAS READ EMERGENTLY	
Date Read	Title
BOOKS THE CHILD HAS READ CONVENTIONALLY	
Date Read	Title
Other observations:	

Source: Sulzby, E. (1993). *Teacher's Guide to Evaluation: Assessment Handbook.* Glenview, IL: Scott, Foresman/Addison Wesley. Copyright © 1993 by Scott, Foresman. Reprinted by permission of Pearson Education Inc.

FIGURE 9–5 Learning center writing rubric

LEARNING CENTER DEVELOPMENT GUIDE SHEET

Objective(s): _The student will use descriptive language_

Materials: _paper, pencils, markers, pens_

Duration: _1 week_

Addressing different levels and assessment:

Level	Activity/Expectation	Assessment
Pre-writer	The student will describe a picture using words	Rubric uses pictures May copy letters or words Can write some familiar words
Developing Writer	The student will describe a picture using sentences. • upper and lower case letters • some punctuation	understands sound-symbol relationship uses indented spelling Can read own writing
Experienced Writer	The student will describe a picture using sentences in a paragraph • Capitals used correctly • Correct punctuation	using conventions of print in spelling Demonstrates sentence sense Can use correct punctuation and use of upper and lower case letters

LEARNING CENTER DEVELOPMENT GUIDE SHEET

Objective(s): _____

Materials: _____

Duration: _____

Addressing different levels and assessment:

Level	Activity/Expectation	Assessment

ANALYZING PORTFOLIO ASSESSMENTS

Periodically, the teacher, child, and parents review portfolio contents to determine the child's progress and how appropriate experiences should be planned for further growth and development. To prepare for discussions, the teacher first conducts an analysis based on established learning objectives, indicators of developmental progress, and other criteria that demonstrate learning accomplishment. Work samples, interview results, checklists, rating scales, rubrics, teacher-designed assessments, and performance tasks are studied to determine what the child has learned. The child's work as presented in the portfolio is evaluated in terms of developmental domains, sequences of skills, and objectives established by the teachers and school. Using such preestablished criteria, the teacher is able to develop a pro-

FIGURE 9–6 Teacher interview form

Interview with Child
Name _____ Date _____
1. What are your favorite things to do at home? _____
_____
2. Do you have your own books at home? _____
_____
3. What is your favorite book? _____
_____
4. Do other people at home like to read? What do they read? _____
_____
5. Who reads to you at home? _____

Source: Polakowski, C. (1992). Literacy portfolios in the early childhood classroom. In *Student portfolios.* Washington, DC: National Education Association, p. 56. Copyright © 1992 by National Education Association. Used by permission.

file of the child's strengths and weaknesses, as well as the interests and creative expressions revealed in various types of work samples.

The teacher and child can then use the portfolio as a vehicle for the child to reflect on progress and interests. Parents can also interact with the teacher and child on accomplishments and discuss future plans and goals together (Smith, 2000). More about analysis and summarization of child development and learning will be discussed in chapter 10.

STRATEGIES FOR DEVELOPING SUCCESSFUL PORTFOLIOS

Teachers who have used portfolios in their classrooms offer suggestions from their experience in getting started with portfolio assessment. Larry Buschman, a second-grade teacher in Jefferson, Oregon, uses portfolios. He uses student conferences at the end of every quarter to assess how his students are doing. His students help to create and maintain their portfolios and choose most of the work samples that are included in their portfolios. Buschman makes the following suggestions to teachers who are beginning the process (Buschman, 1993):

- Start small and emphasize quality, not quantity
- Use photographs, drawings, and reflective descriptions to document projects that don't fit inside the portfolio
- Make sure each portfolio has a table of contents
- Be sure students date their work
- Select a few work samples yourself
- Give parents the opportunity to review their child's portfolio (p. 24)

FIGURE 9–7 A reading and writing rating scale

K-2 READING/WRITING SCALE
Development of Children's Strategies for Making Sense of Print

1. EARLY EMERGENT

Displays an awareness of some conventions of writing, such as awareness of front and back of books and distinctions between print and pictures. Sees the construction of meaning from text as "magical" or exterior to the print. While the child may be interested in the contents of a book, there is as yet little apparent attention to turning written marks into language. Is beginning to notice environmental print.

2. ADVANCED EMERGENT

Engages in pretend reading and writing. Uses reading-like ways that clearly approximate book language. Demonstrates a sense of the story being "read." Uses picture clues and recalls storyline. May draw upon predictable language patterns in anticipating (and recalling) the story. Attempts to use letters in writing, sometimes in random or scribble fashion.

3. EARLY BEGINNING READER

Attempts to "really read." Indicates beginning sense of one-to-one correspondence and concept of words. Predicts actively in new material, using syntax and storyline. Establishes small, stable sight vocabulary. Displays initial awareness of beginning and ending sounds, especially in invented spelling.

4. ADVANCED BEGINNING READER

Starts to draw on major cue systems: self-corrects or identifies words through use of letter-sound patterns, sense of story, or syntax. Reading may be laborious especially with new material; new readings require considerable effort and some support. Writing and spelling reveal awareness of letter patterns and conventions of writing, such as capitalization and full stops.

5. EARLY INDEPENDENT READER

Handles familiar material on own, but still needs some support with unfamiliar material. Figures out words and self-corrects by drawing on a combination of letter-sound relationships, word structure, storyline, and syntax. Strategies of re-reading or of guessing from larger chunks of texts are becoming well established. Has large, stable sight vocabulary. Understands conventions of writing.

6. ADVANCED INDEPENDENT READER

Reads independently, using multiple strategies flexibly. Monitors and self-corrects for meaning. Can read and understand most material when the content is appropriate. Conventions of writing and spelling are—for the most part—under control.

Scoring:
NA = Not Applicable
Points 0-6

Note 1: The scale focuses on development of children's strategies for making sense of print. Evidence concerning children's strategies and knowledge about print may be revealed in both their reading and writing activities.
Note 2: The scale does not attempt to rate children's interests or attitudes regarding reading, nor does it attempt to summarize what literature may mean to the child. Such aspects of children's literacy development are summarized in other forms.
Rating scale developed by South Brunswick, New Jersey, teachers and Educational Testing Service staff, January 1991.

Source: Polakowski, C. (1992). Literacy portfolios in the early childhood classroom. In *Student portfolios.* Washington, DC: National Education Association, p. 55. Copyright © 1992 by National Education Association. Used by permission.

FIGURE 9–8 Science assessment checklists

	Children													
Behaviors														
Makes groups consistently when given a basis for classification.														
Names basis for classifying.														
Devises basis for classifying.														
Makes subclassifications.														
Other														

A checklist for classifying skills.

	Children													
Qualities														
Applies information.														
Conveys information clearly.														
Represents creative work.														
Neatly made.														
Clearly explained (as applicable).														
For group projects, was project work shared?														
Was work cooperative?														
Other														

A checklist for evaluating projects.

Source: Cliatt, M. J. P., & Shaw, J. M. (1992). *Helping children explore science.* Upper Saddle River, NJ: Prentice Hall. Copyright © 1992. Reprinted by permission of Pearson Education, Inc.

FIGURE 9–9 Organizing my portfolio

Name _____   Date _____
Teacher _____   School _____

Organizing My Portfolio

I have looked at all the things in my portfolio.
1. This picture or writing tells about the thing I like best.

2. Here is the work I have the most of.
   Here is my picture or writing about it.

3. This is the work I would like to have more of.
   Here is my picture or writing about it.

Source: Excerpt from the *HBJ treasury of literature portfolio assessment, teacher's guide, grades K–8* by Roger C. Farr, copyright © 1993 by Harcourt, Inc., reprinted by permission of the publisher.

ADVANTAGES AND DISADVANTAGES OF USING PORTFOLIOS TO REPORT STUDENT PROGRESS

The advantages of using portfolios for assessment and reporting were discussed earlier. Portfolios permit a wide range of assessment methods and a variety of ways that children can demonstrate mastery and growth in development. They allow for flexibility in how the teacher documents student progress; at the same time, they provide parents with extensive information about their child's experiences in school that facilitate learning and accomplishments.

Portfolios provide evaluation above and beyond letter grades on a report card. Children can be tracked on a continuum of development. In addition, assessment can be used for diagnostic purposes, as well as to document learning. Teachers can meet the individual needs of each child by examining portfolio contents and discussing progress and problems with the child through interviews and conferences.

Portfolios include input from the child, making the child an active partner in the evaluation process. The child not only makes selections for portfolio contents, but also participates in the assessment process. This participation includes discussing progress with parents during parent–teacher conferences.

The most obvious difficulty in organizing and maintaining portfolios is the issue of time. Time is needed by both the teacher and the children to implement and maintain portfolios. It is important for the teacher and the children to work regularly with portfolios, review contents, discuss progress, and make changes in what is to be kept in the portfolio. If the portfolios are to be effective, they must be kept organized and current. Time is needed to work with portfolios, and teachers who are enthusiastic about the benefits of portfolios may also be concerned about the time needed to use portfolios appropriately.

Teachers are also concerned about accountability and grading portfolios. If a school district combines the use of portfolios with the evaluation of the child's longitudinal progress, and if the evaluation of that progress is the primary purpose of reporting, teachers can become very comfortable with using portfolios. If, however, portfolios are used to assess and assign grades, the evaluation process is much more difficult when using portfolios. Teachers can be much more anxious about using portfolio assessment when they have to use them to compare the achievement of students with each other. The issue of assigning grades can be one of the biggest challenges teachers face when initiating portfolio assessment.

A major concern when using portfolios for assessment and reporting is validity of the assessment strategies used. Earlier in the chapter, we discussed the need to predetermine standards and procedures that would be used to assess portfolio contents. In addition, steps must be taken to ensure that the assessment strategies have been checked for validity (Goodwin & Goodwin, 1993). Teachers are particularly concerned about their own accountability for the evaluation process. They may be insecure about using portfolio assessment because they are uncertain whether they will be able to grade the child's work appropriately.

The statewide use of portfolios in Vermont (O'Neil, 1993) gives some information about the possible difficulties in establishing reliability. Low reliability coefficients in the 1991–1992 statewide assessment process led Vermont to improve the portfolio assessment process to overcome these technical limitations. Teachers who individually are trying to be accountable for the quality of their assessments are rightfully concerned about the ability to be accountable to parents and administrators about the evaluation process they use in the classroom.

DEVELOPING QUALITY PORTFOLIO ASSESSMENTS

Ensuring the quality of the assessments that are placed in portfolios was discussed in earlier chapters. The development of quality in performance assessments through the use of rubrics and other strategies was discussed in chapter 8. But how is the quality of the portfolio as a whole to be developed? The portfolio is one type of assessment system and must have quality as a system. Six suggestions have been provided to help teachers to establish quality in portfolio assessment (Arter & Spandel, 1992, as cited by Herman, Aschbacher, & Winters, 1992):

- How representative is the work included in the portfolio of what students can really do?
- Do the portfolio pieces represent coached work? Independent work? Group work? Are they identified as to the amount of support students received?
- Do the evaluation criteria for each piece and the portfolio as a whole represent the most relevant or useful dimensions of student work?
- How well do portfolio pieces match important instructional targets or authentic tasks?
- Do tasks or some parts of them require extraneous abilities?
- Is there a method for ensuring that portfolios are reviewed consistently and criteria applied accurately? (pp. 120–121)

Another consideration in developing portfolios that include quality assessments is relevance. They must be purposeful. Hanson and Gilkerson (1999) propose that a meaningful portfolio must meet the following criteria:

- Be clearly linked with instructional objectives.
- Be an ongoing assessment system.
- Avoid becoming a teacher-manufactured document.
- Be performance based; emphasize purposeful learning; be ongoing in all cultural contexts of home, school, and community. (p. 81)

SUMMARY

Education in the United States reflects a history of embracing innovations only to discard them within a few years. Some instructional changes lack the research that can prove or question effectiveness. The introduction of portfolio assessment may suffer from this pattern. As with other innovations, teachers in some schools are asked to implement portfolios without the training needed to make the process successful. Likewise, when training is provided, it is possible that only the positive characteristics of portfolio assessment are stressed, without adequate information about difficulties and cautions that should be observed and followed. A major limitation of portfolio assessment may be this lack of competence and confidence that teachers need to implement the process successfully. It is important that the implementation of portfolio assessment and reporting be accompanied by the training, decision making, and preparation that are required for any type of assessment to be a quality method of assessing and evaluating student progress and achievement.

In this chapter, we have explored some strategies for reporting student progress to parents through performance or authentic assessments. We discussed the inherent limitations in traditional report cards that report only what the child knows. In contrast, performance assessments demonstrate what the child knows and how the child applies that knowledge in a realistic context.

A major focus of the chapter was to describe some alternative methods of constructing an evaluative profile of the child's development and learning that permits the teacher and the child to communicate to the parents broad information about what the child has accomplished. It was stressed that portfolios can contain many types of informal and performance assessment results to support what the child has learned.

Many types of examples of children's work and assessment results can be included in a portfolio. Various organizational possibilities can be used for portfolios as well.

REVIEW QUESTIONS

1. What are the concerns about using report cards with young children?
2. How do authentic assessments and reporting provide a broad picture of children's progress?
3. Describe why curriculum and instruction and reports of performance need to complement each other.
4. How are report cards being revised to be more compatible with current trends in curriculum and instruction?
5. How do portfolios meet the criteria for appropriate performance assessment and reporting?

6. Outline the possible components of a portfolio and briefly describe each.
7. What types of teacher assessments can be included in the portfolio?
8. How can teachers overcome concerns they might have about initiating the portfolio process?
9. How are children actively involved in the assessment process when portfolios are used? How are they a part of the process of reporting to parents?

SUGGESTED ACTIVITY

Design a portfolio to be used with preschool children. Include (1) sections or dividers for the portfolio, (2) the types of teacher assessments you would use, and (3) how you would report the child's progress to parents.

REFERENCES

Arter, J., & Spandel, V. (Spring 1992). Using portfolios of student work in instruction and assessment. *Educational measurement: Issues and practice, 11,* 36–44.

Barbour, A., & Desjean-Perrotta, B. (1998). The basics of portfolio assessment. In S. C. Wortham, A. Barbour, and B. Desjean-Perrotta, *Portfolio assessment: A handbook for preschool and elementary educators* (pp. 15–30). Olney, MD: Association for Childhood Education International.

Batzle, J. (1992). *Portfolio assessment and evaluation: Developing and using portfolios in the K–6 classroom.* Cypress, CA: Creative Teaching.

Buschman, L. (1993). Windows on learning: Taking an integrated approach. *Learning, 21,* 22–25.

Cliatt, M. J. P., & Shaw, J. M. (1992). *Helping children explore science.* Upper Saddle River, NJ: Prentice Hall.

Farr, R. C. (1993). *Portfolio assessment teacher's guide grades K–8.* Orlando, FL: Harcourt Brace Jovanovich.

Gilkerson, D., & Hanson, M. F. (2000). Family portfolios: Involving Families in portfolio documentation. *Early Childhood Education Journal, 27,* 197–201.

Glazer, S. M. (1994, January). Assessment in the classroom: Where we are, where we're going. *Teaching K–8,* 68–71.

Goodwin, W. L., & Goodwin, L. D. (1993). Young children and measurement: Standardized and nonstandardized instruments in early childhood education. In B. Spodek (Ed.), *Handbook of research on the education of young children* (pp. 441–464). New York: Macmillan.

Grace, C., & Shores, E. F. (1991). *The portfolio and its use.* Little Rock, AR: Southern Association on Children Under Six.

Gronlund, N. E. (1998). Portfolios as an assessment tool: Is collection of work enough? *Young Children, 53,* 4–10.

Hanson, M. F., & Gilkerson, D. (1999). Portfolio assessment: More than ABCs and 123s. *Early Childhood Education Journal, 27,* 81–86.

Hebert, E. A., & Schultz, L. (1996). The power of portfolios. *Educational Leadership, 53,* 70–71.

Herman, J. L., Aschbacher, P. R., & Winters, L. (1992). *A practical guide to alternative assessment.* Alexandria, VA: Association for Supervision and Curriculum Development.

Lescher, M. L. (1995). *Portfolios: Assessing learning in the primary grades.* Washington, DC: National Education Association.

Meisels, S. J., & Steele, D. (1991). *The early childhood portfolio collection process.* Ann Arbor, MI: University of Michigan, Center for Human Growth and Development.

Micklo, S. K. (1997). Math portfolios in the primary grades. *Childhood Education, 73,* 194–199.

O'Neil, J. (1993). The promise of portfolios. *ASCD Update, 35,* 1, 5.

Piaget, J. (1952). *The origins of intelligence in children.* New York: Basic Books. (Original work published in 1936)

Piaget, J. (1962). *Play, dreams, and imitation in childhood.* New York: Norton. (Original work published in 1945)

Piaget, J. (1963). *The origins of intelligence in children* (M. Cook, Trans.). New York: Norton.

Polakowski, C. (1993). Literacy portfolios in the early childhood classroom. In *Student portfolios* (pp. 47–66). Washington, DC: National Education Association.

Puckett, M. B., & Black, J. K. (2000). *Authentic assessment of the young child: Celebrating development and learning.* Upper Saddle River, NJ: Merrill/Prentice Hall.

Seidel, S., et al. (1997). *Portfolio practices: Thinking through the assessment of children's work.* Washington, DC: National Education Association.

Smith, A. F. (2000). Reflective portfolios: Preschool possibilities. *Childhood Education, 76,* 204–208.

Sulzby, E. (1993). *Teacher's guide to evaluation: Assessment handbook.* Glenview, IL: Scott, Foresman.

Teaching for Excellence. (1992). Portfolio assessment: A worthwhile testing alternative. *Teaching for Excellence, 12.*

Valencia, S. (1990). A portfolio approach to classroom reading assessment. *Reading Teacher, 43,* 338–340.

Vygotsky, L. S. (1978). *Mind and society: The development of higher mental processes.* Cambridge, MA: Harvard University Press.

Willis, S. (1993). Are letter grades obsolete? *ASCD Update, 35,* 1, 4, 8.

Wortham, S. C. (1998). Introduction. In S. C. Wortham, A. Barbour, & B. Desjean-Perrotta, *Portfolio assessment: A handbook for preschool and elementary educators* (pp. 7–13). Olney, MD: Association for Childhood Education International.

Assessment Systems

Communicating with Parents

CHAPTER 10

Chapter Objectives

As a result of reading this chapter, you will be able to

1. **Understand how narrative reports are used for reporting progress**
2. **Understand how parents can learn about portfolio assessment as a reporting system**
3. **Become familiar with model reporting systems used with young children**
4. **Understand how schools can develop partnerships with parents to benefit the child**
5. **Describe strategies for communicating student progress with parents**
6. **Discuss the importance of parent conferences and how they can be conducted**

Parents have an important role in their child's development and learning. Teachers and administrators in early childhood programs and schools have learned that the child's success as a learner depends on parents as well as teachers. As early childhood education continues in a new century, the importance of having parents as partners with early childhood settings is a goal for quality education. Throughout this book, information related to keeping parents informed and helping parents to understand assessment results has been discussed. In chapter 4, particularly, a section described how teachers can help parents to understand the results of standardized testing. Chapter 9 included information on how portfolios provide parents with a more comprehensive understanding of student progress.

In this chapter, we will focus on how assessment and assessment systems are an important element in reporting what a child has accomplished in the school setting. We will discuss how this applies to portfolio assessment and also to narrative reports. Some model assessment and reporting systems will be described as well.

A major part of the chapter will be devoted to how parents should play a major role in the child's school experience and how schools can develop partnership relationships with parents. Then strategies for communicating with parents about student progress will be discussed to include planning and conducting parent conferences. Throughout the chapter, the emphasis will be on sharing information with parents, soliciting input from parents, and including parents in planning for the child.

DEVELOPING PARENT–SCHOOL PARTNERSHIPS

ROLES FOR PARENTS IN THE CHILD'S DEVELOPMENT AND LEARNING

Parents have always been active in the schools. When my father was an elementary school student in the early 20th century in Austin, Texas, mothers took turns going to the school to prepare lunch for the children. Parents have traditionally helped with school parties and volunteered in the classroom. Parent–teacher organizations have raised money to provide needed books, equipment, and other materials that are not in the school budget. The idea of a partnership with parents goes beyond helping with school programs. The National Association of Elementary School Principals has developed standards for early childhood education that denote the relationship with parents as a partnership. The indicators for this partnership describe new dimensions of parent–school relationships. In the standards, the following statement is made (National

Association of Elementary School Principals, 1998, p. 22): "Parent involvement is of basic importance to the success of all elementary school programs. For an early childhood program, it is crucial and should be a high priority for the principal." Standards descriptors for the partnership include the following (National Association of Elementary School Principals, 1998):

- Parents share development of the school's educational program, and so understand and support it. In meetings, newsletters, conversations, and other ways, the principal and staff provide information about the developmental philosophy of the program and its goals.
- Parents are helped to increase their effectiveness in working with their children, both at school and in the home, through their involvement in the school's work and their participation in classrooms, meetings, and conferences.
- Parent concerns regarding parenting and their individual performance as parents are addressed both formally and informally—through conferences, newsletters, workshops, and in personal conversations.
- Parents are actively involved in the school site council, making decisions about the program.
- A reciprocal relationship is formed and nurtured. Teachers recognize that parents have valuable information to share about their children. All parties seek to make both school and home places where young children feel secure and enjoy success. (p. 22)

The last descriptor declares that parents have valuable information to share about their children. This includes active involvement in the assessment of children's progress in development and learning. Communication with parents is not limited to reporting to parents, but also includes them in the information-gathering process when children are assessed.

ASSESSMENT ROLES OF PARENTS OF CHILDREN WITH DISABILITIES

When parents discover that their infant or toddler has a delay or disability, they soon find out the importance of assessment of the child. They experience conflicting emotions about what the assessment will reveal. One mother described her reaction (Rocco, 1996):

When assessments emphasize deficits and diminished expectations for future success, we parents generally begin to look for a way to thwart these negative prognostications. At the very best, we want a miracle cure. At the least, we want professionals to "fix" our children. . . . We believe that professionals have all the answers, and therefore, all the power. (p. 56)

After parents experience the first stages of screening and diagnosis, they find they have a major role in assessing what the child needs and participate in planning for the child. Once the child has been evaluated and determined to be eligible for services, the ongoing assessment and intervention process centers on parents and the family. The extent of the family's involvement affects the child's performance and the relevance of the child's assessment in guiding intervention services (Berman & Shaw, 1996). Berman and Shaw describe the assessment process as family directed or family centered, with the child and family's priorities and values the most important in planning for the child. The Individuals with Disabilities Act (IDEA) requires that families be involved in assessment, decision making, and activities planned for helping the child.

INVOLVING PARENTS IN THE ASSESSMENT PROCESS

Practices established for parents of children with disabilities serve to involve parents in the assessment process used with all children. Home visits with parents before the beginning of school can initiate the process of gathering information about the child. Thereafter, parents can participate in the assessment process through efforts made by the teacher to solicit information from parents on an ongoing basis, participation in conferences when the child's progress is reported, and contribution of information about the child's progress within the conference, through written responses submitted to the teacher and by telephone or e-mail messages (Gilkerson & Hanson, 2000).

All the assessment strategies discussed in this text apply to children with disabilities. Some types of assessments might have to be modified, especially if children have a cognitive delay or physical disability. Nevertheless, children with disabilities should not be excluded from performance assessments and portfolios. These children should have opportunities to demonstrate what they understand and can use. Teachers and parents will need to be creative in finding ways for children to engage in their own assessment if they are unable to participate in the same manner as children without disabilities. Computer and other types of assistive technologies can be used, as well as photographs, videotapes, and audiotapes. The important point is that children with disabilities should be included in the assessment and planning process to the best of their abilities. Bridging their disabilities with alternative assessment strategies will complete their inclusion as full members of the classroom.

STRATEGIES TO REPORT STUDENT PROGRESS

USING PORTFOLIOS TO REPORT STUDENT PROGRESS

Although portfolio assessment is a valuable system to report student progress, parents must be involved, particularly when teachers are transitioning from traditional reporting, such as report cards to portfolios. Although parents have typically been left out when portfolios are initiated (Hill & Ruptic, 1994), in a partnership relationship, parents are invited to learn about portfolios at the beginning of the transition process. Parent training sessions can be held to explain the purposes and goals of portfolio assessment, followed by opportunities to understand how portfolio entries are selected, the format designed, and how entries will be evaluated (Weldin & Tumarkin, 1998/1999).

USING NARRATIVE REPORTS TO REPORT STUDENT PROGRESS

PURPOSES FOR NARRATIVE REPORTS. Narrative or summary reports are another alternative to report cards for communicating a child's progress to parents. A *summary report* is an evaluation written by the teacher to describe the child's development and learning. A narrative report can stand alone as the periodic evaluation of progress or be combined with other assessment and reporting strategies. A narrative report can be part of a portfolio assessment or another system of assessment and reporting. Purposes for the report are to describe a review of the child's growth over a period of time and to describe that growth in a meaningful way for parents.

A summary report can describe the child's strengths, using developmental categories or subject areas. It (1) can be organized to include projects and integrated curriculum topics, (2) is a profile of development and change over time, and (3) is written with terminology that parents can understand to draw a picture of their child. Using the results of observations, checklists, performance assessments, and other performance strategies, the teacher translates the information so that parents can comprehend what their child has accomplished (Horm-Wingerd, 1992; Krechevsky, 1991; Meisels, 1993).

WRITING A NARRATIVE REPORT.   A narrative report as described by Horm-Wingerd (1992) includes the following:

1. Descriptions of examples of the child's behaviors
2. Examples of what the child can do

3. Concerns the teacher may have about the child's progress
4. Goals and plans for the child in the future

Advocates of written summaries to report child progress express concern that teachers write reports in such a manner that parents have an appreciation of their child and value his or her progress. Strengths, rather than weaknesses, should be stressed. When the child's weaknesses are described or concerns are expressed, the teacher should be careful not to assess blame and to use a positive tone in the report. The goal is to develop reports that promote positive home–school relationships (Horm-Wingerd, 1992). Project Spectrum, described in more detail later, suggests that any home activities described for the parents for use with their child require inexpensive, readily available materials (Krechevsky, 1991).

It is important for teachers to write the narrative report carefully and accurately. It should inform the parents about the child's progress and educate them about appropriate instruction and assessment practices. Horm-Wingerd (1992) suggests the following procedure when writing narratives:

1. Open with an overall statement describing a child's progress in a broad developmental area since the last report or conference.
2. Give a specific example of behavior to serve as evidence for your global description of change and to help parents understand exactly what you are describing.
3. State your plans.
4. If appropriate, note what the parents can do at home to facilitate their child's development. (p. 14)

Horm-Wingerd also provides guidelines for writing narrative reports to ensure that complete and appropriate information is shared with the parents. Figure 10–1 includes specifications, suggestions, and cautions that, if followed, help the teacher to write a quality report to share with parents.

Teachers frequently have difficulty in reporting objectively about some children in their classroom. It is easy to write a very positive report about an attractive child who is cooperative and eager to please the teacher. The teacher may not be aware that the child's progress is being overestimated and reported because the teacher has very positive personal feelings about the child. On the other hand, teachers may have great difficulty in evaluating and reporting objectively on children who pose problems in the classroom. Children who are disruptive, rude to their peers and the teacher, or physically unattractive can have their progress underestimated. The teacher might put too much negative emphasis in the report, rather than stressing the child's accomplishments. The guidelines in Figure 10–1 have strong suggestions for writing positive reports; however, teachers can be unaware that they have subjective perceptions of some of their students. Additional questions a teacher might ask are these: Am I being objective about this child's progress? Are my personal feelings about this child affecting how I write the narrative report? The narrative report should stress positive information about the child first, but even negative information should be discussed in a manner that is accurate and fair.

FIGURE 10–1   Guiding questions for designing, writing, and critiquing narrative reports

Format
- Are organizing categories congruent with philosophy, goals, and curriculum?
- Does it reflect the "whole" child?
- Does it honestly encourage and facilitate parent-teacher communication?

General Content
- Does it blame the child?
- Does it blame the parent?
- How will it make the child feel?
- How will it make the parent feel?
- How will it impact parent–teacher relations?
- How will it affect parent–child relations?

Specific Content
- Does it contain information about the essential areas of development and learning?
- Does it describe patterns of typical classroom behavior over time?
- Does it describe individual growth and progress?
- Does it focus on strengths rather than weaknesses?
- Does it contain specific examples of what the child can do?
- Does it communicate real, authentic, meaningful information?
- Does it let the parents know your plans?
- Does it let the parents know that you are "on the child's side"?
- Does it educate parents about developmentally appropriate practices?

Preparation
- Is the tone conversational, personal, and positive?
- Is it clear and easy to understand?
- Does it contain educational jargon?
- Is it professionally prepared? (Grammar, spelling, handwriting)
- Has it been proofread?

Source: Horm-Wingerd, D. M. (1992). Reporting children's development: The Narrative Report. *Dimensions of Early Childhood, 21,* 15. Reprinted with permission from *Dimensions of Early Childhood,* Southern Early Childhood Association, 8500 West Markham St., Suite 105, Little Rock, AR 72205. 1–800–305–7322

ADVANTAGES AND DISADVANTAGES OF USING NARRATIVE REPORTS TO REPORT STUDENT PROGRESS

Many of the advantages and disadvantages of using performance assessments in general and strategies for reporting the child's performance and development discussed in terms of portfolios are true for narrative reports. Advantages are that they permit the teacher to report the child's broad range of developmental characteristics over a period of time. They can incorporate information from various sources and assessment and recordkeeping strategies when the child's evaluation is reported. A unique aspect of the narrative report is that the teacher can describe in writing what the child has accomplished. Unlike the portfolio, which might be the focus of verbal exchange between the parents and the teacher, the narrative report requires the teacher to think through what is desired in the report and to write it down prior to a conference. If a face-to-face conference is not possible, the narrative report contains the essential information and interpretation the teacher wishes to communicate.

The obvious disadvantage of the narrative report is the time needed to write, edit, and finalize a narrative report in professional form. The teacher must not only collect pertinent information and organize it to reflect the advances made in all developmental or subject areas of the curriculum, but also translate these data into a coherent, comprehensive, concise narrative. The ideal would be to combine the written summary with the portfolio so that contents of the report could be supported with contents of the portfolio; however, each additional component of an evaluation also adds time to the teacher's overall evaluation tasks. Perhaps if the written report is completed at the end of the school year or, at most, twice a year, the teacher would have the opportunity to write down thoughts and descriptions about the child.

MODEL ASSESSMENT AND REPORTING SYSTEMS

Attempts have been made in recent years to develop models of assessment and reporting systems that reflect the strengths of authentic or performance assessments. Educational leaders and measurement specialists for young children have worked toward designing and piloting methods of assessing and reporting children's evaluations in a logical and coherent manner. The goal is to guide teachers in connecting curriculum, instruction, assessment, and reporting via strategies that are natural and meaningful. Three examples of these models are Project Spectrum, the Work Sampling System, and the High/Scope Child Observation Record. Each of these systems seeks to correct the mistakes in assessment that are currently being made with young children. They also focus on strategies for informal and performance assessments differently, but with the same goal of evaluating and reporting child development and learning in a meaningful and constructive manner.

PROJECT SPECTRUM

Project Spectrum was initiated in 1984 at Harvard and Tufts universities to better understand the linguistic and logical bases of intelligence. A major goal of the project was to produce a developmentally appropriate approach to assessment in early childhood. In addition to studying the child's individual cognitive style, the project emphasized the child's areas of strengths often not included in Piagetian approaches to education. The areas of cognitive ability examined in the project included numbers, science, music, language, visual arts, movement, and social development. The assumption was that, by evaluating the young child's strengths in many domains, all children will exhibit performance in some domains.

Assessment is integrated into curriculum and instruction in Project Spectrum. A variety of activities is offered to the children; assessment is conducted through the child's involvement in the activities. Thus, assessment is performance based within both structured and unstructured tasks and teacher observation. Assessment is interfaced with meaningful activities provided in the classroom environment. Assessment is conducted throughout the year and documented through observation checklists, score sheets, portfolios, and tape recordings. Activities used for curriculum and assessment include games, puzzles, and other activities in learning areas such as obstacle courses for movement assessment, a child's activity in reporting for language assessment, and a bus game designed to evaluate the child's ability to make mental calculations and to organize numbers.

Assessment data collected during the year are reported through a Spectrum Profile, a summary of the child's participation in project activities during the year in the form of a narrative report. The child's areas of strength are described, along with suggestions for follow-up activities the parents can conduct with the child.

The child's active involvement in the assessment process and the wide range of developmental domains incorporated into the curriculum are considered to be strengths of Project Spectrum. A concern is that parents might focus only on the child's strengths described in project assessments and focus on these strengths prematurely, thus neglecting the development of other areas (Krechevsky, 1991).

THE WORK SAMPLING SYSTEM

The Work Sampling System was designed as an alternative to the use of standardized tests for the assessment of young children. The system is based on the philosophy that performance assessments are appropriate because they (1) document the child's daily activities, (2) reflect an individualized approach to assessment, (3) integrate assessment with curriculum and instruction, (4) assess many elements of learning, and (5) allow teachers to learn how children reconstruct knowledge through interacting with materials and peers.

The first component of the Work Sampling System is teacher observation by means of developmental checklists. Because learning and instruction are integrated with assessment, the documentation of development and learning also provides information on the curriculum. Checklists cover seven domains: (1) personal and social development, (2) language and literacy, (3) mathematical thinking, (4) scientific thinking, (5) social studies, (6) art and music, and (7) physical development. Guidelines are provided for understanding the process of observation with the checklist indicators.

A second component is portfolios, which provide an assessment process that actively involves the teacher and child. Both the teacher and child select portfolio contents. The activity of organizing the portfolio permits the teacher and child to review progress and plan future activities, thus integrating the teaching–learning process. Items are selected that represent the seven domains covered by the checklist. Essential or core items of work samples are selected several times during the year, in addition to other items selected that represent all domains. The portfolio becomes a tool for documenting, analyzing, and summarizing

FIGURE 10–2 The Work Sampling System

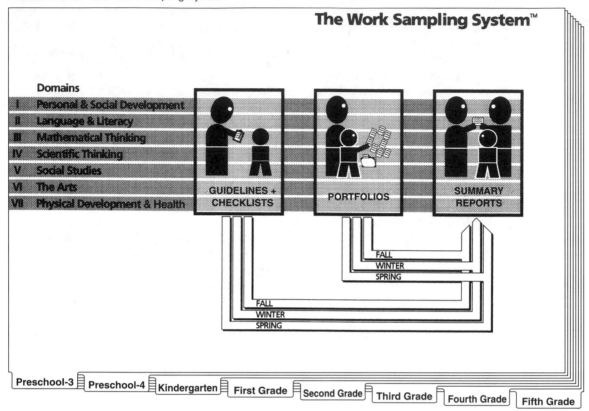

Source: Meisels, S. J. (2001). *Work Sampling in the Classroom: A Teacher's Manual,* p. 4. New York. Copyright by Pearson Education, Inc., publishing as Pearson Early Learning. Used by permission.

the child's learning and development through the year (Harrington, Meisels, McMahon, Dichtelmiller, & Jablon, 1997; Meisels, 1993).

A third component of the Work Sampling System is the summary report completed for each child three times a year. The report summarizes the child's performance by means of specific criteria for the evaluation. Information from the checklists and the portfolios are used to communicate the child's progress to the parents. The child's overall progress is reported, as well as whether the child is making appropriate progress in each developmental category. Figure 10–2 is a diagram of the components of the Work Sampling System and how domains of development serve as the foundation for the assessment and reporting process.

THE CHILD OBSERVATION RECORD

The Child Observation Record, too, is based on observation as the core of the assessment project with young children. The system was developed as an answer to the misassessment of young children, including those in caregiving settings during the preschool years. The goal was to produce an assessment process that is developmentally appropriate, reliable, valid, and user friendly. Also, the purpose of the system is to observe and assess children conducting child-initiated tasks for some of the activities. Because child-centered activities integrate all categories of development, children can be assessed during natural daily activities. Developmental checklists combined with anecdotal recordings of observations form the activities used by the teacher in the assessment process.

The Child Observation Record (COR) system was developed by the High/Scope Educational Research Foundation for use in all developmentally appropriate programs. The system was studied for 2 years to establish validity and reliability. COR assesses six areas of development: (1) initiative, (2) creative representation, (3) social relations, (4) music and movement, (5) language and literacy, and (6) logic and mathematics. The teacher rates the child several times a year on 30 COR items that have five levels of indicators. Anecdotal notes taken on an ongoing basis through observations are used to complete the ratings (High/Scope Educational Research Foundation, 1992; Schweinhart, 1993).

COMMUNICATING WITH PARENTS ABOUT CHILDREN'S PROGRESS

Whatever approaches the teacher uses to assess children, a report is made to communicate with the parents about the child's developmental advances and learning accomplishments. The assessments that have been made are evaluated to determine what will be in the report. Parents are given the opportunity to share their ideas about the child's growth and progress and to respond to the report that the teacher has developed. Although written reports and portfolios are helpful assessment systems to use when sharing information with parents, conferences with parents permit parents and teachers to interact directly. In the following sections, parent conferences will be discussed to include how to prepare for and conduct conferences.

PLANNING FOR PARENT CONFERENCES

The inclusion of parents in the overall assessment is critically important. They need to be involved in more than just the final stage of the process if they are to see all the skills and strategies that their children are developing and to assist their children along the way.

Parent involvement with portfolios can take many forms, including holding three-way conferences that include students, teachers, and parents. Parents may also respond in writing to the work in the portfolio. They can complete a questionnaire about their perceptions of the student's work and provide examples that the parent thinks are indicative of growth. (Lescher, 1995, p. 28)

Prior to conducting a conference with parents, the teacher must prepare the information that is to be shared. Some of the information should involve input from parents. As part of the preparation, the teacher selects the assessments that will be used for reporting progress and develops a profile or some type of encapsulation that will summarize the child's evidence of development and learning.

SELECTING ASSESSMENTS FOR REPORTING PROGRESS. If the teacher uses portfolio assessment, the process of preparing the portfolio contents for the child's evaluation will become the vehicle for reporting. If a portfolio is not used, the teacher will gather and organize examples of the child's work, assessments that have been conducted, and some type of report on the child's evaluation that has been determined by the teacher.

DEVELOPING A PROFILE FOR THE CHILD USING ASSESSMENT RESULTS. Portfolios include the assessments and evidence of the child's work that permit an evaluation to take place. Materials in the portfolio, when combined with a narrative report, provide a profile of progress. A profile can also be developed using checklist assessments, samples of the child's work, and a summary report as is done in the Work Sampling System (Harrington et al., 1997) and the checklist and anecdotal records used in the Child Observation Record System (Schweinhart, 1993). Given the many types of assessments and recordkeeping strategies described in earlier chapters, the teacher has a variety of ways that assessment and evaluation can be organized into a comprehensive profile of the child to share with parents.

PARENT CONFERENCES

Before parent conferences begin, the teacher gathers and organizes all materials necessary to conduct the conference. Once the parents have arrived and the conference is ready to begin, the teacher keeps three guidelines in mind when conducting a successful experience for the parents and the child, if the child is to participate: (1) helping parents to understand evaluation information, (2) helping parents to interpret evaluation information accurately, and (3) soliciting parental input for assessment and planning for the child.

HELPING PARENTS TO UNDERSTAND EVALUATION INFORMATION. When parents encounter a collection of student work and teacher assessments that form the basis for the child's evaluation, they may feel a bit overwhelmed when they compare this type of reporting with a report card. If the teacher and school have prepared the parents for the use of portfolios and performance assessments, they will appreciate understanding how the materials they are seeing form a picture of what the child has learned; nevertheless, they are likely to have questions about assessments and the meaning of the child's work. The teacher needs to be prepared to volunteer information about the assessment strategies used and why the collection of the child's work provides evidence of learning. Parents might have questions such as the following: How are checklist assessments conducted? What kinds of things does the teacher do to acquire checklist information? Why are observation reports important? What does the teacher learn about the child by doing observations? What do the summaries of the child's advances and accomplishments mean when compared with a traditional report card? How does a rubric work? How does the teacher design written tests in the case of primary-grade children? The teacher should be able to

Parents need to engage in the assessment process.

explain how and why assessments are used during the conference so that parents understand the assessment process.

HELPING PARENTS TO INTERPRET EVALUATION INFORMATION. At some point during the conference, parents need to know what the assessment information means. In chapter 4, the point was made that parents need to know how to interpret standardized-test results and how some of the methods of reporting can be confusing as to their meaning and significance.

The same is true of assessment materials shared at the parent-teacher conference. One method of summarizing the child's progress and overall evaluation is to have a summary report or narrative report for the parents. The teacher goes over the report with the parents, helping them to understand the relationship between the assessment resources and the child's overall evaluation. If a summary report is not used, the teacher will need to have an overall evaluation ready to share with the parents. The assessments and work samples must be explained, with their implications for the child's progress and future needs for instructional experiences.

SOLICITING PARENTAL INPUT FOR ASSESSMENT AND PLANNING. Opportunities for parental input into assessment and planning should be built into the conference. If parents do not voluntarily reflect on the child's progress and make suggestions, the teacher should be ready to solicit input. As the teacher completes the evaluation report, parents can give their own views about progress and concerns they might have about the child. As the teacher discusses the next steps in planning for the child, parents can give their suggestions of what might be helpful for the child. Also, the teacher and parents can discuss what the parents might do to help the child at home. The important point is that parents need to feel that they are a vital part of the evaluation process and not mere recipients of the evaluation report. Although the teacher might need to discuss improvements that the child needs to make, parents should also be encouraged to look at problems and suggest solutions. If a true partnership has been established, parents will be able to address the child's needs and help to plan for ways to guide the child without feeling that they are being judged.

SUMMARY: LOOKING TO THE FUTURE

As the 21st century gets underway, assessment in early childhood will include opportunities and challenges. Many of the issues that developed during the latter decades of the 20th century persist at the beginning of a new century.

Assessment of young children that evolved during the 20th century has broadened and intensified over the decades as more has been learned about how young children develop and learn and how variances in development and culture may cause young children to encounter difficulties when they enter school. Tests and measures to assess young children have been developed for children who need intervention services and preschool programs to enhance their academic success when they enter the primary grades.

The development and use of a variety of approaches to assessment of children in the early childhood years are not without problems. Because of the nature and rapidity of development of young children, it is difficult to design measures that are dependable and that accurately measure personal characteristics and other needed information. Each kind of measure designed for use with young children has pluses and minuses. Users of each type of assessment must be informed about the strengths and limitations of the strategies they plan to use. With young children especially, a combination of assessment approaches, rather than a single instrument or method, is indicated.

As school reform decisions increase the use of testing of preschool and primary-grade children for placement, promotion, and retention, teachers will increasingly believe that they are accountable for their role in the decisions made about their students. If they disagree with the grading procedures they are required to use, for example, do they have a responsibility to voice their concern? When they have research-based information that an instrument is being used for the wrong purpose or lacks reliability, should they so inform the personnel who selected the tests? Should teachers press for alternative methods of assessment that include informal strategies and performance assessment?

Parents will want teachers to explain the use of performance assessments and changes in student progress reports that accompany the use of these assessments. Teachers will want parents to have input when the decision is made to move to this type of assessment and the use of portfolios, rather than report cards. In addition, teachers will want to be confident that they have the skills to use and interpret assessment results with parents.

No crystal ball reveals future trends in the measurement of young children. There are certain indicators, however. School reform, which is a national phenomenon, will continue to affect early childhood education. At the same time that the importance of the early years is again being emphasized, the school reform movement continues to force restrictive parameters on the education of young children. The push for quality early childhood programs is in conflict with efforts to raise academic standards. And, as the makeup of early childhood classrooms changes to reflect the presence of more children with disabilities and diverse backgrounds and languages, competence in selecting and using appropriate types of assessments assumes even more importance.

The issues that surround the assessment of young children will not be resolved soon. If present trends continue, improvement in methods of assessment of young children will continue in the effort to improve their potential for optimal development and learning. The ongoing improvement in assessment methods should have a positive effect on the quality of early childhood programs and services as well.

REVIEW QUESTIONS

1. How is a parent–teacher partnership different from roles parents had as school volunteers in the past?
2. How does the concept of parents as partners affect the assessment of the child?
3. Why is assessment especially difficult for parents of children with disabilities?
4. How do portfolios and narrative reports support an active role for parents in contributing to the overall evaluation of their child?
5. What does a narrative report contribute to assessment and evaluation that is lacking in portfolios?

6. How does planning or lack of planning affect a parent–teacher conference?
7. Should the child be a part of the conference with parents? Why or why not?
8. Why is it important that parents understand how assessments are used and the implications of the information gained from assessments?
9. Why do parents need to be involved in planning for the child based on the progress report?

SUGGESTED ACTIVITY

Make arrangements to sit in on a parent–teacher conference in a school that uses portfolios. Observe the strategies the teacher uses to make the parents welcome and comfortable at the beginning of the conference. Note the strategies the teacher uses when sharing portfolio assessment information with the parents. What method is used to summarize the student's progress? What role do the parents have in the conference?

REFERENCES

Berman, C., & Shaw, E. (1996). Family directed child evaluation and assessment under the Individuals with Disabilities Education Act (IDEA). In S. J. Meisels & E. Fenichel (Eds.), *New visions for the developmental assessment of infants and young children* (pp. 361–390). Washington, DC: ZERO TO THREE: National Center for Infants, Toddlers, and Families.

Gilkerson, D., & Hanson, M. F. (2000). Family portfolios: Involving families in portfolio documentation. *Early Childhood Education Journal, 27,* 197–201.

Harrington, H. L., Meisels, S. J., McMahon, P., Dichtelmiller, M. L., & Jablon, J. R. (1997). *Observing, documenting, and assessing learning: The work sampling system handbook for teacher educators.* Ann Arbor, MI: Rebus.

High/Scope Educational Research Foundation. (1992). *Assessment Booklet Child Observation Record (COR).* Ypsilanti, MI: Author.

Hill, B., & Ruptic, C. (1994). *Practical aspects of authentic assessment: Putting the pieces together.* Norwood, MA: Christopher Gordon Publishers.

Horm-Wingerd, D. M. (1992). Reporting children's development: The narrative report. *Dimensions of Early Childhood, 21,* 11–15.

Krechevsky, M. (1991). Project Spectrum: An innovative assessment alternative. *Educational Leadership, 48,* 43–48.

Lescher, M. L. (1995). *Portfolios: Assessing learning in the primary grades.* Washington, DC: National Education Association.

Meisels, S. J. (1993). Remaking classroom assessment with the Work Sampling System. *Young Children, 48,* 34–40.

National Association of Elementary School Principals. (1998). *Early childhood education and the elementary school principal* (2nd ed.). Alexandria, VA: Author.

Rocco, S. (1996). Toward shared commitment and shared responsibility: A parent's vision of developmental assessment. In S. J. Meisels & E. Fenichel (Eds.), *New visions for the developmental assessment of infants and young children* (pp. 55–58). Washington, DC: ZERO TO THREE: National Center for Infants, Toddlers, and Families.

Schweinhart, L. J. (1993). Observing young children in action: The key to early childhood assessment. *Young Children, 48,* 29–33.

Weldin, D. J., & Tumarkin, S. R. (1998/1999). Parent involvement: More power in the portfolio process. *Childhood Education, 75,* 90–95.

Glossary

Achievement test A test that measures the extent to which a person has acquired information or mastered certain skills, usually as a result of instruction or training.

Alternative-form reliability The correlation between results on alternative forms of a test. Reliability is the extent to which the two forms are consistent in measuring the same attributes.

Anecdotal record A written description of an incident in a child's behavior that can be significant in understanding the child.

Aptitude test A test designed to predict future learning or performance on some task if appropriate education or training is provided.

Arena assessment An assessment process whereby a group of specialists in developmental disabilities observes a child in natural play and working situations. A profile of the child is developed by the team, comparing their individual observations of some facet of the child's behaviors.

Assessment software Software that has been developed to enable children to be assessed using a computer. Textbook publishers and developers of early childhood assessment tools make assessment software available as an option to traditional assessment tools.

Attitude measure An instrument that measures how an individual is predisposed to feel or think about something (a referent). A teacher can design a scale to measure students' attitudes toward reading or mathematics.

Authentic achievement Learning that is real and meaningful. Achievement that is worthwhile.

Authentic assessment An assessment that uses some type of performance by a child to demonstrate understanding.

Authentic measure A measure that uses authentic assessments that include performance and application of knowledge.

Authentic performance assessment *See* Authentic assessment.

Behavioral objective An educational or instructional statement that includes the behavior to be exhibited, the conditions under which the behavior will be exhibited, and the level of performance required for mastery.

Checklist A sequence or hierarchy of concepts and/or skills organized in a format that can be used to plan instruction and keep records.

Concurrent validity The extent to which test scores on two forms of a test measure are correlated when they are given at the same time.

Construct validity The extent to which a test measures a psychological trait or construct. Tests of personality, verbal ability, and critical thinking are examples of tests with construct validity.

Content validity The extent to which the content of a test such as an achievement test represents the objectives of the instructional program it is designed to measure.

Contract An agreement between teacher and child about activities the child will complete to achieve a specific objective or purpose.

Correctives Instructional materials and methods used with mastery learning that are implemented after formative evaluation to provide alternative learning strategies and resources.

Criterion-referenced test A test designed to provide information on specific knowledge or skills possessed by a student. The test measures specific skills or instructional objectives.

Criterion-related validity To establish validity of a test, scores are correlated with an external criterion, such as another established test of the same type.

Developmental checklist A checklist that emphasizes areas and levels of development in early childhood.

Developmental screening Evaluation of the young child to determine whether development is proceeding normally. It is used to identify children whose development is delayed.

Diagnostic evaluation An evaluation to analyze an individual's areas of weaknesses or strengths and to determine the nature and causes of the weaknesses.

Diagnostic interview An interview to determine a child's learning needs or assess weaknesses. May be part of a diagnostic evaluation.

Directed assignment A specific assignment to assess a child's performance on a learning objective or skill.

Direct performance measure A performance measure that requires the student to apply knowledge in an activity specified by the teacher.

Electronic management of learning Resources available to early childhood programs for instructional experiences using the computer. The materials can include creative, skill development, and assessment software.

Enrichment activity In the context of mastery learning, the enrichment activity is a challenging activity at a higher cognitive level on Bloom's taxonomy than the instructional objective described on a table of specifications.

Equivalent form Alternative forms of a test that are parallel. The forms of the test measure the same domain or objectives, have the same format, and are of equal difficulty.

Event sampling An observation strategy used to determine when a particular behavior is likely to occur. The setting in which the behavior occurs is more important than the time it is likely to occur.

Formative evaluation Evaluation conducted during instruction to provide the teacher with information on the learning progress of the student and the effectiveness of instructional methods and materials.

Formative test A test designed to evaluate progress on specific learning objectives or a unit of study.

Game In the context of authentic assessment, a game is a structured assessment whereby the student's performance progress is evaluated through engagement with the game.

Grade equivalent The grade level for which a given score on a standardized test is the estimated average. Grade-equivalent scores, commonly used for elementary achievement tests, are expressed in terms of the grade and month.

Grade norms Norms on standardized tests based on the performance of students in given grades.

Graphic rating scale A rating scale that can be used as a continuum. The rater marks characteristics by descriptors on the scale at any point along the continuum.

Group test A test that can be administered to more than one person at a time.

Inclusion The process of including children with disabilities into a classroom where they would have been placed if they had not experienced a disability.

Indirect performance measure A measure that assesses what a student knows about a topic. The teacher's assessment is accomplished by observing a student activity or examining a written test.

Individualized instruction Instruction based on the learning needs of individual students. It may be based on criterion-related evaluation or diagnosis.

Individual test A test that can be administered to only one person at a time. Many early childhood tests are individual tests because of the low maturity level of the examinees.

Informal test A test that has not been standardized. Teacher-designed tests are an example.

Instructional objective *See* Behavioral objective.

Integration Relates to facilitating the participation of children with disabilities into the classroom with peers who do not have disabilities. The child is integrated with other children and the needs of all children are met without treating some children as "special."

Intelligence quotient (IQ) An index of intelligence expressed as the ratio of mental age to chronological age. It is derived from an individual's performance on an intelligence test as compared with that of others of the same age.

Intelligence test A test measuring those developed abilities considered to be a sign of intelligence. Intelligence is general potential independent of prior learning.

Interest inventory A measure used to determine interest in an occupation or vocation. Students' interest in reading might be determined by such an inventory.

Internal consistency The degree of relationship among items on a test. A type of reliability that indicates whether items on the test are positively correlated and measure the same trait or characteristic.

Interview A discussion that the teacher conducts with a child to make an assessment.

Item analysis The analysis of single test items to determine their difficulty value and discriminating power. Item analysis is conducted in the process of developing a standardized test.

Learning disability A developmental difference or delay in a young or school-age child that interferes with the individual's ability to learn through regular methods of instruction.

Mainstreaming A process of placing children with disabilities into regular classrooms with children who do not have disabilities for part of the school day. Mainstreaming is being replaced by inclusion or integration, in which the child with disabilities is not singled out as being different.

Mastery testing Evaluation to determine the extent to which a test taker has mastered particular skills or learning objectives. Performance is compared to a predetermined standard of proficiency.

Mean The arithmetic average of a set of test scores.

Minimum-competency testing Evaluation to measure whether test takers have achieved a minimum level of proficiency in a given academic area.

Multiple choice A type of test question in which the test taker must choose the best answer from among several options.

Narrative report An alternative to report cards for reporting a child's progress. The teacher writes a narrative to describe the child's growth and accomplishments.

Neonatologist A physician who specializes in babies less than 1 month old.

Normal distribution The hypothetical distribution of scores that has a bell-shaped appearance. This distribution is used as a model for many scoring systems and test statistics.

Norm-referenced test A test in which the test taker's performance is compared with the performance of persons in a norm group.

Norms Statistics that supply a frame of reference based on the actual performance of test takers in a norm group. A set of scores that represents the distribution of test performance in the norm group.

Numerical rating scale A series of numerals, such as 1 to 5, that allows an observer to indicate the degree to which an individual possesses a particular characteristic.

Obstetrician A physician who specializes in pregnancy and childbirth.

Pediatrician A physician who specializes in the development, care, and diseases of young children.

Percentile A point or score in a distribution at or below which falls the percentage of cases indicated by the percentile. The score scale on a normal distribution is divided into 100 segments, each containing the same number of scores.

Percentile rank The test taker's test score, as expressed in terms of its position within a group of 100 scores. The percentile rank is the percentage of scores equal to or lower than the test taker's score.

Performance assessment   An assessment in which the child demonstrates knowledge by applying it to a task or a problem-solving activity.

Performance-based assessment   An assessment of development and/or learning that is based on the child's natural performance, rather than on contrived tests or tasks.

Personality test   A test designed to obtain information on the affective characteristics of an individual (emotional, motivational, or attitudinal). The test measures psychological makeup rather than intellectual abilities.

Play–based assessment   Assessment for children with disabilities that is conducted through observation in play environments. Play activities can be spontaneous or planned. Play-based assessment can be conducted by an individual or through arena assessment.

Portfolio   A format for conducting an evaluation of a child. Portfolios are a collection of a child's work, teacher assessments, and other information that contribute to a picture of the child's progress.

Preassessment   An assessment conducted before the beginning of the school year or prior to any instruction at the beginning of the school year.

Project   An authentic learning activity that can also be used to demonstrate student achievement.

Rating scale   A scale using categories that allow the observer to indicate the degree of a characteristic that the person possesses.

Raw score   The number of right answers a test taker obtains on a test.

Readiness test   A test that measures the extent to which a student has the prerequisite skills necessary to be successful in some new learning activity.

Reliability   The extent to which a test is consistent in measuring over time what it is designed to measure.

Rubric   An instrument developed to measure authentic and performance assessments. Descriptions are given for qualitative characteristics on a scale.

Running record   A description of a sequence of events in a child's behavior that includes all behaviors observed over a period of time.

Scaled score   The score obtained when a raw score is translated into a score that uses the normal curve for points of reference. Examples of scaled scores are IQ scores, percentiles, T scores, and Z scores.

Scope (sequence of skills)   A list of learning objectives established for areas of learning and development at a particular age, grade level, or content area.

Specimen record   Detailed observational reports of children's behavior over a period of time that are used for research purposes.

Split-half reliability   A measure of reliability whereby scores on equivalent sections of a single test are correlated for internal consistency.

Standard deviation   A measure of the variability of a distribution of scores around the mean.

Standard error   An estimate of the possible magnitude of error present on test scores.

Standardized test   A test that has specified content, procedures for administration and scoring, and normative data for interpreting scores.

Standard score   A transformed score that reports performance in terms of the number of standard deviation units the raw score is from the mean.

Stanine   A scale on the normal curve divided into nine sections, with all divisions except the first and the last being 0.5 standard deviation wide.

Structured interview   A preplanned interview conducted by the teacher for assessment purposes.

Structured performance assessment   A performance assessment that has been preplanned by the teacher to include specific tasks or activities.

Summative evaluation   An evaluation obtained at the end of a cycle of instruction to determine whether students have mastered the objectives and whether the instruction has been effective.

Summative test   A test to determine mastery of learning objectives administered for grading purposes.

T score   A standard score scale with a mean of 50 and a standard deviation of 10.

Table of specifications   A table of curriculum objectives that have been analyzed to determine to what level of Bloom's taxonomy of educational objectives the student must demonstrate mastery.

Test-retest reliability   A type of reliability obtained by administering the same test a second time after a short interval and then correlating the two sets of scores.

Time sampling   Observation to determine the frequency of a behavior. The observer records how many times the behavior occurs during uniform time periods.

True score   A hypothetical score on a test that is free of error. Because no standardized test is free of measurement error, a true score can never be obtained.

Unstructured interview   An assessment interview conducted by the teacher as the result of a naturally occurring performance by a child. The interview is not preplanned.

Unstructured performance assessment   An assessment that is part of regular classroom activities.

Validity   The degree to which a test serves the purpose for which it is to be used.

Work sample   An example of a child's work. Work samples include products of all types of activities that can be used to evaluate the child's progress.

Z score   A standard score that expresses performance in terms of the number of standard deviations from the mean.

A Selected Annotated Bibliography of Evaluation Instruments for Infancy and Early Childhood

1. *AAMR Adaptive Behavior Scale, School Edition (ABS-S:2)*
   Authors: K. Nihira and N. Lambert
   Publisher: American Association on Mental Retardation
   Publication Date: 1993
   Type of Test: Behavior rating scale
   Uses for which the test is recommended: Assesses the behavioral and affective competencies of individuals from 3 to 69 years of age. It is intended to be used with individuals with mental retardation and emotional maladjustment.

2. *Adaptive Behavior Assessment System—Infant and Preschool*
   Author: T. Oakland
   Publisher: Psychological Corporation
   Publication Date: 2002
   Type of Test: Adaptive skills
   Uses for which the test is recommended: Assesses strengths and weaknesses in adaptive skills in infants and preschoolers. It is intended to identify and diagnose intervention for children with developmental delay.

3. *AGS Early Screening Profiles*
   Authors: P. Harrison et al.
   Publisher: American Guidance Service
   Publication Date: 1990
   Type of Test: Developmental screening
   Uses for which the test is recommended: Provides a comprehensive instrument for screening children from ages 2 through 6 for developmental delay. The test provides profiles for cognitive, language, motor, self-help, and social development.

4. *Battelle Developmental Inventory*
   Authors: J. Newborg et al.
   Publisher: Teaching Resources
   Publication Date: 1988
   Type of Test: Early childhood screening and diagnosis
   Uses for which the test is recommended: Identification of the developmental strengths and weaknesses of children with and without disabilities in infant, preschool, and primary programs. Because it also has a screening test component, it can be used for general screening of preschool and kindergarten children at risk for developmental delays.

5. *Bayley Scales of Infant Development—Second Edition*
   Author: N. Bayley
   Publisher: Psychological Corporation
   Publication Date: 1993
   Type of Test: Infant development
   Uses for which the test is recommended: Measures infant development and includes a mental and motor scale of development. An infant behavior record also provides a systematic way of assessing and recording observations of the child's behavior when examined.

6. *Boehm Test of Basic Concepts—Third Edition*
   Author: A. E. Boehm
   Publisher: Psychological Corporation
   Publication Date: 2000
   Type of Test: Individual or group screening of concepts
   Uses for which the test is recommended: Intended for use in kindergarten through second grade for screening and teaching. It measures knowledge of various concepts that are thought to be necessary for achievement in the first few grades of school.

7. *Bracken Basic Concept Scale—Revised*
   Author: B. A. Bracken
   Publisher: Psychological Corporation
   Publication Date: 1998
   Type of Test: Concept development
   Uses for which the test is recommended: Measures knowledge of basic concepts acquired in preschool, kindergarten, and primary grades.

8. *Brigance Screens*
   Author: A. H. Brigance
   Publisher: Curriculum Associates
   Publication Date: 1998
   Type of Tests: Diagnostic and screening inventories
   Uses for which the test is recommended: Screens are designed to be used for children from birth through grade 6. The screen for early years assesses psychomotor development, self-help skills, speech and language, general knowledge, and comprehension. The screen for elementary students is designed to assist teachers in adjusting curriculum and instruction for inclusion of children with disabilities.

9. *California Achievement Tests—Fifth Edition*
   Publisher: CTB/McGraw-Hill
   Publication Date: 1992
   Type of Test: Norm-referenced achievement tests
   Uses for which the test is recommended: Provides information for use in making educational decisions leading to improved instruction in the basic skills. Measures prereading, reading, spelling, language, mathematics, and reference skills.

10. *Denver II*
    Authors: W. K. Frankenburg et al.
    Publisher: Denver Developmental Materials
    Publication Date: 1990
    Type of Test: Developmental screening
Uses for which the test is recommended: Measures development: gross motor, fine motor, language, and personal-social. Used to identify children from birth to 6 years of age with serious developmental delays.

11. *Developmental Indicators for the Assessment of Learning—III (DIAL).*
    Authors: C. D. Mardell-Czundowski and D. S. Goldenberg
    Publisher: American Guidance Service
    Publication Date: 1998
    Type of Test: Individual screening
Uses for which the test is recommended: Assesses motor, concept, and language skills for children ages 2 to 6. It is intended to screen the range of abilities from severe dysfunction to potentially advanced.

12. *Early Screening Inventory—Revised*
    Authors: Meisels et al.
    Publisher: Pearson Early Learning
    Publication Date: 1997
    Type of Test: Developmental screening
Uses for which the test is recommended: To screen children for developmental delay in early childhood year. Assesses all developmental domains to identify children who need further testing for developmental delay.

13. *First Step: Screening Test for Evaluating Preschoolers*
    Author: L. J. Miller
    Publisher: Psychological Corporation
    Publication Date: 1993
    Type of Test: Preschool screening test
Uses for which the test is recommended: To screen preschool children for developmental delays. Higher scores represent average performance.

14. *Kaufman Assessment Battery for Children*
    Authors: A. Kaufman and N. Kaufman
    Publisher: American Guidance Service
    Publication Date: 1983
    Type of Test: Individual intelligence, achievement
Uses for which the test is recommended: Intended for use in schools and clinical settings to measure intelligence and achievement for children ages 2 to 6 through 12 to 15.

15. *McCarthy's Scales of Children's Abilities*
    Author: D. McCarthy
    Publisher: Psychological Corporation
    Publication Date: 1983
    Type of Test: Cognitive abilities

Uses for which the test is recommended: Measures the cognitive abilities of children from 2½ to 8½ years of age. Can be used for the assessment of young children with learning problems or other exceptional conditions. Measures intellectual functioning, including verbal ability, nonverbal reasoning, number aptitude, short-term memory, and coordination.

16. *Neonatal Behavioral Assessment Scale*
    Author: T. B. Brazelton
    Publisher: J. B. Lippincott
    Publication Date: 1984
    Type of Test: Neonatal rating scale
Uses for which the test is recommended: To identify mild neurological dysfunctions and variations in temperament. Measures temperamental differences, nervous system functions, and the capacity of the neonate to interact.

17. *Peabody Picture Vocabulary Test—Revised*
    Authors: L. Dunn and L. Dunn
    Publisher: American Guidance Service
    Publication Date: 1997
    Type of Test: Receptive vocabulary
Uses for which the test is recommended: To evaluate the hearing vocabulary or receptive knowledge of vocabulary of children and adults.

18. *Stanford–Binet Intelligence Scale—Fourth Edition*
    Authors: R. L. Thorndike, E. P. Hagen, and J. P. Sattler
    Publisher: Riverside Publishing Company
    Publication Date: 1986
    Type of Test: Intelligence
Uses for which the test is recommended: To assess the cognitive ability of young children, adolescents, and young adults. Subtests may be used to identify children with learning disabilities, to assess brain damage, and to measure the cognitive skills of children with hearing impairment or visual–spatial or mathematical talents.

19. *Wechsler Intelligence Scale for Children—Revised*
    Author: D. Wechsler
    Publisher: Psychological Corporation
    Publication Date: 1991
    Type of Test: Intelligence
Uses for which the test is recommended: For clinical and psychoeducational work. Useful in the assessment of brain—behavior relationships. Intended to evaluate children's intellectual ability.

20. *Wechsler Preschool and Primary Scale of Intelligence*
    Author: D. Wechsler
    Publisher: Psychological Corporation
    Publication Date: 2002
    Type of Test: Intelligence
Uses for which the test is recommended: To assess the cognitive abilities of preschool and primary children. Includes developmental data that can be used for program planning.

A Selected List of Internet Assessment Resources

COMMERCIAL PUBLISHERS OF STANDARDIZED TESTS AND RESOURCES

Brooks Publishing Company
www.brookspublishing.com

The Psychological Corporation
www.PsychCorp.com

Pro–Ed
www.proedinc.com

American Guidance Service
www.ags.com

INFANT ASSESSMENTS

General
www.riverpub.com/products/early/html

Parent–Infant Assessments
www.bapta.com/early–child.htm

Tracking Infant Development
www.shrs.pitt.edu/facets/FALL–01/0T_F01.pdf

Infant Behavioral Assessments
www.wri–edu.org/infant

Infant Head Start Assessment
www.acf.hhs.gov/programs/core/ongoing–research/ehs/local–research/births–utah.html

Infant Neuromotor Assessments
www.cidg.com/–marienF/K/i/n/m0065.htm

EARLY CHILDHOOD ASSESSMENTS

Recommendations for Early Childhood Assessments: National Goals Panel
www.negp.gov/reports/prinrec.pdf
www.negp.gov/pages9–3.htm

Improvements in Determining Readiness for School
www.ed.gov/legislation/GOALS2000/TheAct/sec207.html

Purposes and Standards for Early Childhood Assessments
www.ocd.wa.gov./info/csd/waeceap/ChildAssessments

Issues in Early Childhood Assessments
www.naeyc.org/childrens_champions/readiness.asp
www.ncrel.org/Sdrs/areas/issues/students/earlycld/ea500.htm

Early Literacy Assessments—CTB/McGraw–Hill
www.ctb.com/products/category–homejsp?FOLDER%3C%3E

Books on Early Literacy and Assessments
www.fetchbook.info/Early–Literacy–Assessment.html

Early Childhood Performance Assessments
www.cms.ag.ohio–state.edu/4DACTION/WEB–InventoryIndividualDisplay/0319G

Index

A

AAMR. *See* American Association on Mental Retardation
ABC analysis, 104
Ability, 39
Achievement, 39, 183. *See also* Achievement test
Achievement test, 33, 39–40, 45, 82, 181. *See also* Standardized test
    example, 63–64
    group test, 45, 48, 65, 69, 70
    using, 74
Activity. *See also* Performance assessment
    performance assessment of, 13–14
Adaptive Behavior Assessment System—Infant and Preschool, 41, 42*f*
Adaptive Behavior Scale—School Edition-S:2, 42, 44
Addison-Wesley Mathematics, Teacher's Edition, 162, 163
Age. *See also* Development
    chronological age and behavior, 4, 105
    mental age, 4
    reliability and validity increases with, 23
Aggression, 103, 108. *See also* Behavior
AGS Early Screening Profiles, 42, 44
Alpern, G.D., 65
Als, H., 40, 41
Alternative assessment, 13. *See also* Assessment; Authentic assessment
    in general, 203
    letter grade/report card limitations, 204–205
    using, 203–204
American Association on Mental Retardation (AAMR), 42
American Guidance Service, 39, 45
American Psychological Association (APA), 48, 55
Americans with Disabilities Act (IDEA) (PL 101-576), discussed, 9
Anastasi, A., 56
Anecdotal record, 97–98, 191–192, 238. *See also* Observation
Angaran, Joseph, 82
APA. *See* American Psychological Association
Apgar Scale, 26, 40, 42*f*
Apgar, V., 26, 40
APIB. *See Assessment of Preterm Infants' Behavior*

Aptitude test, 39, 40. *See also* Standardized test
Arena assessment, 95. *See also* Assessment; Play-based assessment
Art activities, 209
Arter, J.A., 13, 224
Aschbacher, P.R., 146, 149, 181, 224
Asians, 12
Assessment. *See also* Assessment strategies; Assessment system; Authentic assessment; Informal assessment; Play-based assessment; Portfolio assessment; Teacher-designed assessment
    at beginning/end of school year, 33
    child study movement, 4–5
    concerns about testing young children, 11–12
    concerns about testing young children with disabilities, 12–13
    defined, 2
    diagnostic evaluation, 65, 67, 89, 161
    evolution of, 4–9
    in general, 2–4, 34
    Head Start and War on Poverty, 6
    learning objectives, 174
    national, 48
    ongoing, 31, 33
    PL 94-142, 7-8, 65
    PL 99-457, 8-9
    PL 101-576, 9
    preassessment, 33
    prenatal, 2
    principles, 22–25
    process, 26–28, 32–33, 34
    profile, 238
    at reporting periods, 33
    results, 31–32
    self-assessment, 207, 215
    software for, 31
    standardized test, 5–6
    technology-based, 31
    trends in a new century, 9–10
Assessment of Preterm Infants' Behavior (APIB), 41, 42*f*
Assessment strategies
    alternative, 11
    checklists, 30, 131
    informal, 29–31

C

California Achievement Test (5th Edition) (CAT/5), 70
Campbell, D.T., 103, 112
Carlisle, A., 97
CAT/5. *See California Achievement Test*
Chambers, D.L., 91
Charles, R., 162
Check, E., 82
Checkley, K., 182
Checklist, 15, 45, 188, 191, 192, 193, 215. *See also* Rating scale; Recordkeeping
  advantages/disadvantages, 131–133
  curriculum checklist, 124–127
  design, 122–127, 129–131, 148
  developmental checklist, 30, 120–121, 124
  discussed, 30, 105
  evaluating, 128
  learning checklist, 127
  misuse of, 92–93
  observation and, 127–128
  organization of, 130
  purposes of, 120
  rating scale and, 105
  recordkeeping, 130–131
  as scope or sequence of skills, 30
  using, 120–121, 122–127
  in work sampling system, 235, 238
Chicago, 102
Child. *See also Child Observation Record;* Infant; Parents
  in assessment setting, 34
  assessment should benefit, 21–22, 23
  involvement in assessment process, 7, 22, 207
  self-concept, 108–109
Child care, 8
Child Observation Record (COR), 45, 46, 88
  discussed, 236–237, 238
Child study movement, discussed, 4–5
Cicchetti, D., 8, 42
Clark, E.A., 8
Clark-Stewart, A., 103
Clark University, 4
Class report, 75. *See also* Report
Classroom assessment, 154, 162. *See also* Teacher-designed assessment
Clawson, A., 45
Clay, M., 101
Cliatt, M.J., 215
Clifford, R., 88, 134

Clinic of Child Development, 5
Cohen, D.H., 94, 98
Cohen, J.H., 141, 144
Columbia University Teacher's College, 5
Communication and Symbolic Behavior Scale (CSBS), 41, 42*f*
Comprehensive Tests of Basic Skills, Fourth Edition (CTBS), 70
Contract
  discussed, 184–185
  using, 186
Copple, C., 83, 91
COR. *See Child Observation Record*
Correctives, designing, 166, 173
Cress, K., 90
Criterion-referenced test, 14–15, 91. *See also* Standardized test; Test
  compared to norm-referenced test, 62–64
  individualized instruction, 69
  mastery testing, 68, 164
  minimum-competency testing, 69
  test scores, 80
  using, 65–70, 88–89
Cronbach, L.J., 5, 6, 45, 54, 56, 71
Cryer, D., 88
CSBS. *See Communication and Symbolic Behavior Scales*
CTBS. *See* Comprehensive Tests of Basic Skills, Fourth Edition
Culture, concerns about testing with cultural differences, 11–12, 22
Curriculum. *See also* Learning objectives
  assessing progress in learning, 95–96
  assessment and, 31–32, 65, 70, 74, 78, 89, 90, 183
  checklist, 120, 122, 124–127
  designing learning experiences, 172
  evaluation, 23, 32, 45–48, 62
  evaluation, diagnostic, 89
  evaluation, formative and summative, 89
  Guidelines for Appropriate Curriculum Content and Assessment in Programs Serving Children Ages 3 Through 8, 13
  individualized instruction, 69
  measurement-driven instruction, 82, 91
  objectives, 161
  state-mandated, 162
  "thinking curriculum," 176
Curriculum Standards for the Social Studies, 10
Cystic fibrosis, 26

D

Darwin, Charles, 4
Day-care, 45
Deiner, P.L., 9
Denver Developmental Screening Test, 27
Denver II, 41, 42f, 65
Desjean-Perrotta, B., 208, 213, 215
Development. *See also* Age; Developmental
    checklist; Developmental delay;
    Developmental disability
    assessment of, 2, 27, 29–30, 83, 93
    cognitive development, 109–110, 209–210
    defined, 105
    evaluating, 94–95, 183
    fine motor skills, 107, 209
    gross motor skills, 107, 209
    language development, 110–111
    observation of, 105–111
    physical development, 107–108
    research into, 5
    social and emotional development,
        108–109, 210
Development Profile II, 66
Developmental checklist, 30, 120–121, 124.
    See also Checklist; Developmental
    screening
Developmental delay, 41, 42, 63, 121. *See also*
    Developmental disability; Developmental
    screening
Developmental disability. *See also* Disability
    assessment of, 27
    developmental checklist, 30
    Early Intervention Program, 8
Developmental Indicators for the Assessment of
    Learning (DIAL III), 42, 44
Developmental screening, 26, 45, 65, 67
Dewey, John, 4
Diagnosis. *See also* Diagnostic evaluation
    analytic rubric, 144
    professional requirements for, 8
    role of assessment in, 2–3
Diagnostic evaluation, 65, 67, 89, 161
DIAL III. *See Developmental Indicators for the*
    Assessment of Learning
Diana vs. California State Board of Education, 12
Dichtelmiller, M.L., 93, 124, 127, 130, 182,
    183, 189, 191, 236, 238
Directed assignments, 31. *See also* Interview;
    Performance assessment
    discussed, 185–186

Disability. *See also* Developmental disability
    affecting assessment, 34, 95
    affecting testing, 43, 45
    assistive technologies, 230
    auditory disability, 8
    concerns about testing young children with
        disabilities, 12–13
    emotional disturbance, 8
    learning disability, 8, 26, 45
    legislation for children with, 7–9
    parents of children with disability, 229
Dossey, J.A., 91
Driscoll, L.A., 97
Dulay, H.C., 45
Dunn, L., 45, 49, 64
Durkin, D., 80

E

Early Childhood Environment Rating Scale
    (ECERS), 88, 134
Early Childhood–Head Start Task Force, 10
Early Head Start, 10
Early Intervention Program, 8
Early School Inventory, 45, 47
Early Screening Inventory–Revised, 67
ECERS. *See Early Childhood Environment Rating*
    Scale—Revised Edition
Education for All Handicapped Children Act
    (PL-142), discussed, 7–8
Education of Man, 4
Education of the Handicapped Act
    (PL 99-457)
    discussed, 8–9
    Early Intervention Program, 8
    Federal Preschool Program, 8
Eicholz, P.E., 162
Electronic management of learning (EML), 31.
    See also Learning
Emergency School Aid Act, 6
Emile (Rousseau), 4
EML. *See* Electronic management of
    learning
Emotional problems, 8, 40
Emotions, social and emotional development,
    108–109
Engel, B., 184
Enrichment activities, 166
Event sampling, 104–105. *See also*
    Observation

N

O

P